# The
# Jewish Brigade

*An Army
With Two Masters
1944-1945*

# THE JEWISH BRIGADE

## An Army with
## Two Masters
## 1944–45

by

Morris Beckman

*2047703*

**SARPEDON**
Rockville Centre, NY

*00 - 40835891*

Published in the United States by
SARPEDON
49 Front Street
Rockville Centre, NY 11570

First published in the UK in 1998 by
Spellmount Limited,
The Old Rectory, Staplehurst, Kent TN12 0AZ

Cataloging-in-publication data is available from the
Library of Congress

ISBN 1-885119-56-9

Typeset in Palatino by MATS, Southend-on-Sea, Essex
Manufactured in Great Britain

10 9 8 7 6 5 4 3 2 1

# Contents

| | |
|---|---|
| Acknowledgements | vii |
| Foreword by Edmund de Rothschild | viii |
| List of Plates | ix |
| Prologue | x |
| Map of Northern Italy | xvi |
| Chapter One | 1 |
| Chapter Two | 12 |
| Chapter Three | 23 |
| Chapter Four | 34 |
| Chapter Five | 42 |
| Chapter Six | 51 |
| Chapter Seven | 61 |
| Chapter Eight | 74 |
| Chapter Nine | 85 |
| Chapter Ten | 96 |
| Chapter Eleven | 107 |
| Chapter Twelve | 117 |
| Chapter Thirteen | 128 |
| Chapter Fourteen | 139 |
| Appendix I Roll of Honour | 149 |
| Appendix II Awards won by Brigaders | 149 |
| Appendix III 'To our fellow British soldiers!' | 151 |
| Appendix IV Registration for the Jewish Brigade Group | 153 |
| Appendix V Hebrew words of command | 155 |
| Index | 157 |

# Acknowledgements

I have come across only three books about the Jewish Brigade. Written just after the end of the war, they are *Wheels in the Storm* by Major Wellesley Aron MBE, *The Brigade* by Hanoch Bartov, and *With the Jewish Brigade* by its Senior Chaplain, Rabbi Bernard Caspar. Later, I read *On Parade*, the much acclaimed book by Armoury Sergeant Major Len Sanitt, Warrant Officer 1st Class, who, recovering from wounds, transferred to the Brigade and wrote about his experiences. Other key sources were *Promise and Fulfilment*, and *Scum of the Earth* by Arthur Koestler, *Forged in Fury* by Michael Elkins, *The Living Bridge* by Shimon Behar, General Secretary of the League of Israeli War Veterans, *Soldiers from Judea* by Rabinowitz, *I Shall Live* by Henry Ohrenstein, *With Zionists at Gallipoli* by Colonel James Patterson, and *The Jewish Military Effort, 1939-1944* by Michael J.Cohen.

The Public Record Office provided the following War Diaries of the Palestine Regiment: WO/169/10312-10340; WO/169/16311-16313; WO/170/3870-3976; WO/170/4488-4492, and WO/170/5056-5058. It also supplied the Routine Orders issued by the Jewish Brigade HQ staff, which were more revealing still than the War Diaries.

Newspapers: every issue of *The Jewish Chronicle* from 1940 to 1945; excerpts from *The [Manchester] Guardian*, *The [London] Times*, *The Jerusalem Post*, the *Daily Mail*, and the Hebrew *Davar*.

Reports and magazines; the *Zionist Review*; fax from Gerald Smith dated 16 July 1995; *Israel's Secret Wars*; 'An Italian Pilgrimage' by Martin Sugarman, 'The Jewish Brigade fought for its goals' by Erita Oyserman, 'The Jewish Infantry Brigade' by Sergeant Myer Goldblum; *The Canadian Jewish War Contribution*; *The Forgotten Ally*.

I received invaluable support from The Association of Jewish Ex-Servicemen, and was thus able to interview British Jews, such as Eric Nabarro and Cyril Lebor, who had served with the Brigade. Towers of strength along the way were Mark Hyatt and Martin Sugarman – they corrected and advised me unstintingly. Above all I owe most to the late David Spector, who transferred from the Eighth Army to the Jewish Brigade and was appointed Staff Major. During his last months of life he was so keen on a book about the Brigade that, ill as he was, I visited him four times at his nursing home in Brighton. He gave me letters, published articles and first-hand information that was like gold dust.

Morris Beckman
London, 1998

# Foreword

I am indeed privileged to write a Foreword to this excellent book that Morris Beckman has written on the Jewish Infantry Brigade Group, formed during World War II, and the difficulties created by those who were very opposed to it. There were many famous names indeed who did prevent a large body of willing men combat Nazi Germany.

Morris Beckman has written a fine account of the help given by the Brigade to those who wished to enter Palestine.

I commend this book as an important record of the events that took place during those years.

Edmund de Rothschild

# List of Plates

1. Recruiting poster for the British Army, Tel Aviv, November 1941 (*Ajex*)
2. British Army volunteers parading in the streets of Tel Aviv, 1940 (*Ajex*)
3. German soldiers leaving the synagogue in Genoa after cleaning it under the supervision of Jewish Brigade soldiers (*Major David Spector*)
4. Brigaders of the Royal Army Service Corps dancing a *hora* with refugees adopted by the unit, Giovinazzo, Italy, 1944 (*Ajex*)
5. The front line, Italy, 1945. A Jewish Brigade patrol prepares to go out (*Ajex/Myer Goldblum*)
6. Brigade staff, Italy, 1945. Left to right: Captain David Spector G3, Major Jackson G1, Brigadier Benjamin GOC, Captain Goodman IO (*David Spector*)
7. Open-air speech given before the attack on the Senio front, April 1945. Captain Norman Cohen RAMC is in the foreground (*David Spector*)
8. Commonwealth War Graves Commission cemetery at Ravenna, Italy, containing the graves of Jewish Brigaders of the Palestine Regiment (*Martin Sugarman*)
9. 'A' Company, 1st Battalion Palestine Regiment's victory parade, Faenza, Italy, 1945 (*Ajex*)
10. Guard duty, Tarvisio, Italy, 1945 (*Ajex/Myer Goldblum*)
11. Announcement of a football game between the Brigade and Belgian Maccabi, Brussels, 14 October 1945 (*Ajex*)
12. Brigader M Goldblum with his truck, May 1946. Note the Brigade insignia on the mudguard (*Ajex/Myer Goldblum*)
13. Foreign Representative of the Jewish Agency, Moshe Shertok, presenting the Brigade standard at Fiuggi, northern Italy (*Ajex*)
14. The Jewish Brigade at Tarvisio after the war. The soldiers are being addressed by the Jewish Agency on the task of finding and rescuing Jewish survivors (*Ajex*)

# *Prologue*

By the summer of 1944, 1.3 million Jews were fighting with the Allied forces against the Germans and the Japanese. They included 600,000 Americans, 500,000 Soviets, 70,000 British and Commonwealth servicemen, and 15,000 Polish free forces. There were also several thousand in the free forces of the other European territories under Nazi occupation. Thousands more, who had escaped from concentration camps, death trains and the Nazi search-and-murder *Sonderkommandos*, were fighting alongside the Maquis and partisans in Europe's marshes, forests and mountains. All of these Jews fought under the flags of their countries of birth. In addition, some 35,000 Palestine Jews fought as volunteers in a variety of units in Europe and the Middle East. They wore British uniforms and fought under the Union flag. Classified as colonial troops, they wore the Palestine shoulder flash. Because Palestine was a mandated territory, the British could not conscript its young men for military duty. This did not matter as, at the outbreak of war, 120,000 young Palestine Jewish men and women rushed to join the British forces.

A high proportion of the volunteers were European escapees from the Nazis. Predominantly Germans, Poles, Austrians and Czechs, they were worried sick about the fate of their families, and their hatred of the Nazis was intense. From day one of the war they wanted only to be combat-trained and to be given a chance to fight against Germany. However, for four years, the pro-Arab bias of the Palestine government and the British Foreign Office, and their fear of upsetting the Arabs by allowing the creation of a Jewish combat force, diverted the volunteers into service, support and guard-duty units. How wrong they were. At that time, the Arabs would not have cared a damn if a Jewish fighting force had come into being as long as it did its fighting against Germany and well away from Palestine. The Arabs had only one objective – an end to British and French colonisation of their lands.

Despite being implacably opposed, the Palestine administration and the Jewish Agency were pragmatic enough to meet when military necessity dictated. These were cagey, adversarial encounters that reflected the mistrust felt between the administration and the Agency. One factor above all others soured relations – something which the British failed to grasp – the Palestine Jews were the only Jews in the world who owned the pockets of land that were theirs alone. Their sense of identification with this *Eretz Yisroel* (Land of Israel) was so strong that it transcended narrow nationalism. When they flew the Jewish flag over their buildings, no mandatory power on earth could make them lower it. To the Agency the formation of a Jewish combat force, fighting under the Jewish flag, was no more than their entitlement. But it was a thorn in the flesh of the Palestine mandarins and the Foreign Office in London. Upset tens of millions of Arabs, with their oil, the Suez Canal and strategic geographical position to appease a mere half million Jewish settlers? Unthinkable!

War makes demands, especially periods when the appetite for personnel is voracious. After the fall of France in 1940, British servicemen were rushed home from the Middle East and Africa to defend their own country. They left a vacuum which had to be filled. There was a particular need for air force ground staff, and the Palestine Jewish community was an obvious source. With the common aim of defeating the Third Reich, the British and the Jewish Agency met again. And it was at this point that the Agency changed its stance. It realised that every Jewish man and woman recruited into the British forces would receive invaluable military training and experience, and strengthening Britain's lone stand against the Axis powers was of paramount importance. The Agency continued to press its demand for the creation of a Jewish force, fighting under its own flag, but in a lower key and less frequently. And of course the demand continued to be denied, even ignored altogether.

However, the Agency began to note support in sections of the British press and from several parliamentarians. More than anyone, Winston Churchill gave them hope. In 1940 he angrily declared in the House of Commons that it was nonsense for Britain to reject the offer of a fighting force of 40,000 Jews when the nation was so hard pressed to contain the Axis powers. Churchill continued to press this point and, by the late summer of 1944, he had lost patience with the Foreign Office and the War Office, and demanded action. He got it. By now revelations of the true horrors of the Holocaust were stunning the civilised world, and virtually the whole British press was demanding that Jews should not be denied the opportunity to confront in combat the murderers of their people.

When, in early March 1945, the Jewish Infantry Brigade took its place in the Allied line south of the Senio river in Italy, and faced seasoned German paratroops and a Jaeger division, the news galvanised Jews throughout the world. The Brigade had 5,500 men. All of its ancillary units had seen active service in the Western Desert and Italian campaigns. Its three infantry battalions, mortar and artillery units had undergone three months of the most gruelling training in bitterly cold weather and icy conditions in the Italian mountains.

The Brigade formed a component part of the British Eighth Army. Every man felt privileged, the large number of academics and intellectuals making all the soldiers aware that they were making history. As he gazed at the German positions, no Brigader would have wanted to be anywhere else. Morale was sky-high. They knew that news of the Brigade's formation had filtered into those parts of Europe where their co-religionists were in dire straits, and had given them hope. Other Jews in the Allied forces watched and waited to see how the Brigade would acquit itself. In a services club in Rome, a young American Jewish infantryman said to a Palestine ATS woman, 'Well, lady, I guess they'll just have to perform.'

History records that they performed well. Flanked by free Italian and Polish units, they attacked with an elan fuelled by pent-up frustration and an unquenchable thirst for revenge. In an 'up-and-at-'em' mood, they fixed bayonets and rushed the German positions. The Germans in their sector melted away in a retreat that developed into a rout of the once mighty *Wehrmacht*. The war ended and the Brigade fetched up at Tarvisio, where the borders of Austria, Italy and Yugoslavia met. Here, though still under the command of the Eighth Army, their attention turned to their hidden agenda, laid down by their political master in Tel Aviv.

The prime remit was to reach out into Europe in small well armed convoys, to find and rescue as many Jewish survivors as they could, and to take them to shelters being set up by Brigaders in Italy. Here, the emaciated, broken human wrecks would be physically and mentally rehabilitated, then driven south to be put onto boats bound for Palestine, where they would once again live normal lives. The soldiers set about their task with inspired zeal and humanity.

Another priority was retribution, though this was a very hush-hush subject. All the Brigaders I have spoken to admitted that 'things did happen', but very few would spell out what these were. A paragraph in the Brigade's 'Routine Orders' stipulated that, during fighting, infantrymen should not execute Nazis taken prisoner as they were needed for interrogation. British Jews who served with the Brigade confirmed that when appalling stories were told of the gas chambers and ovens, and the mass slaughter of Jews, emotions often became uncontrollable. The Agency knew that in the post-war confusion, thousands of top SS officers, who were guilty of the most atrocious crimes, would attempt to escape punishment, often in Spain or South America, along the Odessa escape route. The Brigade was chosen to ensure that at least some of these top-ranking SS officers would answer for their crimes against humanity. Armed with intelligence supplied by the Agency and Jewish survivors, revenge squads, with three or four soldiers to each vehicle, went out all over Germany and Austria to exact revenge. There was no shortage of volunteers for the task. In the London *Times* of Thursday 13 July 1995, there appeared an obituary of Meir Zorea who had died on 24 June, aged 72. He had been an Israeli army general and a member of the Knesset. As a second lieutenant in the Jewish Brigade he was awarded the Military

Cross for leading his patrol through intense enemy fire, allowing spotters to pinpoint German positions. Zorea had been a member of a revenge squad and he recalled:

> We only eliminated those directly involved in the slaughter of Jews. At first we put a bullet through their heads. Then we strangled them. With our bare hands. We never said anything before we killed them. Not why or who we were. We just killed them like you kill a bug.

These were the first post-war executions of selected top Nazis. There were certainly several dozen revenge squads operating; the highest estimate of executions was 1,500. The exact figure will never be known. Those targeted were picked up in their home cities and towns, many plucked from the homes they had come back to before leaving with new identities for safe havens.

Taking precedence over all else was the Brigaders' awareness that it was now time to prepare for the approaching struggle that would have to be waged to ensure the survival of the Land of Israel. By 1945, unrest in Palestine and the conflict between the British forces and the Haganah, the uncontrollable right-wing Stern Gang, and the Irgun Zvi Leumi groups had escalated to the point where it became certain that Britain would give up the mandate and pull out of Palestine. When this happened, the Jewish community would be attacked by an overwhelming number of Arabs intent on its destruction.

Hitler had achieved one victory – he had rendered central and eastern Europe Jew-free. He had murdered six million; the surviving one million were physically and mentally shattered by what they had been through. They were rootless, totally disoriented and without hope as they wandered aimlessly, or rotted in the hastily established displaced persons camps. The suicide rate was alarmingly high. No one wanted to take them in – with one exception, the Jewish community in Palestine. But to get there they would have to run the gautlet of the British army, navy and air force, engaged in an attempt to satisfy the obsession of the British Foreign Secretary, Ernest Bevin. He had vowed to crush Zionism. With utterances such as, 'It's them or us', he had turned world opinion against Britain. He had also succeeded in turning the British press, as well as parliamentary and public opinion against his sledgehammer policies in Palestine.

So, when one war was scarcely ended, the Jewish Brigade threw its energy into preparing for the next one. They stepped up the rescue of their suffering co-religionists from the hell of Europe and their passage south to the Palestine-bound boats and salvation. They increased the smuggling of arms to be hidden on farms and kibbutzim throughout Palestine. They picked out the fittest, young, male refugees and took them into the Italian mountains for weapons and fieldcraft training. Brigaders boarding ships in Antwerp and Marseilles to take them home to be demobilised in Palestine gave their uniforms and papers to these now trained refugees, who would take their place.

When the Brigade contingent took part in the impressive post-war victory parade in London, many of its members were still trying to come to terms with the loss of their families. They marched proudly, but unlike those around them, they had their minds focussed on the struggle that lay ahead.

On 29 November 1947 the General Assembly of the United Nations recommended the partition of Palestine. From that day, the British stood aside and watched, until they withdrew their entire military force and their administration on 15 May 1948. On the day following the UN pronouncement, Arabs opened fire on buses, ambushed cars and lorries, set fire to the commercial heart of Jerusalem, went on strike, rioted, attacked and murdered isolated Jewish settlements. The British did not intervene. But the Haganah, aware that it was now the sole protector of the Jewish community, fought back ferociously. On 15 May 1948, David Ben-Gurion proclaimed the birth of the state of Israel.

Only one day later, the armies of five Arab nations, overwhelming in numbers, well armed, and totally confident, attacked with the aim of wiping out the new democracy. No one outside the region expected the Jews to survive. The world held its breath. But with the Holocaust a still fresh memory, and embedded in the souls of the Jews, they fought back with a ferocity that stopped the invading armies in their tracks. The enemy crumbled and scurried back to the safety of their own borders. In a single week the Jews doubled the amount of land that had been awarded to them by the United Nations.

The Jewish Brigade, which subsequently provided thirty five generals for the Israeli defence forces, helped to establish the foundations and the structure on which the state of Israel built the most formidable defensive military machine in the Middle East.

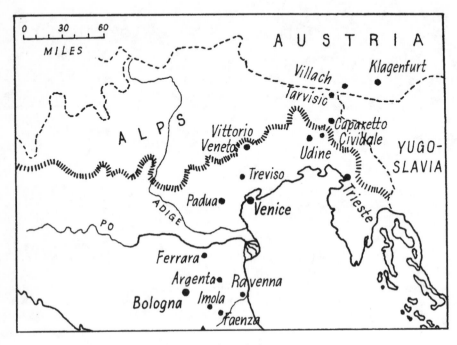

*Northern Italy*

# Chapter One

This is the story of the odyssey of a people who never gave up hope. It lasted for nearly 2,000 years. It took them through a seemingly endless dark age when rootlessness and persecution was their everyday lot. It began in AD135, when the Roman legions under Hadrian crushed the Judean rebellion, and it ended in 1948, when the descendants of those defeated Judeans won their war of independence in that same land.

When the Romans crushed Bar Kochba's revolt, they vowed it would be the last by their most troublesome subject people who, rather than worship Roman gods instead of their own One God, Jehovah, preferred to die in battle. The Romans were pitiless. They razed towns and villages, and put the people to the sword. They sacked Jerusalem and destroyed its magnificent temple, leaving only the western (Wailing) wall standing. Then they scattered the surviving Jews to the four points of the compass. The long, fraught journey had begun.

Wherever the remnants of the Jewish community landed up, they clung to four things for comfort: their concept of the One God, their ethical beliefs, their traditional family values, and the Hebrew language. Their strange and reclusive behaviour did not go down well with the indigenous peoples among whom they settled. And they quickly became the focus of blame, lies and grotesque propaganda. They made a ready target for anyone who saw advantage in stirring up and exploiting anti-Jewish prejudice. Over the years, that has not changed.

The aggressive spread of Christianity compounded the isolation of the Jews. Because Judaism was at the time the only other monotheistic religion, Christian leaders saw it as a rival, and even a threat to their power and authority. Attempts to convert Jews to Christ ran into the brick wall of Jewish stubbornness. The next logical step was to demonise these strange people in their midst. It worked. To the unsophisticated masses, the persecution of a Jewish minority became an acceptable, even commendable, activity. The deadliest myth of all, and one that never truly died, was that the Jews had killed Jesus. This enormous lie, accusing the Jews of deicide, was so prevalent across the ages that, even in the twentieth century, Jewish students, taking scripture lessons in enlightened schools, would have to suppress the urge to leap to their feet and protest that it was not their people who were responsible for the death of Christ.

1

As the centuries passed, there was no let up in the scapegoating of Jews. They were used as catspaws and then discarded, even put to death, when their usefulness ended. They were harried and murdered by Crusaders en route to Palestine to fight the Saracens, and for sport. On the whim of rulers, they were incarcerated in ghettos, and expelled from countries where they had lived for generations. In the Iberian peninsula, they were burnt at the stake for refusing to convert to Catholicism. They were subjected to malicious anti-Jewish laws, pogroms, and physical and verbal abuse. They endured an endless flood of anti-semitic literature in every European language. They suffered so many humiliations, it was not surprising that deep in every Jew's psyche lay the longing that one day the Jewish people would be able to live a normal life in their own land, free of fear and apprehension.

This yearning was found in every Jewish family throughout the world. At gatherings to celebrate the festival of Passover, the final toast of the Seder night services, commemorating Moses' leading the Hebrew slaves out of Egypt, was, 'And, the next year in Jerusalem'. The toast was proclaimed with the most heartfelt emotion. My father, who fled from Polish pogroms at the turn of the century, would shake his head and say sadly, 'It's a pipe-dream. When? Where? How? Forget it.'

As Jews repeated the toast during the 1930s and '40s, the end of the awful odyssey was near. For young Jews, if not for the still cautious and even servile elderly Jews with their appalling memories, the walls of Jericho were within sight. The coming of the Messiah would not take the form of an old, venerably bearded man with a charismatic appeal and the eloquence of a Shakespearean actor, but as young men and women carrying guns, driving tanks and flying warplanes.

Historically, Jews have always taken up arms to defend their countries of birth or adoption. Yet, this has never protected them from anti-semitism, whether intellectual, as in France, brutal, as in eastern Europe, or psychopathically beyond the pale, as in Nazi Germany.

After the 1914-18 war, many Germans, unable to accept that their much vaunted military machine had been defeated, blamed German Jews for having stabbed the country in the back – a difficult feat for the 22,000 killed fighting for the Fatherland. In Britain, also after the First World War, ugly murmurings needled Rabbi Michael Adler DSO, SCF, BA into compiling *The British Jewry Book of Honour*, a four-inch thick tome published in 1922 and listing the community's 9,000 casualties and tally of 1,596 decorations, including five Victoria Crosses.

There were very few instances of Jews in the diaspora forming their own units. The first recorded was in 1794, when Berek Yoselovitch formed a Jewish regiment in Poland as part of General Tadeusz Kosciusko's army to overthrow the oppressive overlordship of Russia. This fought in Polish uniforms, and under the Polish flag. Most of its officers and men were killed trying to contain successive Russian attacks. The survivors went home to endure the Poles' endemic hatred of the Jews.

Jewish longing for a National Home has always been a buried seed waiting to germinate. It needed an inspiration to fertilise it. In France, in 1894, that miracle happened. It arrived in the shape of a young Hungarian Jewish journalist, Theodore Herzl, who was covering the Dreyfus trial for a Vienna newspaper.

Although Jews enjoyed full civil rights, France then was a country in which anti-semitism was rife. It broke the surface with a splash when Captain Albert Dreyfus, a Jewish officer on the General Staff, was found guilty of espionage and was sentenced to life imprisonment on the dreaded Devil's Island. His conviction set off a flurry of anti-semitic articles in the press. Fortunately, however, there were some Frenchmen who thought something about the affair stank. Among these was the famous novelist, Emile Zola. He took up the cudgels on Dreyfus's behalf and penned his famous piece, 'J'accuse'. When it was printed in *L'Aurore*, all hell broke loose as France split into those who damned the Jewish traitor, and those who were convinced of his innocence.

Then, out of the blue, the real traitor, Major Ferdinand Esterhazy, walked into a London newspaper office and confessed his guilt. Even then, the French government was reluctant to reopen the case. Too many prominent people had been involved in the murky business of false accusation. But five years later a new government ordered a new trial. Again the court, part of the establishment, condemned Dreyfus; later, quietly, the court's findings were set aside. The president pardoned the Jewish officer, and Dreyfus was reinstated into the French army.

The trial of Dreyfus affected Jewish minds as nothing else had. It struck Herzl, the young journalist, like a flash of lightning. Until then, he had considered the assimilation of Jews as a viable solution. Suddenly the ground shifted under his feet. He became completely obsessed with the future of the Jewish people, and he saw that the only real solution was the establishment of a Jewish National Home. From that moment, all of his energy and efforts were concentrated on achieving it. He travelled ceaselessly, seeing anyone and everyone who was prepared to listen. Amazingly, these included presidents, politicians, the pope, the sultan of Turkey, as well as countless Jews, from the influential upper crust to the lowliest worker. He wrote pamplets, the best known of which was 'The Jewish State', and a book, *Old-New Land*. Herzl and his growing band of supporters called themselves 'Zionists', and in 1897 he convened the first Zionist Congress in Basle, Switzerland. The Zionist movement was officially founded. It proclaimed a single aim – the establishment of a legally secure homeland for Jews in Palestine.

Herzl worked tirelessly and literally burned himself out in his endeavours to realise his dream. He died at only 44; 7,000 people attended his funeral on 7 July 1904. Among them, following the cortege, was the famous author, Stefan Zweig, who wrote:

> This gigantic outpouring of grief from the depths of millions of souls caused me to realise how much passion and hope this lone and lonesome man had borne into the world through the power of a single idea.

It could be argued that Herzl was as great a leader of the Jewish people as Moses who led the Hebrew slaves from Egypt to freedom in the Promised Land. Over 2,000 years later, Herzl established that this same Promised Land had to be the new Jewish National Home, and he founded the movement that united Jews to achieve this goal. Furthermore, he persuaded them that they could and would achieve it.

In 1905 the Tsar's troops crushed a revolt in Russia and vicious, widespread pogroms followed. Disillusioned Jews, with no bread to eat nor a kopek in their pockets, decided to leave Russia. Herzl's Zionism now proved its worth. It gave them direction, a sense of where to go. Between 1905 and 1914, some 35,000 made the trek to Palestine. They burned with the zeal of pioneers and planned to create a socialist paradise. They were desperately poor, inured to hardship, and ready to work their fingers to the bone to build new lives for themselves. They settled on land purchased for them by the Jewish Agency. They found the going harsh. From sunrise to sunset and beyond, they drained swamps and cleared desert of stones and scrub. They dropped from heatstroke and malaria. They died of exhaustion and malnutrition. A doctor advised a young Polish student to return to Europe or he would die. That student, David Ben-Gurion, ignored the advice, and forty years later became Israel's first prime minister.

In 1909 Tel Aviv was founded on the dunes of Jaffa beach. Kibbutz Degania was built. Herzl's dream was becoming reality. The two vital ingredients needed to make a country are land and the people to work it. Until the First World War, Jewish colonising in Palestine took place with Arab cooperation. Arab effendi and landowners sold their land to the Jewish Agency, demanding exorbitantly high prices for what they considered barren areas – and to their gratification they were paid.

Inevitably the determined efforts of the settlers meant they began to enjoy a standard of living denied their Arab neighbours. New orchards produced fruit and olives. Well planned irrigation systems and good husbandry saw grass grow on new soil. There were cattle, chicken runs, and a range of produce. But the settlers were sniped at. Their vehicles were ambushed. Those required to work in the open carried rifles along with their spades and sieves. The *Hashomer* (watchmen) erected tall observation towers manned round the clock, and encircled the settlements with barbed-wire stockades. Here lay the beginnings of what would one day develop into the powerful Israeli armed forces. In the late 1930s, the British introduced legislation to reduce the sale of land. But still the Arabs sold and the Jewish Agency bought, and European refugees and idealistic Zionists from the western democracies and South Africa continued to trickle in.

In 1914 war broke out. Jews in the countries involved donned their national uniforms and fought alongside their fellow citizens. The Tsar, however, took it into his head to accuse the Jews of disloyalty. Thousands were deported to Siberia. Few returned. Palestine Jews felt an affinity with Britain and the Allies, and offered to form Jewish units to support them. Their offer was turned down. A leading writer and orator, Vladimir Jabotinsky, refused to accept the Allies' denial of a Jewish regiment to fight the Turks. Later, he swung to the extreme right and founded the Zionist Revisionist Party. An energetic dreamer with a cause, Jabotinsky sat down at a meeting with other Zionist leaders in Egypt in March 1915. Among these was a Russian Jew, Joseph Trumpeldor, who had lost an arm fighting for Russia against Japan in the war of 1905. He had been awarded the Gold Order of St George four times for gallantry, and had been taken prisoner by the Japanese. He was killed in 1920 defending the kibbutz of Tel Hai.

At that meeting in March 1915 Trumpeldor displayed his forceful personality. General Maxwell of Cairo HQ Staff would not accept Palestine Jews as fighting troops because they were foreign and not Empire nationals, though he was prepared to use them as a mule corps, for specific purposes. All the delegates at the meeting turned down this suggestion, declaring that they did not wish to join a donkey battalion. Trumpeldor took a different line. With passion he declared, 'On which front we start is a matter of tactics. Any and every front leads to Zion. We have to smash the Turks.' He prevailed and the Zion Mule Corps (ZMC) was formed. With 737 volunteers, mostly Russian Jews who had been expelled to Egypt, it was equipped with twenty horses and 750 pack mules. The men had rifles, bayonets and ammunition. For three weeks before embarking for Gallipoli, they underwent intensive training. Their commander was Lieutenant-Colonel Henry Patterson DSO, a tall and elegant veteran of the Boer War. He was of Irish Protestant origin, and immediately established a sympathetic rapport with his men. He even fought against unfriendly attitudes in high places to secure for them kosher food and matzo (unleavened bread) for Passover.

On 15 April 1915, the ZMC on HMT *Dundrennon* approached Cape Helles at the extreme southern tip of Gallipoli. Under intense enemy artillery and machine-gun fire they landed and went straight to work. They were officially classified as a line-of-communication unit. Two hundred mules were unloaded at W Beach, and the others at V Beach. Then they were continuously in action under fire supplying the line troops with food, water and ammunition. On one occasion, terrified mules with their chains clanking panicked and careered into Turks creeping forward for a surprise attack. This alerted the British, who halted the attack with intense fire. On 5 May Private M Groushkowsky exposed himself under fire to prevent his mules stampeding. Although wounded in both arms, he delivered his ammunition to the trenches. General Stopford personally awarded Groushkowsky the Distinguished Conduct Medal.

Three days later the ZMC reached the Inniskilling Fusiliers with supplies as they, depleted in numbers by many casualties, prepared for a counterattack. The ZMC fixed bayonets to their rifles and, led by Corporal Hildesheim, joined in the charge. On 20 May the ZMC suffered losses – men killed and wounded, horses and mules – under intense Turkish artillery fire. Private Nissel Rosenberg brought his laden mules through to the front line under intense fire and was recommended for a DCM and promoted sergeant. Sergeant-Major Erchkovitz was awarded the DCM.

By the end of July the ZMC was down to half its original strength owing to casualties and sickness. Over a hundred mules had been killed. On 25 July Patterson and Trumpeldor sailed for Egypt, and in the main Cairo synagogue raised 150 volunteers for the Corps. They were referred to as the Cairo troop of the ZMC. By now, news about the ZMC had aroused great interest among Jews everywhere and generated pride that they were performing so well. Patterson recorded that he had received dozens of letters from senior officers testifying to the fearless work of his men. On 29 November Patterson had to be evacuated to Alexandria with an illness that laid him low. Trumpeldor was appointed CO in his place, was wounded by a bullet in the shoulder, but refused to be evacuated and stayed with the ZMC until it was pulled out in January 1916.

In Egypt the ZMC were told that they were to be ordered to Ireland to help to quell a revolt. To a man they refused, declaring they had joined up to fight Turks not Irish patriots. The ZMC was disbanded.

Patterson, whose name is still revered in Israel, fought like a tiger to secure for the ZMC its name, Star of David badge, and flag. It is suggested that his resistance to the views of higher ranking army prejudice did his career no good. The ZMC soldiers volunteered for one simple reason. Most had been driven from Palestine by the Turks, and wanted to help defeat them so as to be able to return to their homes and farms.

Enter another remarkable Jewish patriot, Dr Chaim Weizmann. Born in Pinsk, Russia in 1874, he was a brilliant chemist who lived in England during the First World War. In 1916 the British army in France faced a serious crisis. It ran short of shells and, during battle, they had to ration the number they fired. This led to higher casualties and a dangerous situation for the British. The shortage was partly due to the drying up of supplies of acetone, essential in the manufacturing of explosives.

Weizmann was called upon to help. He speedily discovered a new formula for producing acetone cheaply and in large quantities. His was such an important contribution to the war effort that Britain offered Weizmann anything he wanted. Payment? Honours? Anything. He refused them all. Instead he asked that, if Britain regained control of Palestine, Jews should be allowed unlimited immigration into that land. This led to James Balfour, the British Foreign Secretary, sending a letter to Lord Rothschild on 2 November 1917, which read:

> His Majesty's Government view with favour the establishment in Palestine of a National Home for the Jewish People, and will use their best endeavours to facilitate the achievement of this offer.

This was the famous (or infamous to Arabs) 'Balfour Declaration'. Would the British keep to it? – perhaps the wrong question. Would Britain be able to keep to it? As it happened, the pressure of events that kept the cauldron of the Middle East at boiling point turned the once desirable mandate of Palestine into a poisoned chalice. Who could then foresee the rise of Hitler and Nazism in the 1930s, and the devastating genocide of European Jews?

Meanwhile, that ferociously dedicated dreamer of a cause, Jabotinsky, was in England. He was the moving spirit behind the formation of Jewish volunteers into an infantry unit that became the 38th Battalion of the Royal Fusiliers. Many were immigrants who could barely speak English, although they were fluent in two, three or even four other languages. They were commanded by a British officer. Jabotinsky pleaded for the soldiers to be allowed appropriate Jewish insignia on their uniforms, but he was turned down.

Early in 1918, from a large reservoir of Jewish volunteers, another battalion was raised in the United States. They underwent training in Nova Scotia, and were transported to Palestine where they fought as the 39th Battalion of the Royal Fusiliers. Persistence by the Jewish Agency nudged Britain into allowing a third battalion to be raised. But behind-the-scenes procrastination meant it did not reach the front before the war ended. This became the 40th Battalion, Royal Fusiliers.

The 40th was made up entirely of Palestine Jews. They were Jews working Jewish land and, in their eyes, defending it against a Turkish enemy. Flying their own flag was to them of paramount importance. On 30 June an extraordinary incident underlined their condition of bondage. On the eve of their departure for Egypt, the 40th Battalion assembled outside the main synagogue in Tel Aviv. Amidst great enthusiasm, Weizmann presented them with a large Jewish flag, sewn by the women of Tel Aviv. Of course, the Battalion could not fly this flag in place of the Union flag, but the event brought closer the inevitable day when Jewish soldiers would be able to fight under their own flag.

With the war over, the Balfour Declaration was incorporated into Britain's charter for administering its mandate in Palestine. Arabic, English and Hebrew became the country's three official languages. Arab landowners continued to sell land to their one and only customer, the Jewish Agency, at ridiculously inflated prices. The Agency knew that every square metre would be needed, and that the immigrants, both the penniless refugees and the idealists, would be ready to break their backs to make things grow.

Then a new factor emerged. Those selling the land started to worry that the evident increasingly high standard of living enjoyed by Jews would start to give their poor Arab neighbours ideas above their station. Furtively, but unambiguously, they began to add their voices to those of Arab politicians speaking out against the Balfour Declaration.

Throughout the 1920s Jews immigrated to Palestine. These were mainly the destitute hewers of wood and drawers of water who had left Europe and its endemic anti-semitism behind. But increasingly, they were joined by a new breed of idealistic Zionist from the western democracies. Many of these came from comfortable middle-class families who were well educated and came on *aliyah* (emigration to the land of Israel) through sheer conviction. They joined the conventional farm villages (the Moshavim) and the socialist collectives (the Kibbutzim), and mucked in with a will to help build up what was now their new country. They were often the first to pick up rifles to repel Arab attacks.

In the twenties the United States passed a bill severely curtailing immigration from southern and eastern Europe. This came as an unexpected blow to middle-class Russian and Polish Jews who had decided to make a new life in America. Instead they made their way to Palestine, bringing with them many professional and artisan skills. Education was always one of the top priorities, and in 1924 the Israel Institute of Technology opened in Haifa. A year later, Lord Balfour opened the Hebrew University on Mount Scopus.

By 1930 there were 250,000 Jews in Palestine. The Histadrut (General Federation of Workers) had developed a labour economy with its own network of institutions to cater for the needs of the Jewish working class. It became a bedrock of stability with its health schemes, trade schools, cultural centres, theatres, newspapers, and sports facilities.

In 1929 Sir Herbert Samuel, the first professing Jew in the British cabinet, was made High Commissioner of Palestine. His first act was a mis-cue. He appointed Mohammed Amin El Husseine as Mufti of Jerusalem. The Mufti was a virulent Jew-hater, and, until the British expelled him some time later, he never ceased to stir up trouble against the Yishuv. He was helped in this by the widening gap between the Arab *fellahin's* (peasants') standard of living, with its use of traditional tools and a general acceptance of their lot, and that of the Jews who were reaping the benefits of industriousness and access to modern farm machinery.

Within months the Mufti announced that the Jews had destructive designs on Moslem holy places, and in August 1929 Arab mobs launched attacks against Jews in Jerusalem. Violence spread. Attacks were made on Jews in Haifa, Tel Aviv and Jaffa. In Hebron seventy Jewish men and women were killed. In Safed eighteen were killed and scores wounded. Settlements and farms fought against heavy odds and British troops had to restore order. Politically, the British response was to appease the Arabs by whittling away at the Balfour Declaration. The Jewish response was an immediate strengthening of the Haganah. Passions ran high, and in 1931 the Jabotinsky-oriented right wing split away to form the Irgun Zvi Leumi.

Elsewhere, other forms of pressure were building. In Germany, the Nazis opened the first concentration camps, passed a string of anti-Jew laws, and made the persecution of German Jews legally acceptable. Life for them went from bad to worse. On 15 September 1929 the Reichstag at Nuremberg legalised racial hatred. Now, if a German wanted to beat up an elderly Jew, verbally abuse him, or throw fire-bombs through the windows of his home, he knew the law would be on his side. Germany had slipped back into the dark ages and anti-semitism was given full rein.

For Jews Germany had become dangerous, a hell on earth. The smell of death was everywhere. Those who could got out. Between 1933 and 1937 some 170,000 German and Austrian Jews reached Palestine, legally and otherwise. Every skill was represented, giving a tremendous boost to the Yishuv. Many would become soldiers in the Jewish Infantry Brigade.

Palestine became a land of erupting turbulence. The British were in a no-win situation. They tried to appease the Arabs by promising to clamp down on Jewish immigration. But the Yishuv went from strength to strength. More and more settlements and towns were established and expanded. Food production was well into surplus. The new immigrants set up manufacturing plants and provided much needed services. In 1937, in a desperate ploy to satisfy both Arabs and Jews, the Peel Commission proposed the partition of west Palestine into a small Jewish, and a larger Arab state. Acutely aware of the plight of their co-religionists in Europe, the Jews accepted the plan, but the Arabs rejected it and kept up their attacks on the Jews.

Into this cauldron stepped another remarkable character, Charles Orde Wingate. A British army officer, he was a slight man with unbreakable and unusual convictions. He was a Christian Zionist and a keen student of the Old Testament. He firmly believed that the Jews were 'People of the Book' who had a mission to establish their own Homeland in Palestine. He was astonished by the pro-Arab bias of his fellow officers. While some were attempting to master Arabic, none was bothering to study Palestine's other language, Hebrew. Wingate set about learning to speak and read Hebrew, and he made many Jewish friends along the way.

When Wingate learned that the Arabs had a penchant for after-dark sniping at anyone or anything that moved in the Jewish kibbutzim, he asked to be allowed to train special night squads of Jews to tackle this problem. And, although he was considered rather odd by his fellow officers, his request was granted. By now, word of his genuine interest in the fate of the Jews had spread, and he was trusted by them. He was well received when he visited settlements. When he asked for volunteers in the Haganah for his night squads, he was overwhelmed by the number of young men who, tired of defending, longed to have a chance to attack the marauders. In time, those who joined Wingate came to worship him.

His enthusiastic recruits learned quickly and learned well. The night squads achieved such success against the Arab raiders that the marauding stopped. However, when Wingate put in his reports, they were read by higher authority and then buried. His glowing testimonials to the courage, discipline and fighting qualities of the settlers unnerved the top brass at GHQ. In 1940, when a Jewish Infantry Brigade to serve with the British forces was proposed, the Jewish Agency asked for Wingate to lead it. This optimistic request was turned down with a thump. Later in the war, Wingate was killed in an air crash in Burma. His name is revered in Israel. He raised morale in the Yishuv by showing the Jews that they were not without friends in a hostile world and, that when they had their own army, they had the calibre to make it the best.

During the last years of the 1930s, the cauldron of Palestine bubbled away. Arab attacks on Jews waxed and waned. Over four hundred Jews were murdered in random acts of violence between 1937 and 1939. Arab extremists captured police stations and, in October 1938, they held the Old City of Jerusalem, all except the well defended Jewish quarter. The British drove the Arabs back out of all the areas they had gained. In mid-1939 the Arab revolt petered out when Prime Minister Neville Chamberlain made it known that Britain would have to appease the Arabs lest they side with the enemy when the now inevitable war broke out. The flame that kept the cauldron bubbling was the issue of Jewish immigration.

The noose around the neck of European Jewry was finally tightened in 1939, when Britain and France signed a pact with Adolf Hitler. Effectively this signed their death warrant. European Jews knew it; Jews worldwide knew it. The rest of the world knew it too, yet they closed their borders against a dreaded influx of Jewish refugees. Here and there the consciences of the more sensitive appeared to be pricked. US President Franklin D Roosevelt convened an international conference to discuss ways of saving European Jews. The conference, held at Evian-les-Bains, was a total failure. The delegates spent a pleasant week wining, dining, playing tennis, dancing and sightseeing – all this while the Jews whose fate they were supposed to be discussing were being dragged from their homes, incarcerated in concentration camps, and murdered.

On 9 November the world washed its hands of the problem. Britain announced the abandonment of the plan to partition Palestine. Instead Jews and Arabs were invited to a conference in London. They came, the Arabs refused to sit down with the Jews – no talks, no agreement.

Jews, wherever they were in the world, now knew of the tragedy befalling their co-religionists in Europe, and that they had no way of helping them. Only in Palestine was the impulse to help translated into action. The newly formed Mossad mounted an operation called Aliyah Bet. Its task was to save as many European Jews from the Nazis as possible, and bring them to their National Home. Young men and women of the Haganah set out for Germany, Austria and Italy, to find Jewish men, women and children and bring them to the ports of southern Italy where they would be put onto boats, many decrepit and unseaworthy, for the hazardous voyage to Palestine. The Jewish Agency provided the funds for the hire or purchase of the boats. Many did reach the Holy Land. But others foundered and their passengers drowned. Some were intercepted by the British navy and turned back. In the final few months of peace, Aliyah Bet safely delivered some 15,000 souls into the welcoming embrace of the Palestine Jews.

In 1939 Malcolm McDonald, the British Colonial Secretary, published a white paper. Intended to satisfy Arab demands, it severely restricted the sale of land by Arabs to Jews. Jewish immigration into Palestine would be restricted to 10,000 a year for five years. After that, any further influx would require Arab agreement. But a fourth stipulation was, for Jews, the most ominous. It stated that an independent Palestine state, with strong links to Britain, would be established within ten years.

Immediately Jews were up in arms. The white paper went against everything set out in the Balfour Declaration. There were mass demonstrations in towns, villages and kibbutzim. A general strike was called. The hitherto moderate Haganah now attacked government railways and installations. The Arabs, on the other hand, felt that the white paper did not go far enough. At the time, the British had no inkling that, eight years later, they would be forced to give up the mandate and quit Palestine, lock, stock and barrel.

With the outbreak of war on 3 September 1939, all regional conflicts were overshadowed. The Jews never doubted that they would give their allegiance to Britain and the Allies, but the white paper had angered and confused them. David Ben-Gurion cleared their minds with his famous advice:

> We will fight the white paper as if there is no war and fight the war as if there is no white paper.

# Chapter Two

When World War II broke out, Palestine roasted under a fierce autumn sun. The 500,000-strong Jewish community wondered what part Britain would allow them to play against the Axis powers. In every other major war, Jews had fought other Jews, each in the uniforms of their respective countries. But in this war, Jews everywhere wanted only to take up arms against the German and Austrian Nazis. This was especially true of the many Jews in Palestine who had escaped the lethal clutches of Nazism, but had left their next of kin behind. With the outbreak of war, they knew their families would not now escape to freedom. They were under no illusions and dreaded the fate that awaited them. Consequently they made up a large proportion of those Palestine Jews who registered in September 1939 to fight with His Majesty's forces. But they never imagined that, for the next four years, British diplomatic priorities would deny them the right to confront in combat the murderers of their people, under their own Jewish flag.

Nothing about the Palestine diplomatic whirligig was ever straight-forward or less than complex. Some leaders of the Yishuv (the Jewish Homeland and its citizens) were so outraged by the immigration white paper that they voted against Jews joining the British forces. Others were more pragmatic and long-sighted, and realised that every volunteer who was accepted would receive valuable military training and experience. They had set their hearts on a Jewish force fighting under the Jewish flag. They argued that it would increase resolve in the national consciousness, and they were determined to make it happen.

Britain at this time could not contemplate ever giving up its mandate in Palestine. And if the need to appease the Arabs meant allowing the enthusiastic availability of Jewish volunteers to go by the board, so be it. So, although the British continued to oppose the creation of a Jewish fighting force, the Agency never let up in its promotion of the idea. On 29 August Dr Weizmann wrote to the British Prime Minister:

Dear Prime Minister,
In this hour of supreme crisis I wish to confirm the declarations
that I and my colleagues have made during the last months, that
Jews stand by Great Britain and will fight on the side of the

12

democracies. We wish to do so in a way entirely consonant
with the general scheme of British action and place ourselves
in matters big and small under the co-ordinating direction of
His Majesty's government. The Jewish Agency is willing to
enter in immediate arrangement for utilising Jewish manpower,
technical ability and resources.

The Jewish Agency has recently had differences with the
Mandatory Power. We would like this difference to give way
before the more pressing necessities of our time. We ask you to
accept this declaration in the spirit with which it is made.

On 2 September 1939, the Prime Minister replied as follows:

Dear Mr Weizmann,
I should like to express my warm appreciation of your letter of
the 29th August. It is true the differences exist between the
Mandatory Power and the Jewish Agency as regards policy in
Palestine, but I gladly accept the assurances in your letter. I
note with pleasure that when those things we hold dear are at
stake Britain can rely on the whole-hearted co-operation of
the Jewish Agency. Your public spirited assurances are welcome
and will be kept in mind.
Yours sincerely,
Neville Chamberlain

And that was that. In fact, Britain's resolve to achieve a lasting settlement
with the Arabs was set in concrete. Whitehall, GHQ Middle East in Cairo,
and the Palestine administration had a mortal fear of antagonising the
Arab world by raising an identifiably Jewish fighting force. This was a
mistake compounded by historical and personal bias. The Jews were too
thrusting, too clever, untrustworthy. The Arabs on the other hand
understood the rules of the game. A garrison here, a few bombs dropped
there soon brought them into line.

In spring 1941, when Britain was fighting the Axis powers alone, and
was stretched to the limits, the Mufti of Jerusalem and Hitler's puppet,
Rashid Ali, called for a holy war against Britain. His revolt in Iraq was
quickly crushed. But the lingering 'Lawrence of Arabia syndrome'
tempted the British to over-egg the military prowess, and even the
glamour of the Arab, and fed the bias against the more down-to-earth and
unimpressionable Jew. And the Agency's offer to raise a Jewish fighting
force to support the British war effort continued to be rebuffed.

In Britain, however, there were those who took a different view to that
of the Arab-oriented mandarins. Among the most prominent was
Winston Churchill, who never ceased to deplore the War Office's refusal

to accept the offer of a Jewish fighting force. On 12 February 1940, in the House of Commons, he proclaimed:

> They are our only friends in Palestine. The sound policy for Britain would be to build a strong Jewish force in that country. We should then be able to use elsewhere the large and costly cavalry force due to replace the eleven battalions locked up in Palestine. It is extraordinary that, at a time when the war is emerging into its most dangerous phase, we should station in Palestine a garrison one quarter the size of the garrison in India.

The attitude of the Palestine administration towards the country's Jewish community bordered on the paranoid. This manifested itself in a fierce clampdown on the reporting of news of Jews aiding the war effort in any way. The ultimate absurdity was the recruitment of Jews in their National Home on the grounds that they were not Jews, but Palestinians. No credit could be given to the Jewish community for any successful military action against the enemy. Information about the Agency's recruiting office, and the 120,000 volunteers signed up was ruthlessly suppressed.

In his book, *The Forgotten Ally*, published in New York in 1943, Pierre van Passen wrote that the best kept secret of the war in the Middle East was the contribution made by Palestine Jews. Ultra-strict censorship had seen to that. In September 1940, Weizmann had a private luncheon with Churchill, by then Prime Minister, in Downing Street. Weizmann offered the services of a Jewish division of 10,000 men, 4,000 from Palestine, the rest from elsewhere. America was an untapped reservoir of young Jews eager to join the fight against Nazism. Churchill accepted Weizmann's offer, and it was agreed that, after training in the UK, the division would be transported to the Middle East. Weizmann went away a contented man, and in February 1941 he was introduced to Major-General A Hawes, who had been chosen to command the division.

The Jewish Agency had asked that Orde Wingate be appointed to command the Jewish division, but the War Office knocked this idea firmly on the head. Suddenly Lord Lloyd, who had been Colonial Secretary and implacably opposed to the formation of a Jewish unit, died. He was replaced by Lord Moyne, but he too, influenced by Generals Wavell and Barker, followed the Lloyd line. On 15 October 1941, the War Office informed Weizmann that there was no prospect of his offer being taken up, and cited a shortage of equipment in explanation. Weizmann, a man of complete integrity, took this vapid and dishonest excuse hard. In Palestine, Jewish leaders such as the pugnacious Ben-Gurion became even more determined that the Palestine Jews would have their own army and their own country.

Because of his close association and rapport with the Palestine Jews,

Wingate had been posted out of the way to Abyssinia (now Ethiopia). But he was still anxious to hear news of what was happening in the Holy Land. In a letter to his cousin, Sir Reginald Wingate, one-time High Commissioner in Egypt, he wrote: 'I have seen young Jews in the settlements. I tell you they provide a better soldiery than ours. We have only to train them.'

Wingate's pro-Jewish stance was a constant irritant to the pro-Arabists, especially the military top brass. But the war's voracious appetite for personnel forced reluctant hands. Early in 1940, Cairo GHQ authorised enlistment for the Auxiliary Military Pioneer Corps. Its officers would be British; the soldiers would be classified as colonials, and would wear the Palestine shoulder flash on their uniforms.

At first, the Palestine government ordained that Jews and Arabs must be recruited in equal numbers. This unrealistic condition was quickly dropped. As the ratio of those enlisted was on average six Jews to every Arab, parity was unachievable. Also, the majority of the Jews had come from Europe and were still frantic with worry about their families, and so were extremely keen to fight the Nazis; the Arabs had a rather different attitude. There was an unbridgeable gulf between Arab and Jew, in temperament, tradition, language and culture.

The first Pioneer Unit to be formed was around ninety per cent Jews, fit young men who wryly referred to themselves as 'pick and shovel warriors'. The unit was quickly despatched to Europe to join the British Expeditionary Force in France. British army training and discipline stood them in good stead, and during the great retreat they were issued with rifles and ammunition for use when the occasion demanded. As many had previously been members of the Haganah Defence in Palestine, they needed no instruction in how to use these. Several Pioneers were lost during the retreat to the French coast, but most managed to reach St Malo, from where they were safely evacuated to England. They were then very quickly shipped via the Cape back to Egypt.

The Jewish Agency now let up in its requests for Palestine Jews serving in HM forces to be allowed to wear their own identifiable shoulder flash and Jewish emblems. The first reports of the systematic slaughter of Jewish men, women and children in Europe were beginning to reach them, and nothing seemed as important as helping the Allies to defeat the Nazis and win the war as quickly as possible. And reports of the Pioneers' achievements in France strengthened the view that the more Palestine Jews there were serving with the British forces, on land, at sea, or in the air, the more effective the Jewish fighting force of the future would be.

In the late summer of 1940, the Battle of Britain began. RAF ground personnel were hastily recalled from the Middle East to Britain, and were replaced by 1,700 Palestine Jews. They quickly demonstrated their competence in all the essential tasks – engineering, mapping, vehicle and aircraft maintenance, medical services, driving, and guard-duty against damage and pilferage at airfields and the docks. They were later to serve in other theatres of war. In moments of crisis, when Britain needed something, British and Haganah leaders continued to meet. Fifty young Jewish men and women, members of the Haganah, were parachuted into the occupied Balkans on espionage and sabotage missions. As they had all once been nationals of the countries into which they were dropped, none had any problem with the local language. Fewer than half survived the war.

Young settlers in northern Palestine, also Haganah members, crossed the border into Vichy Syria and spent several days mapping out the lie of the land. Then, they led the Allied forces in an attack on the pro-Axis Vichy forces, establishing an excellent rapport with the Australian troops who followed them. During this campaign, one young officer was wounded. He lost an eye and, ever afterwards, wore a black eye patch. This became the world famous trademark of Moshe Dayan who, as a general in the Israeli army, helped to mastermind Israel's victory over Jordan, Egypt and Syria in the Six Day War of 1966.

German-speaking Jews volunteered for commando operations in the Western desert. They went into action with outfits such as Popski's Private Army, an audacious search-and-destroy unit led by the Polish Colonel Popski. Dressed in captured Afrika Korps uniforms, they used their fluent German to lull and then kill bored German sentries guarding selected targets.

The Palestine government's attempts to suppress news about Palestine Jews on active service were becoming farcical, not to say desperate. Words such as 'Zionism' and 'National Home' were censored in the local press. On 30 July 1941, Mr Lipson MP asked the following question in the House of Commons: 'Does His Majesty's government still adhere to the policy of establishing a National Home for the Jews?' Prime Minister Churchill replied: 'There has been no change of policy with regard to Palestine.'

Censors in Palestine deleted reports of this exchange from both the local and the imported British press. In 1941 a Palmach (strike force) unit was formed with British officers. The NCOs were a mixture of British and Palestine Jews. All other ranks were Jewish. This fact was erased from all reports. Meanwhile the Arabs, not at all concerned about Jews fighting alongside the Allied forces, were content to watch Nazi successes spell the end of British and French dominance in their region.

Back in Britain, the anti-Jewish prejudice of the War Office and Cairo GHQ did not go unnoticed. In November 1941, a truculent editorial in *The Times* claimed that there was no evidence that the Arabs objected to the raising of a Jewish fighting force outside Palestine. The *Manchester Guardian* chipped in, declaring that there was no justice in refusing to let Jews have their own identifiable fighting force when Churchill had reaffirmed a policy of establishing a National Home in Palestine. A parliamentary committee, chaired by Colonel Victor Cazalet, campaigned ceaselessly for the raising of a Jewish combat division.

In 1937 a young English Jew, Wellesley Aron, had suggested to General Wavell that when, not if, war broke out with Germany, it would be wise for factories and workshops in Palestine to be geared up to produce the equipment that would be needed by the British forces in the Middle East. He pointed out how much shipping capacity would be saved. Wavell, convinced that war was inevitable, passed the idea on to London. The Jewish Agency sent Aron to London to put the idea to Hore Belisha, the Minister of War. Himself a Jew, Belisha in turn referred the proposal to the Palestine High Commissioner, Sir Harold McMichael. Although McMichael was cold towards the suggestion, Wavell was more clear-sighted and endorsed the plan. When war broke out, small factories across Palestine were producing much needed equipment and spares for the Allied forces.

Aron was a tall, lean, remarkable man with a quiet but forceful way of getting things done. He gained a degree at Cambridge, and in 1926 went to Palestine where he taught English at the Gymnasia Herzlieh in Tel Aviv. What he saw won him over to Zionism. He made his mark, impressing Dr Chaim Weizmann, then President of the World Zionist Organisation, who asked him to go to London to be the Organisation's Political Secretary in Holborn.

One of Aron's main tasks was to interest young English Jews in Zionism, and to encourage them into Aliyah (emigration to Palestine). Things got off to a slow start. Jewish parents were not keen to see their sons and daughters, destined for university and the professions, go instead to Palestine to break stones and dig ditches. Aron visited the boys' clubs at Cambridge, Brady, Stamford Hill, Oxford and St George's, Hackney and West Central. It was a difficult mission. He reported back that the boys were only interested in sports, social activities, table tennis, and girls. Charles Rubens, a South African who had taken Aron round the clubs, suggested he hold back on Zionism and instead talk to the boys about Jewish history and culture. But Aron was single-minded and would have none of this. His heart was set on a Jewish National Home in Palestine. Then he came up with a novel idea. He was an admirer of Baden Powell's Boy Scouts movement, and decided to form a Jewish equivalent, and he would imbue its members with the ideal of Zionism.

So, Aron founded the Habonim (Builders) Movement. He designed a uniform consisting of khaki shorts, navy stockings, and a navy blue shirt with a breast-pocket badge depicting a pioneer beneath a palm tree with his rifle and spade. He wrote the Habonim handbook which set out the Movement's ideals, with emphasis on aspirations, rules of conduct, and

Zionism. Mainly due to Aron's unflagging enthusiasm, the Movement was up and running by the early thirties. The rise of Hitler, and Nazism's increasing power and anti-Jew laws boosted the attraction of the Zionist ideal. Habonim opened branches in major English cities, such as Leeds and Manchester. The early recruits found themselves giving up western comforts and, after working on farms and going through agricultural college, were now heading for Palestine. Having got things off the ground, Aron returned to Tel Aviv with his wife and child, and a cheerful, energetic Londoner, Joe Gilbert, took over. Right up to the outbreak of war, a steady flow of young British Jews emigrated to the farms and kibbutzim of their new country.

Back in Palestine, Aron helped to set up the Tel Aviv Hospitality Committee, which promoted a much needed understanding between the British forces and the Jewish community. On 7 October 1939 Aron himself enlisted in HM forces, becoming the first Palestine Jew (as he saw himself) to be commissioned in the British army, as a second lieutenant in the RASC (Royal Army Service Corps). A friend, South African-born Harry Joffe, duly became the second Palestine Jew to be similarly commissioned in the RASC. Very quickly Aron won a reputation for never giving less than 150%. In his book, *Wheels in the Storm*, a Foreword by Major-General Paul Cullen CBE, DSO, Commander of the Australian Infantry, states:

I first met Wellesley Aron in Haifa in 1940 when he was a captain in the RASC of the British Army. He was very British, correct and very clear in his mission in life – to bring about the creation of a Jewish state. His loyalty to Britain was absolute. He saw no divergence in that and his dream for Israel. He put into his war effort, with its dual aims, all the energy of two ordinary men. I next met him in Tobruk when still with the Australian 6th Division. We had just captured it and his Jewish RASC Company was working wonders. Later I learned of the prodigies of his valour and achievement with inadequate improvised means before and during the defence of Tobruk. He was untiring and inspiring. He was a practical and achieving idealist.

Herzl, Jabotinsky, Trumpeldor, Weizmann, Ben-Gurion, Moshe Sharret, the Sabras (Palestine-born Jews), and the immigrant Nazi-haters were all putting their weight behind a future that promised both hope and pain. The first three did it by example. For the others, a growing sense of security and of their increasing military prowess spurred them on. Aron was at the cutting edge.

Circumstances and perhaps a touch of common sense were conspiring to create a tacit accommodation between the Jewish Agency, Cairo GHQ, and the Palestine government. The administration kept up its frantic suppression of any news about Palestine Jews fighting alongside the forces; the Agency, for its part, kept quiet about Jewish servicemen serving under their own flag, and with their own distinctive shoulder flashes and emblems. It saw more and more Palestine Jews being sucked into service with the British armed forces, and being trained in the skills of modern warfare. The tide was running their way. The Palestine government had dropped the idea of Jews and Arabs serving in the same units. Whereas Jewish recruits filled the cadres as soon as they were created, the British instructors complained that they had to wait weeks before they had a sufficient quota of Arabs.

Aron was posted to 285 Company RASC at Sarafand in the autumn of 1940. He reported to the CO, Major Babcock RIASC. The intention was to turn 285 Company into a Jewish unit, and over a period of ten weeks, 500 English drivers were replaced by Palestine Jews at the rate of fifty a week. Aron was then ordered to take a course in weapons training. He qualified after six weeks and reported back to the company. When he arrived he found 500 Palestine Jewish personnel learning to drive, and handle and maintain magnificent new 10-ton diesel lorries.

Apart from one Jewish sergeant, Moshe Caspe, and a sprinkling of lance corporals, all the NCOs were British. Tempers frayed in the sweltering heat as the NCOs' orders were not obeyed because of linguistic misunderstandings. Aron cracked down on this problem immediately – essential commands were learned and given in Hebrew and English by all.

Thirty selected drivers from among the Palestine Jews were given intensive training and became NCOs. The fastest learners were given a crash course in English, and later became officers and senior NCOs.

On 27 December 1940 the entire company, apart from one section, was ordered to Egypt, driving via the Sinai desert. Corporal Ben Chanoch (later to become a captain in the Jewish Brigade) telephoned Dov Hos, a prominent member of the Federation of Jewish Labour. Dov arrived and, during a short but emotional ceremony, he handed over to the company the first Jewish and British colours to be awarded to a Jewish unit in World War II. Major Babcock, the company commander, entered into the spirit of the occasion, and thanked Dov Hos for his interest in the unit. As the convoy of 150 vehicles headed south, the Jewish settlers of Rishon-le-Zion and Rehovoth lined the road and cheered their own troops on their way to war.

On 1 January 1941 the company was ordered to Suez to clear the docks of a mass of equipment. Valuable experience was gained, manoeuvring large Leyland and Foden trucks through the narrow, twisting streets. But Aron noticed a depressing change. While they were on their own, the atmosphere became more relaxed; military smartness and discipline dropped away, and what remained was a collection of Jewish drivers wearing British uniforms. Accidents became more frequent. Kit was lost, and tents were left untidy. The privates even argued with their NCOs. Aron realised that, if this situation was allowed to continue, the raising of further Jewish units would be jeopardised. Not mincing his words, he slammed into the men, reminding them that how they performed should set an example to be admired and respected. His angry words hit home, and there was an immediate return to smartness, discipline and punctuality. The men buckled down, and within three weeks were ready to go into the desert on active service.

Aron was summoned to Cairo where he was told that a new unit, the Palestine Motor Transport Works Services Company, was to be formed. And it was to proceed immediately into the Western Desert. The new CO was Major W A Belk. Aron requested the transfer of his whole section, still at Suez, and this was agreed. The next day, his D Section drove into Cairo, and a delighted 280 Palestine Jewish drivers moved into the lines of the newly formed company. Equipment and arms were drawn. Four British officers, a regular army sergeant-major, corporals and technical NCOs arrived. On the following day, the senior RASC officer commanding at the Abbasia barracks in Cairo inspected the company. For the first time, a company made up entirely of Jewish other ranks paraded in full marching order. The colonel's satisfaction at their smart turn-out was passed on to the men. As a result of Aron's uncompromising outburst at Suez, they never slacked again.

In the same week, the British corporals were promoted sergeants and put in charge of sections. Selected soldiers became corporals. Major Belk ordered Aron to put up his badges of captain's rank right away, and Aron became his second-in-command. The unit was ordered to catch up with the British advance on Tobruk, and the men, exhilarated at the thought of meeting up with the German enemy, sang and danced the *hora*. But the British officers and NCOs were uneasy. They felt themselves attached to an inferior colonial unit, and wondered how their men would acquit themselves in action. However, their fears diminished as the men's competence at driving, handling and maintaining their vehicles became evident. All ninety vehicles reached the crossroads in Tobruk, but here the first men were lost, with four killed in an air raid.

Tobruk was a shambles. Rubble and ruins were everywhere. The soldiers found a badly damaged synagogue which, with the help of Jews serving with various Australian infantry units, they managed to clear out and partly repair. And local Jews, who had hidden and survived, joined in. On their first Friday there, they held an evening consecration service, attended by the soldiers of the company and Jews serving with other Allied units. This was the first of many such emotional evenings, when liberating troops could express their sense of responsibility for the well-being and safety of their less fortunate co-religionists. In Derna they found 500 Jewish men, women and children and offered their protection as long as they were there. Captain Wellesley Aron fully supported his men in this, and a pattern was established. Whenever Palestine Jewish soldiers moved into liberated towns and cities, they made it a priority to meet the needs of their wretched and emaciated co-religionists.

Unexpectedly, the unit was ordered to hand over its ninety vehicles. This came as a blow to the men who were told to find replacements from among the hundreds of abandoned Italian vehicles littering the desert. They found Lancias and Spas and cannibalised them in a large workshop. Twenty Italian motor mechanics were roped in to help repair and make roadworthy some 150 vehicles. Many drivers dared to paint the blue and white Jewish flag, with the Star of David centred, on wings and doors, but no British officer or NCO objected. Palestine Jew and Briton had developed a mutual respect and pride in their company.

During the siege of Tobruk, which began on 13 April 1941, the men became seasoned veterans. Despite bombing, shelling and strafing, they shuttled between the docks, loading their trucks with stores, ammunition and rations, and delivering them to various sectors of the perimeter. On many occasions, armed with four old Lewis machine-guns, captured Breda light and heavy machine-guns, and a Fiat quick-firer, they played an active role in the defence of Tobruk. And it was here that the first meeting between Jewish soldiers and captured Germans took place.

Sergeant Giladi, who was from Vienna, explained to the Germans that the Shields of David emblems on their vehicles indicated that these were Jewish soldiers. One German asked:

'Are those hard-faced, tough men really Jews?'

'Yes,' replied Giladi who was later promoted captain.

The Germans stood to attention and said, 'All honour to you.' Giladi walked away. He had been born in Vienna and escaped to reach Palestine before war broke out. He was worried sick about his parents and sisters, and could only fear the worst. Later, he discovered, as so many did, that the worst had happened. The last thing he wanted at this confrontation was a friendly exchange with a man he hated.

An English sergeant told Aron that some of the men who had escaped from Nazi Germany and Austria were worried about being taken prisoners-of-war. He suggested that they be taken to Sollum before the escape route was cut. Aron refused. Nothing would be allowed to undermine morale, but he was of course aware of the wider Palestine Jewish scene. The barrier to Palestine Jews seeing active service was crumbling at a satisfying pace. By early 1941, the 1039 Port Operating Company, with British officers and Palestine Jewish soldiers, was ensuring the smooth transfer of vital war supplies to where they were needed. A sapper unit was operational in Egypt. Commando 51 was in Eritrea, and fought well at Kern. However, the news was not all good. In the disastrous Greek campaign, 1,500 Palestine Jewish stevedores and sappers were taken prisoner at Kalamata, and in May 1941, 170 Palestine Jews were captured in Crete.

In Palestine, the British miltary top brass, and the administration were still managing to keep reports of the Palestine Jewish community's war effort out of the Middle East media. The Jewish Agency by now regarded this farcical cover-up with amused resignation, no longer worth bothering about. The war would last for a long time. Jewish combat units, fighting under their own flag and wearing their distinctive shoulder flashes, would continue to be a major requirement, and every Palestine Jewish volunteer accepted for active service weighed the scales in favour a little more. So did the glowing reports coming in of Aron's company's conduct under fire.

# Chapter Three

Sometimes, on special occasions, an intense feeling of Jewishness welled up. During the siege of Tobruk, Squadron Leader Israel Brodie, Senior Jewish Chaplain to the forces in the Middle East, visited Aron. He stayed with him in his dugout for a week. During this time, Brodie toured the perimeter, taking air strikes and shelling in his stride, as he visited the Jewish Anzac soldiers in the front line. They gave him letters and messages which he promised to get to their families. On Friday night, in the wadi occupied by Aron's men, Brodie conducted a most moving outdoor service. Soldiers from the Anzac and other armies, including a few from British units, were present. There were a couple of naval ratings, and surviving local Jews. Above, steel-helmeted soldiers kept guard as artillery roared and Stukas dive-bombed. The congregation stood its ground, and at the end sang a fervent rendering of the Jewish national anthem, Hatikvah (The Hope). When the congregants dispersed, they did so in silence, each man immersed in his own thoughts and emotions.

Before Tobruk was completely encircled by the Afrika Korps, drivers from the Motor Company moved Jews out of embattled areas such as Benghazi, Derna, Barce and Tobruk to Egypt, where they handed them over to welfare organisations. This misuse of military vehicles in a war zone could have merited harsh punishment. But the culprits got away with it. They were protected by most of the officers, NCOs and soldiers knowing about it, and supporting the rescue of endangered Jewish civilians.

On 23 April 1941 Major Belk was ordered back to Egypt to take up an appointment at base. He had been a popular commander, particularly sympathetic towards his soldiers' fears and concerns about their families left behind under Nazi occupation. He was proud of the way they had performed, which he made clear in a farewell speech. He appointed Aron major and company CO, although Aron was still the only Jewish officer. Later the same month, Aron reported to Fortress HQ and was ordered to take command of No. 6 Motor Transport Company, sister company to No. 5 MT, which he had left in Tobruk. Harry Joffe, who had joined up with Aron and who was also now a major, was given command of No. 5 MT Company. On 22 July, after seven months in battle, the now seasoned No. 5 Company was evacuated from Tobruk by the Australian destroyer, HMAS *Stuart*.

23

During the great retreat before Rommel's advancing Afrika Korps which ended on the borders of Egypt, Aron and his No. 6 MT Company were in non-stop action. They often found themselves driving west, against the flow of the British retreat, taking explosives and demolition gangs to the forward positions. On the return journey they would pick up stragglers who had become separated from their units and who had resigned themselves to capture. On one occasion, they found a hundred British lorries immobilised along the roadside, having run out of petrol. Each truck in the Motor Company always carried a surplus of filled jerrycans. With these, they were able to refuel the stranded vehicles.

Meanwhile, back in Palestine, minds were concentrated by the possibility that Rommel would sweep through Egypt to the Suez Canal. With German troops in the Caucasus, the threat of a German pincer movement snapping shut on Palestine became real. Until now, the Palestine High Commissioner, Sir Harold McMichael, had stubbornly adhered to the policy of parallel Jewish and Arab recruitment to all Palestine units. GHQ Cairo became increasingly exasperated by this restriction on the recruitment of skilled Palestine Jews at a time when HM forces in the Middle East needed technical personnel more than ever. Unlike the politicians with their biased views, the military had to be pragmatic. And the latter were constantly being reminded by London, especially Winston Churchill's office, that the only available source of local trustworthy manpower was the Palestine Jewish community. Consequently, training depots at Sarafand expanded considerably during 1941, and the intake now included Jewish girls joining the PATS (Palestine Auxiliary Territorial Service).

In 1940 Palestine Jews had suddenly been permitted to enlist in all-Jewish companies. These were attached to the East Kent Regiment (the Buffs). By the end of 1942, fifteen such companies had been raised. They made up three infantry battalions in the newly established Palestine Regiment. Most of the officers and NCOs were British. Other ranks were mostly Jews, with a handful of Arabs. At first the Palestine Regiment was confined to Palestine, where they lacked proper equipment, and were mainly deployed on guard duty. This was a state of affairs which inevitably led to disappointment, a lack of motivation, and trouble. In 1943 they were shipped out of the way to Cyrenaica (a former province of eastern Libya), and Egypt. But here too they lacked equipment, were assigned to heavy guard duties, and chafed at not being given proper combat training, and a chance to fight the enemy. The ranks included intellectuals and high-ranking professionals, who were very aware of the political situation. This awareness made their sense of frustration worse. What they could not know then was that the day when they would join combat under a Jewish flag was just round the corner.

It was in December 1941 that a Palestine Jewish unit had reached

Benghazi. This was No. 5 Water Transport Company, which was destined to become an ancillary unit in the force that would come to be known as the Jewish Brigade.

Major Aron took a long leave in Palestine, during which he met Moshe Shertok of the Jewish Agency, and Joshua Gordon. Gordon was a feisty young Russian Jew who emigrated to America and immediately enlisted in the Judean Battalion that went to Palestine and fought under General Allenby during his 1917 campaign that drove out the Turks. The three men decided to oppose the Jewish labour leaders, who did not want any more Jews to join HM forces on the grounds that the Yishuv was not a populous community and could not afford to be drained of its best young men and women.

The argument put up by Aron and Shertok was that every Jew had the right to fight against Adolf Hitler. Gordon was a sick man and, against medical advice, he plunged into an intensive recruitment campaign. Several weeks into the campaign, he collapsed and died in the hotel room he was using as his headquarters.

During 1941 Nos 5 and 6 Palestine Motor Companies were expanding, and were replacing British NCOs, and to a lesser extent officers, with Palestine Jews. Aron persuaded Pinchas Rutenberg, Chairman of the Palestine Electric Corporation, to release twenty-four bright young men who were likely to make senior NCOs and officers in the RASC. All exceeded expectations, and by the end of the year Hebrew was supplanting English as the principal language in communications and in the mess. By the end of March 1942, both PMT companies had undergone a radical change. Virtually all the NCOs were Palestine Jews. Some were sent to training centres to instruct new recruits.

Tobruk was holding out. But the Afrika Korps was consolidating its territorial gains and advancing eastwards. The Palestine Jews, many European-born, were preoccupied by horror stories seeping out of Nazi-occupied areas – the Babi Yar massacre, the growth in size and numbers of the death camps, the extermination experiments on Jews in specially designed gas wagons, the mass shootings of Jewish communities in captured towns and cities, and so on and on. Their very inability to help their suffering brethren filled them with guilt and anger.

To assuage their bitterness and agitation, Aron and Joffe arranged for their men to be given weapons training. During the ensuing quiet weeks in the Western Desert they learned to handle a variety of modern arms. This was an astute move by the two generals, and the enthusiasm engendered by the handling and firing of weapons restored an esprit de corps. The day when they would have a chance to open fire on Nazis seemed much closer.

Although Cairo GHQ did not ease the ban on the flying of the Jewish flag, it was nevertheless flown, along with the RASC flag, by both Motor

Transport companies on ceremonial occasions. To the British, this was the Zionist flag; to the troops, it was the Jewish flag – a distinction the British could not comprehend. Not all Jews were Zionists, but every Jew wanted a National Home to take in the needy and the persecuted. The Star of David was painted on many vehicles alongside divisional insignia. British officers and NCOs attached to Palestine Jewish units quickly developed a rapport with, and understanding of, their men. And some, especially those who had been in action in the Western Desert and at the siege of Tobruk, became quite proud of their company's emblem.

The end of April 1942 saw Rommel's invigorated and reinforced Afrika Korps push Cunningham's and Auchinleck's armoured forces east towards Cairo. There, GHQ was calling for more recruits. The Jewish Agency supplied them. They underwent intensive training and were quick learners. They were soon despatched to join the two RASC companies, and Major Aron's unit became 178 GT Company, while its offshoot became known as GT Company No. 468. Under an English commander, Major Wallis, it left for the Canal zone, spent one year in Palestine, and then met up with Aron's company in Malta. From there it went to Italy, and eventually became part of the Jewish Brigade. Joffe's company became No. 179, while its offshoot was designated GT Company No. 462.

The two units afforded scope for many a promotion. Bankover's promotion to Armoury Sergeant-Major was followed by that of many lance corporals and corporals to sergeant, and of privates to corporal. Among the new intake of NCOs and other ranks were a number of well trained and experienced members of the Haganah. As David Spector, who was later to be a brigade-major of the Jewish Brigade, told me when I visited him in his Jewish care home in Brighton in 1995, many of the Brigade's lower ranks were not quite what they seemed to be. When the Brigade finally saw action against the Germans, they fought like tigers. But it was apparent that they were there to fulfil a hidden agenda in preparation for when the war ended, and perhaps even before. As David put it:

> It was best not to ask them questions, so we didn't. As part of the British Eighth Army they were smart, highly disciplined and raring to get at the Germans. So, tacitly, we went along with the cordon sanitaire they erected between us.

Intensive field training under Sergeants Eliahu Cohen and Evitza became de rigeur. Live ammunition was used. New recruits to all units were flung into training as soon as they arrived.

In June the Afrika Korps captured Tobruk and advanced to El Alamein, where it was stopped, right on the Egyptian border. At the same time Germany launched a new offensive in the Caucasus. Increasingly the threat of the German 'pincer' on Palestine looked real. Many Egyptians spoke of welcoming German troops into their country as liberators from British rule. The Jewish Agency learned of secret British plans to evacuate the Middle East and set up a new defence line in India. If this happened, the Yishuv planned to withdraw all Jewish forces into a fortress area based on Haifa, with Mount Carmel as its southern bulwark, where they would stand and fight. Where else could they go? What else were they to do? There was no alternative. It would probably all end with another massacre of Jews, but at least the Germans would be given a bloody nose.

The situation was grim, but the two Palestine RASC companies rose to the occasion. Along with other Palestine Jewish units in north Africa, they set about collecting arms and equipment, and covertly transferring them to Palestine. Here, it was hidden in hundreds of small caches on kibbutzim and farms. Even if British searches unearthed a few, there would still be plenty left to fight with.

Aron and a coterie of his officers and NCOs were up to their necks in acquiring and smuggling arms. Although it invited terrible retribution from High Command, the gamble had to be taken. Motor traffic across the Sinai Desert to Palestine increased. One day Sergeant Cohen returned from Palestine with a radio. It was linked directly to Haganah HQ in Tel Aviv. In most Palestine units, the quartermaster-sergeant was a Haganah man, and each proved to be a key figure in the arms-smuggling operation. As word of the British plan to fall back to India circulated, Jewish soldiers acted instinctively in the interests of defending their community.

Crates, falsely marked with regard to their contents, were loaded on vessels to Aquaba, where they were put onto fast trucks and driven north to the Holy Land. They were met at specified destinations and swiftly unloaded. Trucks were fitted with false floors and forged papers were provided to conceal what was being carried, and to ease the passage through checkpoints. Sergeant Yehihal Taiber and his men accumulated a substantial quantity of captured arms and put them onto trucks at Geneifa. The trucks were handed over to Sergeant Israel Carmi, a tough, daring, German-born immigrant, who had taken part in several commando raids in the Western Desert, and who was also a senior Haganah officer. With papers showing that the shipments he and his trucks carried were for German-speaking commandos being trained at Mishmar-Ha Emek, he delivered them to a kibbutz, where they were quickly squirreled away by the settlers.

Major Aron visited Cairo GHQ where he was known and respected. He persuaded them to release surplus Italian machine-guns, revolvers, grenades and ammunition to 178 Company for 'familiarisation' use. The next day, Captain A Silberstein and Sergeant Arieh Miller led a small convoy of trucks to Alexandria to load up the Italian weapons. Five days later they were being unloaded by the Haganah in Palestine. Whether

Cairo GHQ knew, or even suspected, what was going on is not known. The Palestine Jewish soldiers' performance had earned respect and sympathy among many British personnel. No doubt British officers and NCOs in the RASC units turned a blind eye.

It was at this time that instructions were received from GHQ that all Palestine troops were to wear the Palestine shoulder flash. The Jews were disgruntled. They wanted to wear a distinctive flash carrying the word 'Jewish'. But orders were orders.

In October 1942 Montgomery launched his successful offensive at El Alamein. A build up of troops and armour in the Eighth Army was driving a demoralised Afrika Korps back east. Panic among Egyptian Jews subsided. And among the Egyptian population, ill-concealed jubilation at the prospect of the British being gone as colonial masters died away. The Yishuv in Palestine breathed more easily. The smuggling of arms into Palestine stopped as the GT companies were called to arms again.

Aron's 178 Company was moved into the mobilisation centre at Tahag, and given new vehicles and equipment. But there was a problem. During its long stay at Qena, the company had posted many of its seasoned NCOs back to Sarafand and other bases to train new recruits. Aron needed to get back into the desert quickly to support the victorious Eighth Army. He plugged the gaps through instant promotion from other ranks, including some from the new intake. In the event, they all turned out well.

In November 1942 an event of no real importance occurred, yet it had tremendous psychological repercussions among Palestine Jewish soldiers. A group of exchanged prisoners of war reached Palestine, and described what they had witnessed in the death camps. This was a turning point in a true understanding of the Holocaust. When the war finally ended, Jewish soldiers fighting in the British, Empire and American armies would be demobbed and would go home to their families. But the Palestine Jews who had fled the Nazis would never be able to go back to where they were born, and the likelihood of their seeing their families again was very slight. British officers and NCOs understood the men and their subdued grief. When, in defiance of orders from Cairo GHQ, the men painted their newly adopted unit insignia on their vehicles, no objection was raised. This light-blue disc, with a white Star of David centred, was painted above the radiator, on the doors and on the tailboard.

Now 178 Company sped west to catch up the rapidly advancing Eighth Army. They drove right up to the edges of the action, with stores, rations, water, and ammunition, returning with prisoners of war and salvage. Post-battle debris lay everywhere. Sometimes they returned with salvaged trucks, from both sides, on which they loaded empty oil drums filled with small arms ammunition. Captain Y Sacharov, who later commanded 468 Company in Malta and Italy, oversaw the operation during which these trucks unloaded their cargoes at farms and kibbutzim in Palestine. Supporting the Eighth Army's advance towards Cappuzzo, 178 Company met up with its sister companies, and learned that they too were engaged in smuggling arms to Palestine. As the advance moved west, and the distance to Palestine increased, the smuggling operation became more difficult.

One afternoon, Brigadier Glover, the officer commanding all the RASC units in support of the Eighth Army, paid 178 Company a visit. He complimented Aron on the orderliness of its convoys, and over lunch discussed the policy of fully integrating the Palestine units into the British forces. He said to Aron, 'If you want a Jewish unit to do its best in the field, you must encourage pride of race. In your case that must be Jewish nationalism.' Unknown to him, the well-intentioned Brigadier was preaching to the converted.

With Rommel in full retreat before a jubilant, tails-up Eighth Army, the Palestine RASC units were at full stretch, running supplies to the moving front, and taking back prisoners of war. The tide was turning in Russia. Germany herself was pounded daily by Allied bombing raids. The steady build-up of the Allied invasion force for Europe was gathering momentum. The sweet smell of victory was in the air. Beside a lake in Benghazi, Aron and other Palestine Jewish officers and NCOs discussed the problems they would face when the war ended.

At this time, there was one gentile British officer who repeatedly asked to remain with 178 Company. His name was Lieutenant Ewen. He liked the men and they liked him. He painstakingly learned to speak Hebrew. At Aron's suggestion, Ewen asked the Church of England padre to all Christians in the Palestine units if he would agree to hold a Christmas service in the field. The padre was happy to oblige. On the eve of the Jewish Sabbath, he dined in Aron's officers' mess. He was charmed by the traditional lighting of candles, and the recital of the 'Kiddush', and he expressed his appreciation of the meticulous cleaving to tradition amidst all the turmoil of the hectic advance.

On Christmas Day 1942, with just one Christian officer in 178 Company, the men decided to give Lieutenant Ewen a treat. Mess Corporal Lucasz, a Hungarian Jew, produced a small Christmas tree, decorated with cotton-wool snow, sweets, and candles. On it were gifts from Ewen's fellow officers and NCOs. He was so affected by the gesture, that when he attended church parade at Eighth Army HQ, he could not stop talking about it.

Over four months, 178 Company clocked up some 250,000 miles, taking supplies up to the forward areas of the advance, as far as Tripoli, when it fell to the Allies. The Palestine RASC companies earned a reputation for dependability and running on time, just like the most efficiently run railway service. In Benghazi, where it was based for several weeks, the company reopened Jewish schools, synagogues, and other institutions despoiled during occupation by the Afrika Korps. Drivers and skilled mechanics from various Palestine units set to to repair them, and academics among the troops were soon giving lessons to Jewish children. They picked up Hebrew very quickly, and told the soldiers that they wanted to go to live in the Land of Israel after the war. Aron noticed that, of all the many nationalities of Jews in the unit, the Hungarians found it most difficult to get their tongues round the Hebrew language – even those fluent in several other languages.

It was here, in Benghazi, that the post-war settlement of needy and rootless Jews was given a concrete foundation, a little noticed, but crucial factor, which led on to great events. A new constitution of the Benevolent Fund was drawn up to embrace all serving members of the Palestine Jewish forces. Its aim was to give succour and support to every Jewish man, woman and child they came across. In a secret poll among serving soldiers, 90% wanted membership. Every officer, NCO and soldier pledged one day's pay per month to the Fund. Furthermore, in this work of salvation, all members had equal rights and responsibilities. All Palestine units, however big or small, and wherever they found themselves, were notified, and one by one they all affiliated to the main scheme.

Before they left Benghazi, 178 Company arranged for Jews in other forces – British, Empire, and South African – to carry on their work teaching the children. The pattern was set and, when the north African countries expelled their Jewish communities after Israel won the 1948 War of Independence, the Yishuv were agreeably surprised by the excellent Hebrew spoken by youngsters from Benghazi and other places.

At Passover, in 1943, 178 Company reached Tripoli on the eve of the festival. Rabbi Rabinowitz had gone ahead and arranged a Passover Seder night in an Italian farmyard. The chosen location was surrounded by green fields and orchards. For the first time, Palestine Jews came into contact with American Jewish soldiers. The service was attended by large numbers of South African soldiers and airmen, British Jewish officers and other ranks, and a sprinkling of other nationalities. Among the congregants was Marcus Sieff of Marks and Spencer, who was Port Movement Control Officer in Tripoli at the time. The service closed with the singing of the British and American national anthems, followed by the Hatikvah. Services like these always made a big emotional impact. As one American tank trooper said to a 178 Company corporal, 'It's strange. I feel more at one with you guys than with my own buddies. Singing Hatikvah got to me. The last time I sang it was at a bar mitzvah in Chicago and it was nothing like this.'

After the service, groups of soldiers of different nationalities smoked and chatted. The Palestine Jews told the others of their efforts to save their co-religionists. They all knew that when they went to Europe, they would find many in great distress and in need of help. So far as military discipline would allow, they were determined to do everything they could for these unfortunate souls.

When civilians spotted the Jewish flag and emblems in 178 Company's trucks, they stopped the drivers and told them where they could find Jewish families in need of help, especially food. The soldiers always responded immediately. As a result of one lot of information, the company came across some 300 Jews from Benghazi interned in a concentration camp twenty miles south of Tripoli. Who knows what fate awaited them at the hands of the Germans, but had the Allies not advanced so rapidly, they would almost certainly have been put to death. The company drivers took them home.

In February 1943 a stevedore company of Palestine Jews arrived at Tripoli. They were told about the rescue work being undertaken by other units, and willingly joined the salvation network. The Jewish Agency was aware of what was going on, and had already drafted what became known as the Law of Return. This stipulated that any and every Jew seeking sanctuary in the Land of Israel would be accepted and made welcome. One day their services would be needed. The Agency was never under any illusion.

In May 1943 tragedy struck. 178's sister company, No. 462, embarked for Malta. The ship carrying it was struck by an aerial torpedo off Benghazi and was sunk. One hundred and forty-eight perished. In the military cemetery on Mount Herzl in Jerusalem a memorial was erected bearing their names. The news spread gloom among their RASC comrades. Almost at once 178 Company embarked for Malta. It reached the island in the first troop convoy to arrive there since the blitz when the island had won the George Cross..

The company welcomed the opportunity to settle down and rest in one place. Spit and polish, which had disappeared in the desert except on special parades, reappeared, and a proper NCOs' mess was established. Their sister company, GT 468, replacing the devastated GT 462 Company, now joined them. The two Palestine units enjoyed mixing and relaxing in each other's messes. Vehicles were thoroughly overhauled, painted and made ready for whatever lay ahead.

Major Aron went to Palestine on leave. En route he stopped in Cairo, where he dined privately with Brigadier McCandish of the General Staff. McCandish raised the issue of the drying-up of recruitment among Palestine Jews. Aron reminded him of the early days of the war when the last thing the British wanted was a Jewish force which they feared would antagonise the Arabs. Even though there were an estimated 30,000 plus Palestine Jews serving with the British forces in various theatres of war, McCandish was complaining about a lack of further recruits. Two reasons were suggested. Early in 1943, British police and soldiers had conducted unnecessarily aggressive searches of kibbutzim and moshavim for hidden arms. They caused gratuitous damage and manhandled those who objected. In protest, the Jewish Agency shut down the recruiting offices on 29 April. In addition, Yishuv leaders were expressing increasingly strong opposition to the steady denuding of their community of dependable young men and women. Over their meal, Aron suggested a third reason to McCandish:

'There is growing ill-feeling among the men. They want to fight under their own identity. They want shoulder flashes that have the words "Jewish Force" instead of "Palestine", and they want to fly the Jewish flag wherever they go.'

McCandish replied:

'To fly the flag would provide Jewish units with a status to which they are politically not entitled.'
'It is the status for which we fight. It is our right and one day will be ours,' Aron replied.

The two men did not part on the friendliest of terms. And there was another sore point. Palestine Jews wanted to engage in combat duties. They were disgruntled at being confined to acting as hewers of wood and drawers of water. By and large, British personnel who served with Palestine units developed a respect and liking for the Jewish soldiers, a feeling which was reciprocated. Aron had received several complimentary letters from the commanders of British units with whom they had been on active service in the Western Desert. Unfortunately, in Palestine, the government and civil service mandarins, as well as the police, displayed an arrogance that led to insensitive behaviour, spiced with the intrinsic antisemitism of their type and of the time.

The Mandatory authorities decided to search Jewish settlements for hidden weapons. The raids were carried out by the Palestine CID and police, backed up by military detachments. The heaviest raid occurred at Ramat Hakvesh, an isolated kibbutz on the coastal plain. It had already suffered several attacks by Arabs, and whatever arms the settlers possessed had been used in self-defence, and not to mount raids on Arab villages. Nevertheless, the British went over the top. A number of settlers, men and women, had been hurt, and buildings needlessly vandalised. Homes were damaged.

When the men of 178 and 468 Companies heard about this action, they were outraged. The normally placid and competent Sergeant-Major Bankover lived in Ramat Hakvesh. Seething with anger at the news that his family and friends had been roughed up, he went to Major Aron and stated that, unless an assurance was given that such a thing would never happen again, he and his men would go on hunger strike, and refuse to obey orders, regardless of the consequences. Aron hurried to see the officer commanding Fortress Malta, who was completely nonplussed. He heard Aron out in silence, then said:

'Does this mean that your unit threatens mutiny?'

'In the last resort, this could well be the case,' Aron confirmed.

'In that case I'll give orders for your entire lot to be put on a prison ship and sent back to Egypt.'

'Many of my lot travelled steerage and far worse to get to Palestine. The prospect of a prison ship would not change their view or the merits of the case,' Aron said.

A week later, the commanding officer informed Aron that there would be no repeat of the incident in Palestine. Aron expressed his thanks, and suggested that the companies would benefit from hearing a word from the CO. He promised to visit 178 Company, and after it had completed a weapons training course, he was as good as his word.

In July the Jewish Agency reopened their recruiting office. The 2nd Battalion, Palestine Regiment left for Benghazi, and in Palestine the 3rd Battalion was brought up to full strength. Within the year, the scattered pieces of the Jewish Brigade would come together to fight under the Jewish flag, and the long, long odyssey would be at an end.

# Chapter Four

During 1943 relations between the Yishuv and the British authorities in Palestine deteriorated, sharply towards the end of that watershed year. At the heart of the dispute, as always, was the Jewish demand for a Jewish army, based in Palestine, to protect its own community. The Yishuv wanted the Jewish units that were being formed to be the nucleus of their own army in what they regarded as their own country. The British strongly opposed any link between the Jewish units and Palestine. The once strict censoring of reports of a Jewish contribution to the armed forces had long since slackened. With Palestine Jewish units operating in various theatres of the war, it was in any case common knowledge. To the surprise and relief of the administration in Palestine, the Arabs did not care who or where the Jews fought, so long as it was outside Palestine.

Meanwhile, the volunteers in the infantry battalions were pressing to be sent to the front to fight the Germans. They were growing more and more resentful at being restricted to tedious guard duty. They became despondent and morale plummeted. Discipline suffered. When Jewish soldiers belonging to the Palestine Regiment were caught stealing arms from the British army in Palestine, their battalion, the 2nd, was shipped out to Cyrenaica, and the British decided to move all Jewish units out of Palestine. In September four transport companies were landed at Salerno. The map depot unit was sent to Bari, while the Loaded Light Artillery (LLA) battery was shipped to Cyprus. No. 739 Engineers Company was sent to Italy, and the third infantry battalion was thinned out, with many of its soldiers transferred to other specialised units.

In Benghazi the 2nd Battalion found themselves on the same type of guard duty they thought they had left behind in Palestine. They were allocated dull routine chores, and the likelihood of seeing action seemed as remote as ever. Agitation swept through the ranks, and on the eve of the New Year (Rosh Hashana), the men defiantly hoisted the Jewish flag for all to see. This was a serious breach of discipline, and the British imposed camp arrest on the whole battalion, and confiscated their arms. But then they relented, and the troops were put through a period of intensive training, something they relished. At last, they thought, they were to be sent into action. Not so. The British debated the battalion's future at length, the men grew despondent again and any motivation engendered trickled away.

In November 1943 the Jewish Agency officially renewed its demand for a Jewish fighting force under its own flag. The free world was starting to learn about the true extent of the genocide of European Jewry. International support of the right of Jews to avenge the murder of their people was gaining strength. The Agency now abandoned its view that a new army of volunteers should be formed. Instead, it began to consider the consolidation of existing units into one division or brigade with its own national identity.

On Christmas Day 1943, Aron's 178 Company sailed at dawn and reached Taranto, the southern Italian naval base, at noon. After disembarking, they proceeded north by platoon to a staging site on the road to Bari. Their experiences in the Western Desert and Malta, where the appearance of Jewish soldiers wearing the Palestine shoulder flash had so uplifted the indigenous Jews they encountered, had changed the men. Without exception, they now regarded their prime mission not as fighting the Germans, something they could do on auto-pilot, but as bringing succour and hope to any Jews they came across. The soldiers in their sister units felt the same.

In Bari, Major Aron got out of his staff car and walked slowly behind it. His vehicle sported the light-blue discs on its front wing, door and rear with, in the centre, the unmistakable Star of David. It was not long before an emaciated figure darted out of the crowd and engaged the driver, Corporal Kramer, in animated conversation. Both spoke perfect Yiddish. Aron and Kramer followed their excited new acquaintance down side streets and into a huge apartment in a large old building where he announced that Jewish soldiers from Palestine had arrived. Within minutes, Aron and Kramer were overwhelmed by men, women and children, excited, weeping, unable to take in what they were seeing and hearing. All of them were refugees from central Europe and the Balkans. There were deep emotions. Some clutched at Aron's and Kramer's uniforms as if they were mirages that would dissolve away.

Back at base, the redoubtedly pragmatic Sergeant-Major Bankover took charge. He went to the apartment and announced that all Jews were invited to a tea party that afternoon. The unit's cooks were soon making sand-wiches, cakes, buns and other treats. At teatime, four large trucks left to collect their civilian passengers. There was a poignant moment, when the refugees stood in groups staring incredulously at the 200 seasoned troops in battledress who welcomed them. Then, they mingled and tears flowed, among the soldiers as well as the refugees. One old man caressed a sergeant's shoulder flash, and said in Yiddish: 'You are ours, truly?' 'Yes.' 'We are now safe?' ' Yes . . . yes . . . yes!' Three times the soldier said 'Yes'. The old man burst into tears. The sergeant turned away. Surreptitiously, he drew a handkerchief from his uniform and dabbed his eyes.

At that moment, an indestructible bond was formed between the armed Jewish soldiers, battle-hardened in north Africa, and their wretched guests. Many sobbed uncontrollably as they recounted their harrowing, nightmarish experiences during the past few years. The soldiers assured them that they were now safe from the Nazis, and that they would be able to reach the Land of Israel and be free to begin to lead normal lives. The soldiers gave the refugees food and warm clothing. They also gave them back their self-respect, and something which they thought they had lost forever – hope.

No 178 Company was ordered to up stakes and drive to Foggia. Here they set up camp, and were immediately engaged in transporting equipment and stores to wherever they were needed, especially by the units fighting their way up the Adriatic coast. Foggia had sustained heavy damage from Allied air raids, and was filled with all manner of wretched and malnourished refugees. The emblems on the vehicles attracted keen attention as they passed through towns and villages. Whenever they stopped, Jewish refugees would approach the drivers, who would pick up the most desperate and take them to the base at Foggia, where they were given food, clothing and shelter. They were also given money to spend on the barest necessities. Many of the soldiers devoted all their spare time to helping the refugees, and the teachers among the soldiers gave lessons for the children. Every driver was given a form to carry at all times, and on which he noted the whereabouts of Jewish refugees.

After giving them essential initial care, psychological as well as physical, 178 Company transported the perked-up refugees south to Bari, and into the main and expanding receiving point. Here, other Palestine Jews gave them blankets, toiletries, and fruit and sweets which they bought with their own money for the children. This was the beginning of an organisation called Reshet ('the net'). It spread rapidly across liberated Italy, and later into Germany, Austria and the Balkans. It was the clandestine, humanitarian rescue of thousands of wretched souls in the depths of despair. Many had already committed suicide. The net hauled others from the muddy, lice-infected, guarded camps onto the long journey to a new life in a new land.

In February 1944 the Jewish chaplain at a nearby American Fifth Army air base visited Aron and told him he wanted to organise a religious service for the men. He invited Aron and his officers to attend a Friday night service for American airmen and soldiers. Aron accepted. During the meal, he told the Americans about 178 Company's work with Jewish refugees. Without ceremony, their American hosts pushed aside the Sabbath candles, and covered a large area with dollar bills. It was a spontaneous act of generosity which was to be repeated many times.

It had become bitterly cold in southern Italy. The area lacked coal and timber. For warmth, charcoal burners were installed, in messes, hospitals, administration buildings, and the soldiers' quarters. Meanwhile, the American Fifth Army and the British Eighth Army advanced north into *Festung Europa*. At the same time, the Jewish Agency, and Moshe Shertok in particular, started pressing the British again on the subject of a Jewish force fighting under its own flag. In their favour was a widespread recognition that the Holocaust was proving to be the worst case of genocide the world had ever known. Pressure from their own Allies was mounting on the British to allow the Jews themselves to get to grips with the Nazis. Meanwhile, all the units that it would take to form a Jewish division or brigade were already in action.

All units – 178 Company, No. 1 Palestine Camouflage Company, Royal Engineers, which was based at Luzera under the command of Major E Aronoff, 468 Company RASC, stationed at Barletta just outside Bari, and the Palestine Map Company, Royal Engineers, commanded by Major Z Beretz – did all they could to assist Jewish refugees, and plugged into 'the net'.

Aron and his fellow Palestine Jewish officer assured the refugees quite openly that they would help them get to a new life in Palestine. Such occasions were always highly charged. For many refugees, it was a miracle that they had survived this far. They had seen their families murdered, or brutally kicked into Wehrmacht trucks bound for liquidation. They had been betrayed by those they had considered friends and neighbours. They had been starved, hunted and systematically humiliated. Many were unable to speak about what they had been through. It was little wonder that an alarmingly high suicide rate continued. The soldiers were strikingly gentle with the refugees in their care, metaphorically raising their chins and straightening their backs, striving at all times to restore their self-respect.

One day, a small ship arrived at the Adriatic port of Manfredonia. On its short journey from Yugoslavia, it had been machine-gunned by German aircraft. The decks were strewn with dead and wounded. Aron ordered Captain I Gobernick to go to the ship with a field kitchen, food, stretchers, medical stores, and several men. Among the living, they found thirty Jewish men and women. Captain Gobernick was about to take these off when the British Military Police arrived on the scene, stopped them from being taken ashore, and ordered the ship to sail to Bari.

Aron travelled to Bari overnight, driven by his trusted Sergeant-Major Bankover. They reached the docks at dawn, and watched as the human cargo was brought ashore and loaded onto trucks. They watched as the miserable wretches were herded into a large, empty department store. A strong Military Police guard allowed no one in or out. Aron pondered what to do next. Bankover said, 'Leave it to me, sir', and somehow he managed to get into the store. The first person he found was a small, emaciated man shivering in a thin, patched coat. He told Bankover that he was a German Jew, and had been a lawyer. This man was bright, and rounded up thirty or so Jews, and told them to do exactly what the sergeant ordered. They obeyed, and somehow Bankover spirited them out into the street. How? Bribery played a part. That was all the resourceful Bankover would say about the matter. The Net took over the refugees' welfare, and Aron was informed much later that they had reached the Promised Land, and had settled down to work on the kibbutzim. As far as is known, the Military Police made no attempt to find them. But then, Bari was always full of drifters and refugees.

The soldiers found a considerable number of Jewish children in convents. The nuns had taken them in to save them from deportation to the killing camps. They had been looked after well. On a large, deserted estate outside Bari, the troops found an enormous house with innumerable rooms. Here, they looked after the children, taught them Hebrew, the principles of husbandry, and tried to restore their sense of stability, and their belief in themselves. In due course, the immigration underground put them on ships hired by the Jewish Agency, and they were able to rebuild their lives in Palestine.

The mortar that bound Jewish soldier and Jewish refugee was Judaic tradition. And emerging news of the Holocaust did more than anything to strengthen this bond. Allied Jewish servicemen, who never saw the inside of a synagogue at home, found themselves tugged back to the family fold by feelings bordering on guilt. Which is why, come festivals and high holy days, they attended religious services whenever they found them.

At Passover in1944, Jewish chaplains to the American Fifth Army and the British Eighth Army took over what had been a Fascist gymnasium in Foggia. It could seat a thousand. Palestine Jews decorated the walls with Jewish motifs. Long tables were laid the length of the hall. At the top table there were three large murals, depicting the Land of Israel, flanked on one side by a settler with his spade, and on the other by a helmeted soldier. News of this Seder night spread like wildfire. It would be the first Jewish celebration of an important festival since the Nazis overran Europe.

A senior American officer in the area, a brigadier, attended with his staff officers, as did hundreds of British and American officers and men, a large group from the Free French forces, and a number of Jewish Yugoslavian partisans, wearing their British uniforms and Red Star emblems. There were many Palestine Jewish officers and other ranks, as well as South Africans. And mingling with the soldiers were refugees, taut with suppressed excitement and disbelief. Just as Major Aron was about to open the proceedings, a large, noisy group of Fifth Army pilots and air crews poured in in their sheepskin jackets. They had just returned from a bombing raid on central Europe. This was a night that everyone who was there would remember for the rest of their lives.

In April 1944, 178 Company was ordered up the Adriatic coast to Vasto, a small town overlooking the sea. The retreating Germans had efficiently blown up all the bridges and culverts, as well as long stretches of the asphalt coast road. The bridges had previously carried traffic across the fast-flowing rivers and streams which ran downhill from the Apennine and Abruzzi mountains to the sea. For the first time, 178 Company used that ingenious, First World War, British invention, the Bailey bridge. This saved an enormous amount of time and labour. When the company reached Vasto, they found the Eighth Army was headquartered there. But the staff was greatly depleted by the recall of personnel to the UK in preparation for the coming invasion of Europe.

Aron found various Palestine Jewish units plugging the gaps. They included a sizeable contingent of PATS, Royal Army Ordnance Corps workshops, a signals unit, a field park, and other specialist units. He did the rounds and found that every unit contained members who were plugged into the Net, helping Jewish refugees to recover, body and soul, before they were moved to the ports, where they were put on to bucket ships bound for Palestine.

Inevitably, the British authorities had got wind of the Net's activities, all of which laid the operators open to charges of military indiscipline. Disapproving noises were heard, but there were no arrests, and no punishments. Certainly, the horror stories coming out of Europe about the systematic slaughter of Jews, and the international sympathy that it aroused stayed the justifiable closing of the military fist. When Moshe Shertok later returned from negotiations in London, at which the formation of a Jewish Brigade was finally conceded, he concluded:

> I believe we owe a great deal to the slaughter. For this small thing [the Brigade] we paid with the blood of millions of Jews. The British Cabinet was uneasy hearing people say accusingly, 'Millions of Jews were massacred. There are thousands of Jews who wish to fight and you don't allow them to fight.'

Nevertheless there was still uneasiness, and Aron attended a conference in Naples. Some dozen majors, captains, subalterns, and their senior NCOs attended. Some officers objected to getting involved in illegal activities. Others expressed fears that they would be sent back to Palestine or even court-martialled. There was understanding towards those who dissented. But they were asked not to blow the whistle, nor to impede those in their units who wanted to continue to help the refugees. Everyone agreed to this, and nobody broke his word.

By the end of July 1944, the Normandy invasion was well under way. No. 178 Company was ordered north to the port of Ancona, which was larger than Vasto. Debris was piled high, and bulldozers were working flat out to clear the approach to the docks. The company were at once employed carrying loads from the ships straight up to the forward areas as the Eighth Army advanced on Rimini. They set up their base on a hill south of Ancona, swiftly and smoothly, as befitted a unit that had now been working together for three years. All of the Bedford 3-ton trucks, which had been issued to them before El Alamein, were running smoothly. The unit enjoyed a well deserved reputation for reliability thanks to assiduous maintenance by Captain A Silberstein, his warrant officers, and mechanics. They were constantly on the lookout for spares from shot-up and abandoned trucks, and became experts at judicious scrounging.

One evening, a civilian came into the officers' mess and asked for Major Aron. He was short and dark, and spoke perfect Hebrew. He said that, apart from himself, three old women, and the rabbi's widow, there were no Jews left in Ancona. The late rabbi's synagogue had built up a valuable collection of books and documents which he had kept in his apartment. An Italian tailor had moved in and was using the apartment as a workshop. The rabbi's widow had been shunted off into one small room. The tailor had piled up ancient tomes to support his ironing board, and had ruined many by resting his hot iron on them. Could Major Aron stop this vandalism?

Aron went to the apartment and, just as he had been told, found many ancient, leather-bound books scattered about the tailor's workshop in various stages of disintegration. He then went to the office of the town's mayor, a tall, grey-haired man called Cohen. Aron grinned as they shook hands. It was not long before the rabbi's widow was back in her apartment, and new accommodation was found for the tailor. An American sergeant, who had been a librarian in New York, lovingly set about the task of restoring the damaged books.

The synagogue in Ancona must once have been a beautiful building. It still reflected the past glories of a Sephardic community, noted for its scholarship and learning. The men of 178 Company got down to clearing out the debris, repairing broken glass, restoring shattered woodwork, and cleaning and painting. They finished in time to allow the New Year and Yom Kippur High Holy Days services to be held in the synagogue. It was a mainly khaki congregation, with soldiers officiating and conducting the services. The joy and relief evident among the handful of refugees and the last few surviving Jews in Ancona lifted the hearts of the soldiers. It made them more determined than ever to get at the Germans, push them back, and rescue their co-religionists.

Minds were now turning from how the war was to be won to how to tackle the problems that would arise when it was over. Aron received a summons from Rome where he was to report to a Sir Clifford Heathcote-Smith of the Allied Control Commission at its HQ. This was a large, imposing building in the via Veneto. When he arrived, Aron found two men in khaki in an outer office. One of them, Mr Greenly, an American representative of the Jewish Joint Distribution Committee, was on edge. He said to Aron, 'Heathcote-Smith is no friend of ours.' 'Why not?' Aron asked. Greenly explained: 'He won't censor my reports on the plight of Jewish refugees in Italy. This blocks their despatch to the JDC office in New York.' He pressed a large envelope into Aron's hands, urged him to take it back to his unit, get it cleared by the censor, and sent to New York. Aron put the envelope in his document case, and went in to see Heathcote-Smith, who said:

> When the Allies break through the final German defences, we will find thousands of refugees in camps. We will provide you with a staff car and driver, and carte blanche to do whatever you think fit to get them moving back to their homes.

Unlike Heathcote-Smith, Aron had had many a conversation with refugees, and he knew that no Jew would return to what had once been his home. Henry Ohrenstein had survived four concentration camps and two death marches. At the end of the war, he did make his way back to his home town, Hubricszow in Poland. He had lost both parents, a brother and two sisters. Of the 8,000 Jews who had lived in the town, he found only five. The Poles who had taken over Jewish homes and property were worried that their righful owners might have survived, and would return to claim what was rightfully theirs. Ohrenstein was told that three Jews did come out of hiding in the forest and claimed their homes back. The Poles solved this problem by killing them. In his book, *I Shall Live*, Ohrenstein recounts how the Poles living in what had been his family home threatened to kill him if he did not go away. Later that day, he was sitting on a park bench, when he overheard a conversation between two middle-aged women. One said, 'At least Hitler did one good thing. He got rid of the Jews.' To which the other replied, 'Yes, but he should have finished them all off.' Ohrenstein got to his feet and walked away. He left Poland.

Never in a million years could a man like Heathcote-Smith have understood the impossibility for Ohrenstein and thousands like him to go home. Back with his unit, Aron wrote to Heathcote-Smith. He thanked him for dinner and his offer, but stated his intention of remaining with his unit. Aron was a man who did not change his mind. Far from sending refugees back to the nightmare from which they had escaped, his Zionist impulses made him determined to get as many of them as possible to Palestine and a normal life. And there was another factor – he was devoted to his men, and wanted to see the war out with them.

# Chapter Five

In July 1944 news leaked out that serious negotiations between the Jewish Agency and the British were under way. The rumour mills in the scattered Palestine units were working overtime. Soldiers in the support and ancillary units knew that the infantry, artillery and mortar sections would form their cutting edge. But they would all need support units, and every man wanted his to be one of them.

In Britain, resistance to the setting up of a Jewish fighting force was melting away in the heat generated by the Allies, especially the Americans. Political and public opinion was swinging in favour of Jews being allowed to have a crack at the Nazis under their own flag. The final barrier was removed by agreement between the Agency and the British that a Jewish Brigade would confine its active service to Europe, and would not operate in Palestine.

The Yishuv responded by resuming its support of recruitment for HM forces. Perversely, this time the response was poor. Two reasons have been suggested. Firstly, revelations about the Holocaust raised to fever pitch outrage among the Palestine Jewish community at the rigid enforcement of the white paper that virtually closed the gates of Palestine to Jewish immigration; there was a change of heart among young Yishuv activists, who felt that to have 35,000 of their best, able-bodied young men and women excluded from Palestine was intolerable. Secondly, they did not trust the Arabs not to attack their more isolated and vulnerable settlements, and they no longer trusted the British troops and the Palestine police to protect them.

Pressure was growing strongly in Britain for the formation of the Jewish Brigade, from the press and from more and more politicians, among the most vociferous being Victor Cazalet and Lord Strabolgi. But it was Winston Churchill who finally swung the balance. He snapped. Time and again he had been fobbed off with objections that had no substance. And when the War Office said it would convene yet another commission to consider the matter, he was furious. Knowing only too well how commissions could be used to delay and block projects, Churchill pulled rank. As a result, on 20 September 1944, the BBC broadcast to the world the following announcement:

His Majesty's government have decided that a Jewish Brigade should be formed to take part in active operations. The Infantry Brigade will be based on the Jewish battalions of the Palestine Regiment. The necessary concentration for training is now taking place before despatch to a theatre of war. Supporting and ancillary units to complete the Brigade, based on existing Palestine units, are being prepared and will join the Infantry Brigade as soon as practicable. The Jewish Agency are cooperating in its realisation.

This announcement was followed on 28 September in the House of Commons, when Winston Churchill declared:

The British army in Italy included Palestine units and Honourable Members will appreciate and approve that a Jewish Brigade Group be formed to take part in active operations. There are vast numbers of Jews serving with our forces, the American armies, and throughout all armies. It seems appropriate that a special Jewish unit of a race that has suffered indescribable torments from the Nazis should be represented as a distinct formation among forces.

Amid the torrent of news flooding in from all parts of the globe, this item was but a small splash. But it had a galvanising effect on every Jew who heard it. All, metaphorically, threw their hats in the air. Lingering scepticism among the Palestine Jewish units was replaced by certainty. Many celebrated by singing and dancing the *hora*. The news gave a tremendous boost to the dreamers and supporters of a Jewish National Home. The fabled blue and white collecting boxes of the Jewish National Fund, found in every Jewish home, office, workshop and factory, were filled to overflowing with coins and banknotes. This was the final giant step towards the completion of the painful odyssey.

The Jewish Agency agreed that the Brigade would be administered from London. Prodded by Churchill, the British General Staff speedily got down to work. It earmarked the Palestine units on active service in Cyrenaica, Cyprus, Italy and elsewhere that were to make up the Brigade's ancillary units. It noted where there were deficiencies in personnel, and, as Italy would be the Brigade's theatre of war, instructed Eighth Army HQ fighting in Italy that Jewish officers, NCOs and specialists were to be transferred to the Brigade on request. A large area of scrubby, desert wasteland between Alexandria and El Alamein, called Burg-el-Arab, was chosen for the assembly and training of the three infantry battalions.

In September 1944 Aron's seasoned 178 Company was on the move again. It drove through relentless heavy rains over the mountain passes and down into the soggy valley of the Arno. The river was swollen and in full spate. It was bitterly cold. The drivers were bone-weary, and when they finally pulled up in Florence, they fell asleep at their wheels. Aron wasted no time in reporting to the American Fifth Army Transportation HQ. His company was told to drive to quarters in Astra di Signa. This was a desolate place which had been pulverised by Allied bombing. The rain continued to lash down as the sodden, hungry soldiers trudged across carpets of broken glass to seek shelter in cheerless, damp buildings. Eschewing sleep, they unloaded and put away their stores. Later that day, the cooks beavered away in their field kitchens, and produced a hot meal of soup, boiled beef, potatoes and greens, which was much appreciated by everyone. The Americans greeted the new arrivals, and ran a phone line through to Aron's makeshift HQ. Later, an American major, second-in-command of his unit, and proudly announcing himself to be a citizen of Seattle, arrived for dinner. He brought two bottles of bourbon, and he and Aron quickly established a friendly rapport.

The front line ran across the mountains just south of Faenza and Rimini to the Adriatic. All along the line, the build-up of supplies continued for the final big offensive against the Germans in Italy. Every truck in 178 Company was pressed into service, running supplies from the docks at Livorno up to the Fifth Army's forward positions. The drivers were up before dawn, and drove non-stop. It was gruelling work for drivers and loaders. The Fifth Army had been issued with new General Motors trucks, 6-tonners and twice the size of 178 Company's vehicles. They also had the advantage of front-wheel drive. Colonel Jack Kennedy, commanding the Transportation unit of the Fifth Army, never failed to express surprise at 178 Company's ability to maintain seventy per cent of their vehicles on the road every day. He and Aron became firm friends, and their mutual esteem spread through the ranks.

Off duty soldiers of 178 Company wandered into Florence looking for Jewish survivors. Any they found were given food and money to buy basic necessities. Some told how they had been saved by Italian friends, who hid them in their own homes, at great risk to themselves. The penalty for hiding Jews was death. But it was always the same sad story – of Florentine Jews being caught by the relentless, bloodthirsty Nazi search commandos, and being shot or despatched to Auschwitz. In Florence, Major Y Franklin, in command of a Palestine Water Tank unit, and Aron worked out a plan to comb the city for surviving co-religionists.

One day, a Mr Greenly, sent by American welfare organisations, unexpectedly called on Aron and asked him to go with him on a trip to Livorno and Pisa. They went in Aron's staff car. Aron inspected his men working in the Livorno docks, then decided to find the local synagogue. Bombing had reduced it to rubble. As Greenly and Aron stood looking at the ruins, the local rabbi appeared. He told them that he had been hidden by Catholic friends, and that to his knowledge there were no Jews left alive in Livorno. The Germans had taken away any who had survived the bombing.

The rabbi begged a favour. Under the piles of rubble were buried the synagogue's scrolls of law, silver candlesticks, and valuable liturgical ornaments. Could Aron help to recover them? Without delay, Aron drove back to the docks, where he found several of his soldiers resting from their labours. Once he had explained the situation, the men went back with him to the synagogue, and piled into the work of saving the scrolls and ornaments.

All Palestine Jewish servicemen helping the Net were stunned by the enormity of the genocide they were witnessing. Time and again, in towns where there had been, say, a 2,000-strong Jewish community, they could find only a handful of survivors. Maybe, somewhere, somehow, some had survived, but there was no question that entire communities, many established for hundreds of years, had been wiped out.

In Pisa, which Aron visited with Greenly, they found that the famous Leaning Tower and the nearby cathedral had been spared by Allied bombers. The caretaker of the local synagogue, and two elegant, elderly sisters told them that no other Jews had escaped the German search parties. The women had been hidden and helped by Italian Catholic friends. Greenly gave them his American army-issue tinned foods, including chicken and other meats.

Rumours emanating from London and reaching 178 Company aroused excitement and expectation. They contained some hard information. The Brigade was to be spearheaded by three infantry battalions which would be known as the Palestine Regiment. To them would be added No. 200 Field Regiment Royal Artillery, which would comprise three batteries. Sappers, RASC, RAOC, and REME units would be needed, together with ancillary units such as postal, workshops, and No. 140 Field Ambulance units.

At this time, David Spector was on the staff as Brigade-Major to the embryonic Jewish Brigade. He well remembers the walking-on-eggshells approach to the setting up of the Brigade during negotiations between the Jewish Agency and the British. Spector was born in Shepherds Bush in London. At the start of the war, he enlisted as a private, and served as a gunner in the Royal Artillery. Two years later, he became the youngest ever captain at a military college in Egypt. He served in the Western Desert, and transferred to the Brigade as soon as he knew of its formation. He stayed with it throughout the fighting against crack German forces in Italy and until it was disbanded. Spector remembered the early qualifications laid down for the commanding officer. There were three: he did not have to be Jewish; he had to have battle experience; and, he should not have an aversion to Jews.

First choice was Brigadier E Myers DSO, MC. But he was found to be missing in Greece and Brigadier Ernest Frank Benjamin was appointed in his place. Benjamin was born in Toronto, Canada in 1900, son of Frank Benjamin DSO, a well known and liked Jewish communal worker in Toronto and later in London. He was educated at Clifton College, Bristol, then entered Woolwich and made the army his career, serving in the Royal Engineers. He served in Egypt and, after passing through Staff College, did spells in India and Malaya. He won a reputation for competence and complete dependability. He held his first Staff appointment, as GSO3, in Malaya. He made his mark when commanding the British forces in Madagascar, and ran a brilliant campaign against the pro-Axis Vichy forces, which lasted for 184 days. His men repaired blown-up bridges and roads within twelve hours, and kept pressing the enemy closely.

Benjamin's visible enthusiasm for his new posting made him the perfect choice. The first task he set himself was to learn to speak Hebrew. His men grew to respect and like him, and he took great pains to understand their anxieties. From the start, he made it clear that the Brigade was going to perform well and win the respect of its allied units.

For Aron's 178 Company, the last fulfilling lap in a long, action-packed journey hove into view. It received orders to leave Florence immediately for Rome preparatory to joining the Jewish Brigade. This gave rise to tremendous jubilation among the men. Morale, high even during arduous times, soared. As the long convoy drove through pouring rain, the soldiers sang and called out to one another. Historically, 178 Company became the first Jewish military unit to be quartered in the Eternal City.

The men and their vehicles were accommodated in an enormous empty building at Lungatore, near the ancient Jewish quarter and ghetto. The officers were put up in a number of small hotels. This was the first time they had not had their own mess, which Aron felt was bad for morale and cohesion. After a great deal of trouble, and aided by Colonel Count de Salis, a big, cheerful Irish regular in his forties, Aron succeeded in moving all his officers into an empty, modern villa on a hill overlooking the Carcolla Baths. This spacious building with its many rooms provided 178 Company with a luxurious mess.

The men could not resist sightseeing in Rome, but, at the same time, they kept their eyes open for refugees and any surviving local Jews. Two corporals came across a Displaced Persons camp on the outskirts. It was surrounded by a high fence of barbed wire, and military police strictly controlled movement in and out. The corporals were denied entry, but they did learn that there were many Jewish children in the camp. They were kept fed, but that was about all. The children had sunk into a state of fear and hopeless despondency. It could only be imagined what some of them must have endured.

Aron determined that the children especially had to be returned to a condition of happier normality. After overcoming official resistance, he was allowed to make contact, but his requests for his men to be let in to help the children were denied. Whenever Aron felt a cause was right and just, he became what the Americans called 'a go-getter'. He found a dismaying lack of interest and support around him, and finally turned to his friend, de Salis, a man who seemed to wield an impressive degree of influence in the right quarters. This did the trick. De Salis quickly organised passes into the camp for Aron and his men. They took food, fruit, sweets, and cakes for the children. They gave them warm clothes, as well as dolls for the girls, and balls and games for the boys. They gave lessons in a range of subjects, including of course Hebrew. For the first time laughter was heard in the camp. When 178 Company left Rome, they passed word to the Net and other Palestine Jewish units about these children.

The newly appointed commanding officer of the Brigade, Brigadier Benjamin, paid a flying visit to 178 Company. With him were two British Jews, Major Cecil Jackson and Captain David Spector, who had transferred from their British units. They discussed Brigade training, and the joining together of all the ancillary units and the combat battalions. Two lieutenants, Ugi Shugarisky, a Pole, and Shlomo Shamir, a Palestine-born Jew, joined them. They proceeded to the front to prepare for liaison with other selected Brigade units. Before he left, Benjamin complimented 178 Company on its efficiency, and said that it would be a great asset to the Brigade.

There were still an estimated 9,000 Jews in Rome. The people of Rome detested the Nazis and their murder squads, and many had lost friends and neighbours to the Gestapo snatch patrols. However, the surviving Jews were in a parlous state. The men of 178 Company found there was violent dissension between the lay community leaders and their spiritual leader, Rabbi Zolbi, an abrasive man who later converted to Catholicism. This bitterness at the top paralysed the few remaining institutions. It has to be remembered that the Jews were a minority group compressed into a restricted area, living with the ever-present threat of summary execution or transportation to the death camps. Months after the liberation of Rome, this ancient community was still without cohesion, and remained disintegrated. The soldiers of 178 Company and other Allied units passing through the city took the shattered community under their wing. Meeting their material needs was not difficult; lifting them above the degradation and shame of their fear under German occupation was a much bigger challenge.

Jewish chaplains and officers of the Allied forces stationed in Italy met in Rome to discuss ways of alleviating their plight. A principal speaker at this sombre gathering was a Lieutenant-Commander Bregner of the US

Naval Staff at Caserta. An attorney in peacetime, he had the job of reporting on all displaced Jewish individuals and communities throughout Europe. He informed Aron that Sir Clifford Heathcote-Smith had returned from London with policies for dealing with all displaced people. Heathcote-Smith convened a meeting, attended by Aron and Bregner among others, at which he reported on his talks in London. Briefly, all displaced persons would be transported back to where they had come from whether they liked it or not. And this would apply, after the final breakthrough, to the thousands of refugees in northern Italy. Sir Clifford was in steely, implacable mood. He left no one in any doubt that this order applied to *all* displaced persons, Jews included.

Following the final breakthrough, Heathcote-Smith addressed a large group of displaced European Jews. He told them they would soon be back in their homes. Then he paused, waiting for their expressions of thanks. Instead he was met with an angry outcry that they would never go back to where they had come from. Sir Clifford was choleric with anger. 'What do you want?' he asked. The reply came swiftly: 'We want to go to Palestine.' Then they took up the singing of the Hatikvah, and a furious Heathcote-Smith stomped out of the hall. The gulf between the three-square-meals-a-day Sir Clifford and the starving wretches he had addressed was so wide they might have come from different planets. Those who came up with neat solutions to human problems had no concept of how dire their consequences could be. Equally, it must be said that the Sir Cliffords of the time faced enormous problems.

Two key dates were 17 August, when the War Office in London informed the Jewish Agency that the British Cabinet had approved the formation of the Brigade, and 21 August, when Professor Namier and Mr Linton, negotiators appointed by the Jewish Agency, went to the War Office to discuss how the decision was to be implemented. On this occasion, the atmosphere between the parties had markedly improved. It may not all have been sweetness and light, but the earlier antagonism had gone, to be replaced by a spirit of cooperation. Everyone involved was, at heart, pragmatic.

The Agency was particularly gratified by the support shown among the British media. The *New Statesman and Nation*, for one, said:

Early in 1940 the Zionist Movement won Churchill's assent for the creation of a Jewish Army. Though units of Palestine Jews fought well in North Africa and Italy, the policy of appeasing the Arabs stood in the way. This week the idea is to be realised. The Jewish Brigade Group, with its own infantry, artillery and auxiliary troops, will be formed. Late though this comes we welcome this victory over anti-semitic prejudice.

And from *The Manchester Guardian*:

The announcement that a Jewish Brigade Group will fight with the British Army is welcome, if five years late. One regrets that the British Government had been so slow to seize a great opportunity and to fulfil a generous promise. In the face of official discouragement, about 30,000 Jews volunteered for what they could get, as pioneers, guard battalions, anything. But the one thing they wanted above all else was to fight the Germans.

A Brigade Group is a small number to put against the great armies employed by the Allies, but not a small thing for the Jews. For them, this was a war with life itself at stake. Why, then, was the British Government reluctant to accept their offers? The reason is that the Government and the Palestine Administration feared that to allow the Palestine Jews to fight under their own flag would acknowledge the right to nationhood and would annoy the Arabs. This fear arose through the mishandling of the Palestine Question by successive governments. Jewish enthusiasm was sacrificed by stupidity and a great chance was lost, for a Jewish Division would have been a useful reinforcement during the dark days of 1941 and 1942 and an encouragement to active Jewish resistance throughout Europe. The Jewish Brigade Group may yet prove that the Jews need not always be the hunted and the persecuted, but soldiers in the front of a great and winning cause.

From *Time and Tide*:

The War Office announcement of the formation of a Jewish Brigade is long overdue. It crowns five years of persistent effort to overcome frustration and obstruction, political and technical, by Jewish determination to put their own force into the field. The Jews have had to struggle for each step, first the formation of the Jewish units, then of Battalions and now, at long last, the Brigade. Its formation will lift the spirits of Jews all over the world, for they have the most potent reasons to unite against Nazism. As the Jewish Agency put it: 'May it be given to the Brigade to carry the Star of David with pride into the lands where it used to be used as a badge of shame.'

After spending six weeks in Rome, 178 Company received the orders it had been waiting for. It was to leave Rome and join the Jewish Brigade. The men were well rested and seethed with anticipation. Their vehicles had been meticulously overhauled, with worn parts replaced with new. In early February 1945 the great day came, when the company set off in convoy, between pavements lined with clapping, waving bystanders, mostly refugees and local people they had helped. The soldiers clapped and waved back. They drove through snow-covered hills and bitterly cold weather to Fiuggi. There, they joined up with the three infantry battalions of the Brigade. They were instructed to replace their Palestine shoulder flashes with the new, large, blue and white flashes bearing, in Hebrew and English, the words 'Jewish Infantry Brigade Group'.

# Chapter Six

Winston Churchill had always harboured a warm admiration for Chaim Weizmann. He felt that the ageing Jewish leader had been treated with scant courtesy and some mendacity by the British War Office. Churchill knew what Weizmann wanted and was determined that he should have it. So, when on 12 July 1944 he saw Sir Edward Bridges, he stipulated to the War Minister that four vital points be observed. It was the Germans the Jews wanted to fight, and the Brigade should not be sent to fight against the Japanese; the Brigade should not be split up unless there was exceptional urgency; political, as well as military, consideration would be given regarding the Brigade's dispersal or otherwise when the war was over; and he would consult the King about the proposal that the Brigade have its own flag. He could see no reason why this martyred race should be denied this satisfaction. Things went well. The decision to form the Brigade having been made, the War Office had to support it, just as it supported every other fighting unit of the British Eighth Army in Italy.

It was in January 1943 that the 1st Battalion of Infantry of what would be called the Palestine Regiment was formed. It comprised five companies – A, B, C, D and E. The battalion's war diary for 30 January 1943 listed one warrant officer Class 1, five warrant officers Class 2, five quartermaster sergeants, thirty-nine staff sergeants, fifty-four corporals, and 881 other ranks. Among the other ranks was a five per cent sprinkling of Arabs. The Jewish volunteers came from many countries – Falashas from Ethiopia, Yemenis from the Hadramaut, Adenis, and young Zionist idealists from several western democracies. A sizeable number were European-born young men who had escaped from the Nazis – Poles, Germans, Austrians, Czechs, and Russians. The stabilising element were the Sabras, the Palestine-born, whose parents had fled eastern Europe to work the land from barrenness to fertility. Half of the NCOs were British, because the blocking tactics of the Foreign Office and Cairo GHQ had delayed the training of Palestine Jewish NCOs and officers. Now, this state of affairs began quickly to change.

There were language problems. No British officer or NCO spoke Hebrew. Few of the Jews, apart from the British and Empire soldiers, spoke English. Often a British NCO, exasperated that however loudly he shouted his commands in English they were not understood, raised his arms to heaven looking for guidance. English-Hebrew vocabularies, with the required words spelled out phonetically, were printed and distributed. With the passage of time, this problem lessened. Permission to wear Jewish badges and emblems on uniforms continued to be refused, a sore point with the more Zionist-minded soldiers. At that time, no one believed that the day would come when a Jewish Brigade, with its soldiers sporting Jewish emblems, and flying the Jewish flag, would exist. The realists among them, however, knew that, to survive the coming war against the Arabs, they must absorb every scrap of combat knowledge that the British could teach them. They learned quickly and well.

There were thirty-six officers in the 1st Battalion, an HQ staff of three, and those leading the five companies. The list in the war diaries show how the gaps caused by a lack of trained Jewish officers were plugged by British staff:

Headquarters
Lt-Col. Duggan, OC (Yorks and Lancs)
Maj. Jones (the Buffs)
Capn Keet (General List)

A Company
Capn Cornfield (General List)
Lt Waldman (General List)
Lt Aharon (General List)
2nd Lt Zielinsky (General List)
2nd Lt Thielhaber (Palestine Regiment)

B Company
Maj. Tibor (General List)
Lt Silman (General List)
Lt Werter (General List)
2nd Lt Epstein (General List)
2nd Lt Taubes (Palestine Regiment)
2nd Lt Zeifs (Palestine Regiment)

C Company
Maj. Buchanan (General List)
Capn Nelson (General List)
Lt Izhar (General List)
Lt McHardy (Black Watch)
Lt Barons (General List)
Lt Remas (General List)
2nd Lt Neus (Palestine Regiment)

D Company
Maj. McDonald (Gordons)
Capn Salaman (the Buffs)
Lt Wardle (Foresters)
Lt Platzko (General List)
2nd Lt Kreisel (the Buffs)
2nd Lt Lichtenstein (General List)
2nd Lt Friedenthal (Palestine Regiment)
2nd Lt Grossman (Palestine Regiment)

E Company
Maj. Lazell (General List)
Capn Long (Yorks and Lancs)
Lt Midgeley (Yorks and Lancs)
Lt Foster (South Staffs)
Lt Sarfati (General List)
2nd Lt Corsenty (General List)
2nd Lt Grill (Palestine Regiment)

Two more battalions, the 2nd and 3rd, were formed, with a more or less equal complement, and with the same mixture of nationalities. The 2nd Battalion left for Benghazi in June 1943, and the 3rd completed its establishment in July of the same year. The three battalions made up what was then called the Palestine Regiment, and in October 1944, all three finally assembled at Burg el Arab as part of the Jewish Brigade. Politics still dictated their movements. They were kept away from the front line. They trained, and fulfilled various duties, especially guard duties, but the combat they craved remained tantalisingly out of reach.

During the spring and summer of 1943, the 1st Battalion square-bashed, perfected their drill, and route-marched under a blistering sun. They were given camouflage training at Wadi Saros. They received weapons training, and were instructed in mountain warfare. They learned field firing, battle inoculation, and fieldcraft. They went on night manoeuvres, and mock dawn attacks. And among all this, they stood guard duty at Lydda Airport, Latrun, Haifa and elsewhere.

In the autumn they were sent to Egypt, and were continuously engaged in guard duties along the Canal, where pilferage from the massive quantities of equipment and stores being unloaded was rife. Those not on guard duty went out into the desert for more training, section and platoon landings, platoon attacks and defence, river crossings, house-to-house and street fighting, mine laying, and exercises with live ammunition. Inspections confirmed that discipline and health among the soldiers were satisfactory.

At 1415 hours on 15 February 1944 Private Aboy was killed on a field-firing range. He was buried the next day with full military honours.

The battalion requested the replacement of sixteen Hotchkiss guns with the efficient modern Bren gun. The request was granted. The detested guard duty could be lively – the 1st Battalion's war diary for August 1944 read:

*August 8/9th: Brigade guards opened fire on 2 Arabs stealing a tent. They fled. Tent was recovered. Guards at Post 12 intercepted thieves.*

*August 9/10th: Sentries at no. 12 post Tel el Kebir arrested Arabs stealing engine parts.*

*August 10/11th: 0200 hours thieves fired on posts nos. 1 and 3 at Tel el Kebir. Shots came from nearby village of Qurein. Four sacks of cement recovered by no. 11 post Tel el Kebir when guards intercepted thieves.*

*August 14/15th: 0330 hours Guards at Tel el Kebir wharf prevented Arabs from stealing bags of cement. Guards at no. 12 post prevented the theft of a horse.*

*August 25th: 0420 hours at no. 11 guard a lorry was stopped. When sentry approached he was fired at and the lorry sped off. 50 rounds were fired at no. 1 post.*

*August 31st: 0310 hours a successful ambush at Tel el Kebir. 2 Arabs were killed in exchange of shots as they tried to steal motor transport parts. At the same time a patrol on duty outside was fired upon. It returned fire. 2 more Arabs were killed.*

Then everything changed. The battalion's elation at the War Office announcement, endorsed by Churchill in his Commons speech, and the 1 October order to up sticks and move to the Brigade's assembly area at Burg el Arab was shared by the British officers and NCOs.

When the battalion arrived at Burg el Arab, they found the other two infantry battalions, an artillery battery, and a headquarters office. It was an inhospitable spot where the wind whipped up fierce sandstorms during the day, and where it was bitterly cold at night. But no one cared about the physical discomfort. There was a feeling of 'Well, we have arrived.' From the top of a tall mast in the large parade ground fluttered the Jewish flag with its wide blue and white stripes and the gold Star of David centred.

The senior chaplain, Rabbi Bernard M Caspar, recorded in his book, *With the Jewish Brigade*, that every convoy bringing equipment, guns and all the paraphernalia of war to Burg el Arab was greeted with tremendous enthusiasm. Soldiers lined the roadside and greeted every arrival with singing and cheers. Caspar noted that each soldier considered himself to be the most privileged of Jews. Ben Zion Yisraeli and Motke Chadash were both aged sixty, but on being recruited had given their ages as much less. Found out, they were told they were much too old to join a fighting unit, and they promptly went on hunger strike. Caspar intervened on their behalf. Brigadier Benjamin was sympathetic, and both men were accepted. Later, they were joined by their sons, and all four men fought side by side in the front line.

From the outset, Benjamin made a good impression. His soldierly professionalism and pride at being in command of the first officially sanctioned Jewish fighting force since the fall of Judea to the Roman legions were manifest. And his pride infected every member of the Brigade, and inspired the high morale and smartness in turnout that characterised its men.

British tardiness and reluctance to train Jews for combat exacted its toll. Shertock had asked time and again for a Jewish artillery regiment, and had been denied. Now, the Brigade had to make do with the one all-Jewish field battery in the 200 Field Regiment, the personnel for which was found in the Light Anti-Aircraft Regiment in Cyprus, and coastal defence units in Palestine.

Brigadier Benjamin made himself readily accessible to all, even those with complaints to make. He understood the intense feelings of Jewishness among his soldiers, and Hebrew words and commands were de rigeur on parade and in the mess. Religious services were presided over by Rabbi Caspar. They were well attended, even, it was noted wryly, by men who had not seen the inside of a synagogue for years. The bond between the men was more like that found in a family than in a fighting force.

While they were training, the men heard the news that a flag for the Jewish Brigade had received official approval. Mysteriously, the flag appeared within twenty-four hours. The order forbidding its being flown in Egypt, an Arab country, was still in force, but the men were in no mood to be deprived of their own identity for the sake of political expediency. A flagpole was put up, and the flag flew from dawn to dusk. The official handing over of the flag to the Brigade would take place later in Italy, but meanwhile, wherever Brigaders were to be found, the flag flew. Morale soared when the order then went out that the Palestine shoulder flash would be replaced by a blue and white flash bearing the words 'Jewish Fighting Force'. The men began to lose their fear that the war would be over before they had a chance to see action against the Nazis.

On 31 October the Jewish Brigade left Burg el Arab. At Alexandria they boarded Royal Navy ships bound for Europe. They disembarked at Taranto on to the land of those whose ancestors had so many centuries earlier defeated their own ancestors and driven them into exile.

In the cold, snowbound street of Fiuggi, and in the muddy nearby villages and hamlets, there was a palpable feeling that the Brigade would soon be in action. Hebrew was to be heard on all sides. Signposts and direction indicators were written in both Hebrew and English. Italian children greeted the Brigaders with a cheerful 'Shalom!' All day long, the crack of rifle and machine-gun fire, and the crunch of mortars echoed among the surrounding hills.

Benjamin held daily conferences with his officers at the large-scale map table to work out the details of the move to the foothills facing the Po valley. More Jewish officers had joined the Brigade, but the three lieutenant-colonels commanding the three infantry battalions were British – Lt-Col. Growse, OC 1st Battalion; Lt-Col. F L Cubitt, OC 2nd Battalion, and Lt-Col. J B T Montgomerie MC, MM, OC 3rd Battalion. Col. W A Beal liaised with GHQ.

A new arrival in 178 Company was Captain Leon Shalit RASC, who had completed a special course in ammunition and explosives. He quickly settled down, plunged into learning Hebrew, and was liked by the men. Corporal Moshe Mossinson of Kibbutz Navan was seconded from driving duties to edit and print the Brigade's monthly publication *Ha-Chayal* ('The Threshold'). Sometimes the past catches up with us. When 178 Company was in Rome, a Major Birt from the Welfare Office saw Aron on an urgent matter. A large consignment of welfare stores had arrived from America by sea at Naples. A large concentration of refugees by Lake Bolsena, north of Rome, needed food, clothing, blankets, and medicines from these stores. Birt had no transport and could not find any. He estimated there were some thirty-five tons of essentials, which were required without delay. Could Aron and his men help? It was a tall order. If any mishap occurred along the way, that would reduce the effectiveness of 178 Company, and Aron and any men involved would be for the proverbial high jump. But Aron felt he could not refuse. He put it to his sergeants, absolving his officers of any blame should things go wrong. All the drivers volunteered. The convoy drove non-stop. Each truck had two drivers, plus two loaders who could also drive. They did the job. Aron was a greatly relieved major.

But the episode had not gone unnoticed. In Fiuggi, Staff Brigade Major Cecil Jackson, a London Jew, called on Aron and told him that Brigadier Benjamin wanted to see him at once. When Aron stepped into Benjamin's office, he was told that Benjamin had been ordered by AFHQ Caserta to read a memorandum to him. This concerned the unauthorised task undertaken by 178 Company's vehicles from Rome to Naples and to the refugee camp. It was a damning and undeniable indictment. For a while neither man spoke. Then Benjamin sighed:

'You realise the serious implications?'

'Yessir,' Aron replied. 'I'm prepared if necessary to face a court martial.'

'Are you? Why?' Benjamin asked.

'Because it will always be a satisfaction to me to know that what I did was always in the very best of causes.'

Benjamin said, 'I have heard that 178 Company has done a lot to help refugees in the Western Desert campaign.' He paused. 'From a technical sense I can see no offence has been committed. Furthermore,' tapping a thick buff file on his desk, 'I can see only one real offence, the use of War Department transport for purposes other than that authorised.'

Benjamin asked Aron to sign a statement to that effect, which Aron did. They shook hands, and Benjamin invited Aron to dine with him that evening. Aron accepted and nothing more was heard of the incident.

All units in Fiuggi sent representatives to a conference. They realised that when they broke through into the Po valley, and onwards into Austria, they would find thousands of refugees and survivors who would need help – not only material necessities such as food, water and clothing, but help to regain their sense that life had a purpose. A Brigade Refugee Committee was set up, comprising officers, NCOs and privates. The Committee would liaise with the Net, and would help to build habitable, albeit temporary, shelters. There would be no shortage of volunteers to teach and help with the children, many of whom would be orphans, traumatised by what they had seen and experienced. The children would be a priority, especially getting them to Palestine.

Brigadier Benjamin was a quiet man, intensely aware of his good fortune at being given command of the Brigade and determined that, when it came to action, it would exceed all expectations. Even during the time spent at Burg el Arab, he had placed great importance on peak fitness, having the infantrymen out on ten-mile route marches, and introducing inter-battalion competitions in which every soldier was determined to win against his rivals. Benjamin emphasised the importance of elementary musketry and fieldcraft training, until each man was as comfortable with battle skills as he was brushing his teeth. In the icy mountains of Italy there was no let up.

For four months 178 Company, along with the infantry and the other vital Brigade units, settled into the home allocated to them by Allied Forces HQ. The severe winter weather was particularly hard on the Palestine, African and Yemenite Jews. Captain Danny Lipschitz, commander of the Military Police section, speedily covered the area with the Brigade's insignia – the gold Star of David on the blue and white background, and the name in Hebrew and English. A strong rapport developed between the Jewish soldiers and the local Catholic peasants, hill farmers and villagers. Through the use of convoluted translation from Hebrew into English, then into Italian, and vice versa, the erstwhile kibbutzniks and the locals had many a discussion about their common agricultural vocation.

Most importantly, now that the Brigade was an official part of the British Eighth Army, it was supplied with up-to-date weapons, previously denied it on political grounds. The days were filled with intensive training in which live ammunition was used. The soldiers became fit and hardened, and skilled in weapons use. Their most frequently expressed fear was that the war would be over before they had a chance to see action. Meanwhile the German press and radio indulged in a spell of heavy Teutonic humour, ridiculing the Jewish soldiers, accusing the Allies of letting loose savage, oriental barbarians onto Christian Europe, and describing in some detail what their *Wehrmacht* would do to the Jewish *Plattfuss* (flatfoot) troops. The German media had their fun; German troops, facing the Brigade later, had a different story to tell.

In his book about the Brigade, the senior chaplain, Major Bernard Caspar, recalled the intense Jewishness of the soldiers. The Jewish flag flew over Brigade HQ. Signs on every officers' mess, sergeants' mess, billet, dining room, washroom, latrine, store room, everywhere were in Hebrew only. More and more Hebrew was spoken in the mess. Parade commands were given in Hebrew.

On 20 February 1945, after its long stay in the bitterly cold and gruelling mountains, 178 Company left Fiuggi. Its preparations for going into battle with the infantry and the artillery were complete. Potential wrinkles had been ironed out, and the different sections of the Brigade – the Royal Engineers (RE) 643 Company, the Royal Ordnance (RAOC) unit, the Royal Electrical and Mechanical (REME) workshops, 140 Field Ambulance unit, and the small, but vital, postal unit – liaised smoothly and with complete confidence in one another.

Whenever the Brigaders thought that news coming out about the concentration camps had plumbed the depths of human evil and depravity, stories of even worse atrocities reached their ears. Those whose families had not managed to escape the Nazis prepared themselves for the worst. A new dimension entered their conversation. They were more determined than ever to help Jewish refugees reach Palestine; and their hunger to get at the Germans became insatiable. But now the talk was of revenge, an eye for an eye, against the worst of the Nazis, and of serious consideration of ways and means of achieving it.

The Jewish soldiers and the local Italians parted with mutual sadness. They had grown to like and respect each other – both were warm and emotional by nature. The Italians had taken part in many of the Judaic ceremonies, including the festival of Chanukah, when the giant, symbolic, seven-branched menorah (candelabra) was erected in a dominant position overlooking Fiuggi and was illuminated at night. The local farmers and villagers had given shelter to disoriented wretches, and revived them with healing kindness. Brigade quartermasters ensured that these Italians were well provided with food, camp beds, blankets, and anything else they needed. The Brigaders were made welcome in homes and they, in turn, repaid the hospitality shown them by strengthening fences, repairing buildings, and carrying out any other necessary tasks for their hosts.

When the order came, 178 Company travelled back to Rome. Civilians recognised the Brigade's emblems, and came out to cheer the long convoy on its way. When they reached Ravenna, Aron reported to Eighth Army Advanced HQ, and to his delight was told that his company could draw brand new vehicles. This came as a great relief to Captain A Silberstein,who commanded the workshop platoon. Assisted by Warrant Officer 1st Class 'Tasch' Krichefsky and Staff Sergeant Eidelsberg of the kibbutz Rehebot Haaharon, and the other NCOs and artificers, he had kept the company's vehicles on the road over a record mileage through the Western Desert and Italy. It was touching to see the soldiers pat their old vehicles and bid them farewell just as if they were pet dogs or horses.

At Ravenna Brigadier Benjamin paid 178 Company a visit. He made a thorough inspection, and complimented them on their mobile office and record. He told them that the Brigade was due to move up into the line at any moment. General Mark Clark, commander of the 5th Army Group, convened a conference of senior officers which Aron attended. Clark briefed them on general plans, and then told each formation where it would be positioned. When he came to the Jewish Brigade, he could not but note how eager they were to get into battle. He wished them luck.

The Brigade was assigned to a sector north of Faenza, along a ridge of verdant hills overlooking the south bank of the comparatively narrow Senio river. On 28 February the Brigade came under the command of the 5th Corps, and on 5 March the infantry took over the front line at Alfonsino, north of Ravenna and south of Highway 16. It was an area of dykes and ditches. Water seeped into dugouts and fox holes. The Germans had liberally sprinkled mines on both banks of the river. The Brigaders found themselves up against the Austrian 42nd Jaeger division and 362 infantry division, the latter composed mainly of SS and Nazi Party members. The Brigade's immediate task was to carry out aggressive patrolling, in order to improve their positions, clear the south bank of Germans, and to take prisoners for identification and interrogation. No time was lost carrying out these orders.

They also crossed the river in small-scale attacks to test the enemy's strength and map the lie of its defensive positions. One significant sortie was supported by tanks of the North Irish Horse with aerial backup by fighter bombers. At the briefing, a South African pilot had told the Brigaders to look out for them overhead, and they did indeed see them pound the German positions. The planes flew and attacked in a Star of David formation; it turned out that many of the South African airmen were Jewish and this was their tribute to the Brigade. The infantry attacked with such eagerness in this exercise that they went ahead of the tanks, mopping up forward German positions, and returning with prisoners of war, which greatly impressed the seasoned troops of the North Irish Horse.

The prisoners taken ranged in mood from apprehensive to petrified.

They were really stumped at seeing the blue and white shoulder flash, and hearing a German- or Austrian-born Brigader ask them in their own language if they knew whether the interrogator's family was alive and well, or had been sent to the gas chambers. It was then that the odd prisoner wet himself through sheer terror. Corporal Rosenblum was a Polish Jew who had escaped from Buchenwald. He knew his family had been murdered. When his patrol returned with prisoners, he lifted one German soldier's shirt and saw the giveaway SS mark. He could think only of revenge, but before he could shoot the prisoner, his comrades wrested his rifle from him. The Sabra lieutenant who had led the patrol patted Rosenblum's shoulder and said sympathetically. 'They're needed for questioning. Kill the bastards in battle.'

# Chapter Seven

On 23 March 1945 178 Company received new orders. They were to move up to the line at once, and again the long convoy, with the men eager for battle, took to the road. Eventually they reached their base at the small village of Brisighella. This was an idyllic spot, on a ridge from which they could look across orchards, olive groves and vineyards sloping down to the south bank of the Senio. Confronting their sector was the crack German 4th Paratroop Division. From their hilltop positions on the north side of the river, the Germans could observe the Brigade, especially during daylight hours, when their snipers and light artillery frequently reminded the more incautious Brigaders that curiosity killed the cat.

The Brigade sent probing patrols across the river, to seek prisoners and information. Inevitably these clashed with forward German posts and their patrols. The soldiers of the Brigade more than held their own against the best the *Wehrmacht* could put up, a prime weapon in their armoury being their smouldering, revengeful anger. By now, first-hand knowledge of the fate of fellow Jews in the towns and cities of Italy and north Africa, and in the Holocaust, dominated their thoughts and conversation.

Forty years after the end of the war, a soldierly looking man in a white shirt and tie waited expectantly in a Tel Aviv hotel lobby. His name was Yohanan Pelz, and he was waiting for a retired British colonel, now Mr G P Salmond who duly turned up. The two men greeted each other with genuine warmth. Salmond had commanded a British paratroop battalion before being seconded to the Jewish Brigade in Italy, where he became one of the few remaining British officers with the Brigade. Pelz had been a deputy commander under Salmond, and remembered that Salmond's job had been to whip the Jewish infantry into shape before they moved into the front line. For two full months he worked them rigorously, sometimes to the point of exhaustion, in the bitterly cold Italian mountains. As Salmond put it:

The inexperienced men have to be blooded, not thrown into battle against seasoned Germans and have them killed. After they have been blooded and trained hard with live ammunition then you can send them into the big show.

61

When his men went into the line and were deployed along a drainage canal, they were ready and eager for action. Pelz remembered:

> We were several thousand men with no real battle experience in organised units. For the first time we began to work at the level of platoon, company, battalion and brigade.

Both men recalled how Pelz had badgered Salmond into switching him from administrative to field duties. Pelz went on:

> I learned for the first time how to plan an attack. First, he had me leading night patrols. I did four of them. Each time I came back to report what I had found – minefields or shrubbery and ground depressions which gave cover. The last night I lay right on the German trench and heard them playing 'Lili Marlene' on a phonograph. That's how I learned the song.

A German salient, named La Giorgetta, had been harassing the battalion's lines. Salmond assigned Pelz to lead an attack on it. Although such attacks were normally carried out at dawn or dusk, this one was scheduled for 1000 hours. It may have been a preparatory initiative with the coming 'big push' in mind. Before the attack, La Giorgetta was pounded by artillery, and by RAF and SAAF fighter bombers. Then Pelz led his men in a spirited bayonet charge and they cleared the salient. Pelz recollected with a smile, 'The Germans didn't know what hit them.'

When Pelz returned to Palestine, he and the other ex-Brigaders put their training and discipline to good use in Israel's 1948 War of Independence. He commanded the point company in Operation Nachson, aimed at capturing Jerusalem. His overall commander in that battle was another Brigade veteran, Chaim Laskov, a future Israeli Chief of Staff. For Pelz, that bayonet charge against veteran German troops symbolised the transition of the poorly trained defenders of the Yishuv into what became one of the world's most formidable fighting forces.

The Brigade Major, David Spector, noted that on 31 March the Brigade came under 10th Corps command. The international composition of the Eighth Army was manifested by the fact that the Brigade had the Polish Corps on their right flank and the Italian Folgore Group on their left flank. In the bright spring sunshine, the Brigade's senior chaplain, Bernard Caspar, watched the build up towards the final victorious push against the Germans. He watched the columns of infantrymen moving up in files alongside heavily laden mules. He strolled among groups of resting soldiers thrumming with excited confidence as they discussed a BBC radio announcement on Sunday 25 March that the Jewish Infantry Brigade had been in action, and had taken German prisoners. Now, at last, they had been internationally identified, not as anonymous, colonial or Palestine troops, but as what they were, Jews.

Arguably, 178 Company was now the most seasoned of the Brigade units. It had shown its mettle in the battles of the Western Desert, and had won a reputation for dependability. Within it, Aron created a special section commanded by Captain Shimon Mazo, aided by Captain Shalit, whose job was to ensure that supplies of rations, ammunition and everything else needed by the forward troops flowed through without a hitch. And the workshops achieved an almost one hundred percent performance from the vehicles.

At Passover 1945, Bernard Caspar organised his two junior chaplains into conducting Seder Night services. The quartermasters and RASC catering sections were so well organised that all the soldiers were that week provided with matzo (unleavened bread) and kosher Rishon-le-Zion wine. Caspar recalled how strangely Old Testament it seemed with the troops sitting in a vast semi-circle under the brilliant Italian sun, and with the field artillery ready to spring into action at a moment's notice. Present at the commemoration was Major Edmund de Rothschild, a member of the internationally famous banking family. He commanded 200 Field Regiment RA, which comprised three batteries. He was greatly concerned to alleviate the plight of refugees, and discussed with Aron what practical measures they could take after the approaching battle was over, and the Germans had been cleared out of those parts of Italy they still occupied.

Rothschild had served in the French, Algerian, Tunisian, and Italian campaigns, and was slightly wounded at the Battle of Cassino. It was while he was at Eboli that the call went out for Jewish volunteers for the Brigade. He transferred immediately, and thereafter commanded the Brigade's artillery along with Major Henriques. All their gunners were Palestine Jews. Later, they achieved the distinction of being the only artillery field regiment to cross the Alps. When the Brigade drove to Holland and Belgium prior to embarkation for demobilisation, they kicked their heels at Venlo, engaged in clearing mines and guarding huge store dumps. When his men were given forty-eight hours' leave to visit Paris, Rothschild extended their leaves to two weeks to give them time to search for their families. Only one gunner returned late. He had been struck down with acute appendicitis, and was operated on in a Russian hospital. On being discharged, he was astonished to find at the hospital gates his sister who had survived.

A unique historical event took place on 3 April 1945. The blue and white Jewish flag, with its gold Star of David, was formally raised over Brigade headquarters in Italy. At a simple, quiet and moving ceremony, tears ran down the dust-caked faces of the watching soldiers. They were unashamed. Those who had been forced by the Nazis to wear the star as a badge of shame now saw it as a symbol of fighting honour. The ceremony was held in a grassy meadow near a shell-torn baronial mansion, and to the accompaniment of not-too-distant gunfire.

The flag was presented to the Brigade by the head of the political department of the Jewish Agency. He handed it over to Brigadier Benjamin as the troops snapped to attention. It was unfurled by the oldest enlisted man in the Brigade, Sergeant-Major Sucher Spiegel, whose entire family, apart from an uncle living in New York, had been murdered by the Nazis. There were representatives present from every unit in the Brigade. Shertok addressed the assembly in Hebrew:

At last Jews can see the flag for which they have always fought in their hearts. It represents the Homeland and also the blood of those who in their millions have died without having the chance to fight back.

Brigadier Benjamin, as affected by the occasion as everyone else present, accepted the flag on behalf of the Brigade, and expressed his pride in the fighting qualities of his men. Rabbi Caspar recited a prayer which had been specially composed for the occasion, and ended with a blessing.

Shertok spoke again. He told the Brigaders that plans had been drawn up for the care of veterans at the end of the war when they would be demobbed. He said that the whole question of Jewish armed forces would have to be addressed by the British and Palestine governments, together with the question of the future of Palestine. What the consecration said to world Jewry was:

We are all one nation, the Jewish nation. In times of extreme danger we will need your help. For this we can only depend upon fellow Jews. To them I say that we know that when the occasion arises you will support us.

Aferwards the Hatikvah (the Jewish national anthem) was sung, and everyone quietly dispersed. At the outbreak of war, Shertok had played a prominent part in getting Palestine Jews to enrol in the British army, and he took an almost avuncular interest in the Brigade. Before he left, and against all advice as it was being pounded by German artillery at the time, he insisted on visiting the front line. His aide was pale and nervous. An infantryman by the name of Baruch Orion from kibbutz Matzuba recalled that Shertok kept his cool, asking many questions and apparently oblivious of nearby shell bursts.

Before leaving, Shertok also addressed an assembly of Brigaders. He said:

Everyone in volunteering for the army carried in his heart the dream to see this flag flying over him, accompanying him into battle. That dream has come true.

His statement was greeted with enthusiastic acclaim. But, that week, the Brigade suffered a sharp increase in casualties. The terrain was difficult; they were overlooked and visible to the enemy. Mines took their toll, as did mortar and artillery fire. Patrols now went out every night looking for information and to take prisoners for interrogation. When the Brigade moved on, they left behind thirty-three graves in a small Jewish military cemetery at the village of Mezzano, two miles north of Ravenna. In addition to their probes north of the Senio, the Brigade had aggressively repulsed German attempts to use the low land to the south.

Some time later, the *Jerusalem Post* published a feature written by Sraya Shapro, and entitled 'There and Then'. It was about a young man, Rueven Assor, who volunteered for the British army in 1940. He was assigned to Company 2 of the Buffs, an all-Jewish, non-combatant unit of sappers. Through steady pressure, backed up by a good performance, they were eventually accepted as part of a combat unit and trained as infantrymen. Assor recalled the experience of being in the line at the Senio river during March and April 1945:

Across the river which meandered through a green valley were the Germans, not more than 800 metres away. They shelled our positions regularly, but at noontime one could risk going down to the river, wash and take a supply of water. The air was always misty and calm. As night fell the atmosphere changed abruptly. The general feeling was that it would not be easy. We perspired in our winter uniforms. Some tried to doze, but without success. Some mused about their backgrounds. A strange air of camaraderie prevailed, and all differences of background were obliterated. The common bond was the will to live and return home safely.

A patrol had gone out a long time ago. We all knew what was happening. They were in mud, crawling, firing, being hit. The telephone rings. Some nonsense about laundry. It rings again from a sister company. One dead. Who? We don't know yet. The German patrol had been wiped out. Heavy shelling close by. Again, the phone. Snippets of conversation: 'How many? I'll speak to the colonel right away. We'll do something about it.'

Assor the stretcher-bearer is sent down with two others. They crawl, and then run quickly across an open road visible to the Germans. There are shell craters all around. 'Very unpleasant,' Assor mutters. His whole body tingles with anticipation of German fire. At the McArthur outpost a bloodstained mess tin lies near the door, as does a blood-soaked stocking. It is pitch dark inside the building. Assor trips over something, and hears a heart-stopping scream. There is a distinctive stench, groaning, and somebody grumbles, 'Why have you been so long?' From a corner there is a cry for water.

To carry the wounded up the hill was a strength-draining task. When he reached the top, Assor planted two Red Cross flags in the hope that the Germans would respect them. Sometimes they did; at other times they would open fire at the new targets. It took twenty minutes to reach the jeeps and hand over the wounded to the medics. The sentry at the central outpost said to Asser, 'I don't want to see you here again.' However, two nights later he did. A patrol, led by Sergeant Lazer, went out to check on German movements, and ran into an ambush. Those sent to its rescue strayed into a minefield. It was a problem to haul the wounded over the steep terraces. One badly wounded man kept moaning, 'I can't take it. I can't take it.'

Sergeant Lazer was fatally wounded in the encounter. The signaller, Private Aharon Bar-Kimche, his wireless smashed by a fragment of grenade, carried on as a rifleman. 'He took over command of the patrol and extricated it with great skill,' said the citation in the *London Gazette* announcing his Military Medal.

Along with the other units of the Eighth Army and the American forces, the Brigade, in place and ready, waited for the signal for the final offensive of the Italian campaign.

On 1 November 1944, Armoury Sergeant-Major Len Sanitt, in charge of the REME detachment of the British 53rd Field Regiment, was browsing through a copy of the latest Eighth Army General Routine Orders (which the authorities thought should be widely read), when a news item caught his attention. This announced that a Jewish Brigade was in the process of being formed, that it would be part of the Eighth Army, and that Jewish soldiers serving with British units would be allowed to volunteer. There were two conditions: a suitable vacancy had to occur in the Brigade, and the CO of the British unit had to agree to the transfer.

Sanitt's aptitude at repairing and handling guns and vehicles had helped him to achieve the highest NCO rank in the British army. He was proud of his regiment, and happy with his mates. Suddenly, as if struck by a call from the wild, he felt he had to be part of what he sensed would be a landmark event in Jewish history. Following procedures, he applied through the regimental Chief Clerk to register his request for a transfer.

Four days later, he moved his unit to the small town of Murradi. He immediately had to attend Robert battery, which had several problems including a temperamental gun. When he returned to base, he was told that a Bedford water truck was in urgent need of repair. There were no substitutes for water trucks, and they took priority. Sanitt went out with a corporal to repair the disabled truck and, as they were working on it, the Germans opened up with their multi-purpose 88mm guns. A close shell burst wounded both men, Sanitt in the leg. It was Guy Fawkes Day and, ironically, his transfer to the Jewish Brigade had just come through.

Another armoury sergeant-major had been posted to the Brigade to hold the fort until Sanitt got over his hospitalisation and convalescence. When he eventually travelled north to Fiuggi to join the Brigade, he was greeted cheerily by Staff Sergeant Mark Hyatt, the Chief Clerk and a Londoner, with the cry, 'Blimey, where have you been? We've been expecting you for three months!' Hyatt led Sanitt to a large garage which had been requisitioned for his new command, the REME LAD (Light Aid Detachment) attached to Jewish Brigade HQ.

From the moment he arrived, Sanitt was affected by what can only be described as 'Jewishness' – in the flags, the emblems on the vehicles, and the experience of being in the first identifiably Jewish fighting force in an eternity. The pride, excitement, and eagerness to do well got to him just as much as it did to all the others. In his book, *On Parade*, he recalled an incident he witnessed while at Brigade battalion HQ. Staff officers needed a company to launch an attack that night to iron out a dent in the line. Because all the units volunteered, they held a draw. Sanitt was astonished to see the men who were successful spontaneously dance a *hora* when they knew thay would be making the attack. The sortie succeeded, but there were casualties among the soldiers who had won this particular lottery.

Sanitt had had a long spell with the 8th Indian Division, where English and Urdu were widely spoken among all units. Similarly, in the Brigade, the language mix was Hebrew and English, with chunks of Yiddish thrown in. Routine orders were posted in Hebrew and English, but in the battalions only Hebrew was now used by the NCOs and other ranks.

Fiuggi's water had been renowned throughout Europe. The several modern bottling plants stood empty. Workers from the south had fled the fighting. So, the Brigade had no shortage of billets, and as the various essential units arrived, they melded well, and quickly learned to act efficiently as a coherent fighting formation. Sanitt replaced the Scottish ASM stand-in, who had filled the void until he turned up, and then reported to Brigadier Benjamin. Benjamin told him to use the unit as he saw fit and, should there be any problems, his door was always open. What Sanitt could not get over was the eagerness of the men, from the brigadier to the humblest private, to get into action against the Germans.

Sanitt's LAD unit comprised Sergeant Dan Hoffman from kibbutz Ra-Amanay, a perky soul and an expert motor fitter, who loved to ride motor bikes, and volunteered to act as despatch rider. He often ran into snow and mud in the mountainous terrain, but never complained; there was Corporal David Geller from Haifa, quiet and dependable; Sergeant-

Armourer Eliezer Sheinbaum from kibbutz Beit Oron, Lance-Corporal Shmuel Wiseman from Tel Aviv, a very conscientious storeman and Sanitt's driver, and Nathan Tarachovsky, a member of the Haifa Bus Cooperative. Many Brigaders had been born in central Europe and had already been close to death several times. Also in the unit was a very young man called Moishe Avny. He had served with General Anders' Polish army in the Italian campaign, and had been a cadet officer in Poland when the Russians marched in and captured him. He was taken to a place called Katyn where hundreds of Polish officers were being assembled. Avny and some other cadets were removed from the ranks, and were told that only their youth saved them from being shot in the infamous massacre that followed.

The unit also contained two cheerful young sabras from Tel Aviv, A Klinghoffer and Shimon Sutka; Dov Albert from Haifa, the willing and unassuming Zvi Feude from Kiryat Chaim, and the unflappable Moshe Reichman. By chance, two British non-Jews, Bob Hamilton from Glasgow and Jack Muscroft from Yorkshire, delivered two stores trucks to the unit and stayed, happily blending in with the others.

Prior to Sanitt's arrival, the senior officer in the sergeants' mess was a London Jewish warrant officer 2nd class sergeant-major, a regular, who had spent his life in the service with many years in India. Like others, this leathery veteran, whose Judaism had long been buried by circumstance and inclination, gravitated to fighting with his own kind under their own flag. Staff Sergeant Mark Hyatt, the former London policeman, Sergeant Gerry Cooper, and four sergeants from the battalions made up a compact and friendly mess as they prepared the detachment for action.

Sanitt was issued with a new, 15-cwt Dodge truck for his personal use. In accordance with tradition, he had to give it a name. Not having a wife or girlfriend, he whimsically painted 'Gefilte Fish' on its front bumper. As he chased around Italy, he frequently found himself hailed by soldiers, mainly British and American. One young Royal Fusilier from London's East End, hearing about the Jewish Brigade for the first time, expressed a keen desire to join up. But Sanitt dashed his hopes, pointing out that there were now personnel requirements only in specialist areas. The battalions had full complements of infantry, and there were many men queueing up to enlist.

The men had been affected beyond measure by stories emerging about the Holocaust, and by the wretched, disoriented refugees whose paths they crossed. If a Zionist was a Jew who would fight for a land which these people could call their own, and where they could start new lives, then every Brigader was a Zionist. For the first time in his life, Sanitt delved seriously into the history of Zionism. He started with Herzl's revelation that Jews could only live normal lives in their own land, and found himself inspired by the heroism and determination of the early settlers, by the Zionist Mule Corps, and by men like Trumpeldor, Jabotinsky, and Dr Weizmann. He felt immensely privileged to be part of the Brigade, not only able to participate in its crack at the Germans, but also to assist the Jewish dispossessed of Europe.

Ten days after Sanitt's arrival in Fiuggi, a soldier brought into the workshop a 3-tonner that needed repair. The soldier told Sanitt that the truck was urgently needed to collect Jewish refugees and get them on their way to Palestine. The truck was given priority over all other work, and was repaired and on its way the same day. When Sanitt was told a few days later that trucks were needed for transporting Jewish refugees to the Palestine-bound boats, he signed documents authorising their use, should they be stopped by military police. Entirely fictitious, these papers implied that the trucks were collecting supplies. Sanitt never spoke about these goings on. No one did. But everyone knew what was happening, and every Brigader approved and helped in the process. Sanitt had become part of the Reshet, the network set up by the Brigade and other Palestine Jewish units right across Italy, to bring salvation to their less fortunate co-religionists. For the record, a handful of British non-Jewish officers and NCOs also knew what was happening. Any who ventured an opinion expressed his support, and some even offered to help.

In early February, the Brigade at last moved up to the front line, and the various units took up their allocated positions. Sanitt's LAD, in support of the infantry battalions, settled into the area of Borgo San Lorenzo.

In April 1939, sensing the inevitability of war, the young Eric Nabarro joined the Territorial Army, and on 1 September the same year he was called up. He was posted to the Royal Artillery, and served a two-year stint with his unit in Iceland as one of the force positioned there to thwart any attempted German invasion. He returned to Britain in 1942. Now a lieutenant, he went on to serve in Iraq and the Middle East generally, and in the Italian campaign.

While in Italy, Nabarro would on occasion find his unit placed close to a Palestine Jewish encampment, and he felt drawn to visit their officers' mess, socialise, and play bridge with them. He was a Sephardi Jew, but not a Zionist, and his views were not popular. However, the cumulative effects of what he had seen and heard, revelations about the concentration camps, and the nightmare experiences of disoriented Jewish refugees, transformed his feelings and outlook. Jewishness, if not Zionism, took hold.

In 1944 Nabarro made himself an expert in the counter-mortar system, designed to give gunners an instant bearing on an enemy mortar almost as soon as it was fired. After firing, mortars could be easily and frequently moved to safer spots before they were fired again. The system was specifically designed to stop this. Roughly, this was how it worked: four or five observation posts would be placed well apart facing enemy lines. Each post was manned by a trained soldier. When a mortar was fired, each observer took an immediate compass bearing, and phoned counter-mortar HQ. Collation would pinpoint the enemy position, and this intelligence would be passed to the gunners. Speed of communication from OP to HQ, and HQ to gunners was the key.

A counter-mortar system was allocated to the Jewish Brigade, with a British officer detailed to command the unit. Because he was Jewish, Nabarro was asked to take this officer to report to Brigadier Benjamin. On the way, the British officer gave voice to his reluctance to command the unit, and Nabarro suggested that he take his place. This was amicably agreed, and Nabarro was promoted captain, and became CO of the Brigade's mortar unit.

In early March 1945, this smallest Brigade unit, comprising Captain Nabarro and ten trained men, moved up to take their place in the line south of the Senio river. Nabarro liaised with the Poles on the Brigade's eastern flank, and with the Italians on the west. Their artillery would also accept pinpointed positions to fire at. Telephone lines were set up between the observation posts and counter-mortar HQ, and between HQ and the artillery. Conscientiously, Nabarro chased round visiting the OPs daily, and sometimes also at night. The counter-mortar unit was used in action successfully, until the German army retreated out of contact with the advancing Brigade.

Captain Nabarro related to me one of many encounters between Jewish soldiers and German troops. All Brigade units contained soldiers whose countries of origin were Poland, Hungary, Germany and Austria. While he was in charge of a platoon guarding a bridge over the Po, out of the blue a soldier, immaculately dressed in British army uniform, walked up to the southern end of the bridge. Speaking perfect English, he said he was a war correspondent, and produced papers to prove it. He said he wanted to send back stories about the situation north of the Po, and the sergeant in charge waved him on. As the man crossed the bridge, a Brigade soldier shouted at him to stop, walked up to him, and let loose a torrent of fluent German. Those watching saw the smart, cheerful 'correspondent' crumple before their eyes. The Brigade soldier had been born in Saxony, and, beneath the fluent English, had detected the distinctive accent of that region. The man was a German who had escaped from a prisoner of war camp in Calabria, had walked and bluffed his way through Italy, hoping to reach home. He was handed over to the military police.

When I interviewed Eric Nabarro again, he dug into his memory and recalled another incident. During the hectic chase after the retreating Germans, the Brigaders picked up straggling soldiers and took them prisoner. At this time, stories about the Holocaust were flooding out, and first contact with Germans led to combustible encounters. The Germans' relief at being taken prisoner by what they thought were British troops turned to fear when they saw the Brigade shoulder flashes and emblems, and realised their captors were Jews. Their apprehension was only heightened when German- and Austrian-born Brigaders cursed them in their own language.

Infantrymen of the 1st Palestine Battalion collected a group of Austrian Jaeger troops, who huddled in a nervous bunch. Suddenly, a Brigade corporal, usually a quiet, introverted man, behaved completely out of character. Shouting in German, he started to beat up one of the prisoners. He was hauled off, and interrogated by an officer about his anti- Geneva Convention outburst. The man explained:

It was his accent. He comes from the same part of Vienna where I was brought up. I remember Anschluss Day when the Germans marched in. My parents were pulled from our home and were forced to clean the street just outside where we lived. They were surrounded by a crowd of our neighbours, jeering and laughing. They were given brushes, not brooms, so that had to get down on their knees. They were spat at, even kicked. When they cleared a spot of ground the damned swines tore up newspapers and scattered the pieces over where they had just cleaned. I was made to watch. They're almost certainly dead, along with my two elder sisters. I got out to Palestine. My father insisted on my going. I joined the Brigade because I want to kill Germans and especially Austrians who behaved worse towards their Jews . . .

The young man straightened and concluded, 'I'll take my punishment, sir.' The Polish-born lieutenant studied him for a moment and replied, 'What punishment? I saw no incident.'

Cringing before the tangible hatred of their armed captors, the Austrians huddled together. They were greatly relieved when the British military police came for them.

In late February the Signals unit arrived. It was commanded by a British officer, Major Galbraith. Mark Hyatt remembered a popular British private in the unit because of the infinite variations of his name, which was Jack Clack. After the war, Clack always travelled from his home in Northampton to attend the annual reunion of Brigade veterans.

One by one, the ancillary units assigned to join the Brigade reported to Brigadier Benjamin, and took their places as important parts of the whole. Under the command of a competent, no-nonsense Glaswegian, Captain Jack Shapiro, 140 Field Ambulance arrived. Several of the medical orderlies were drafted in from British units. A British Jew, Captain Cyril Goodman, was in charge of Intelligence. He served in the Field Security unit in 1940. In 1941 he was commissioned in the Intelligence Corps. He was serving in Sarafand, Palestine as assistant adjutant at the training depot for Jewish and Arab units when he was sent to join the Brigade in Egypt. He worked closely with HQ staff, and reported directly to Benjamin especially on the interrogation of prisoners. A Palestine-born Jewish officer commanded the REME workshops, and another commanded 643 Company Royal Engineers. This particular young officer had sailed through a very intensive course of hard training to earn his commission.

The entire Jewish Brigade group, with its fighting, ancillary, and support units, now totalled just over 5,500. Its commander, Brigadier Benjamin, was supported by a British officer, Lieutenant-Colonel P F A Growse, who was the Brigade's second-in-command, appointed by the War Office.

The Brigade's cutting edge were the three infantry battalions. Each had a strength of one thousand, and collectively they were still known as the Palestine Regiment. Diehard Zionists resented this, while others (the majority) did not care. They had their flag, their uniform, and vehicle identity badges, flashes and pennants, and were unofficially known as the Jewish Brigade. Jews had been replacing British officers and NCOs, but when they went into the line, there were still British non-Jews plugging the gaps. Spector recorded that a headcount, made more out of curiosity than anything else, revealed that Brigaders represented fifty-two nationalities.

When the Brigade moved into the front line, the 1st Battalion was commanded by Colonel Gofton-Salmond, and the 2nd Battalion by Colonel Gash, a British officer who had volunteered to join the Brigade. The latter was considered the perfect English gentleman by his men, and was held in high esteem. Colonel Ben-Artze, a Palestine Jew, had climbed the ladder and commanded the 3rd Battalion. Later, he founded the Israeli state airline El Al. From various theatres of war, the selected units – 200 Field Regiment, commanded by Major Edmund de Rothschild, with its four batteries, each with four guns, and the 1st Palestine Light Anti-Aircraft (LAA) battery – reached Fiuggi and reported to Benjamin.

On 28 February 1945 the Brigade came under the command of the 5th Corps. Intensive training had made the men completely at ease with their weapons. They were in peak physical condition. They were also impatient to have a chance to prove themselves in combat. Across the board, the Brigaders were a literate bunch. They devoured news reports, analysing them, buoyed up by the awareness that they were making history. Years later, former Brigaders still remembered the contagious anticipation affecting all units. The worst of the news fuelled their anger and increased their determination to have a crack at the enemy. As one ex-Brigader put it over civilised iced coffee at Eilat:

It was a strange, light-headed elation. Of course, we were utterly devastated by the terrible news from Germany. At the same time we realised that we were the luckiest Jews in the world. Casualties? We didn't think about them. Not ours. But we were so full of what we would do to the Nazis.

# Chapter Eight

For two months the Brigade manned its sector of the front line, playing its part in Allied Command's preparations for the final offensive that would complete the liberation of Italy. As ordered, it kept the south bank of the Senio clear of Germans and German activity. It improved its forward positions, and mounted aggressive patrols across the river, taking prisoners for interrogation, and confusing the enemy about the area designated for the eventual crossing in force.

During this time, the Brigade's 5,500 men grew frustrated at the interminable waiting for the order to launch their attack. Bored men became restless, and the Brigaders sought normal soldierly diversions. Some of these came to light in Staff HQ's Routine Orders for all units, drawn up by Acting Major David Spector:

Routine Orders Serial No. 9

*It must be borne in mind that transfer of territory to the Italian Government is Allied policy to restore responsible government to the Italians. It is the duty of troops to assist local authorities maintain authority and avoid thoughtless action which would undermine the position of the police, the Mayor, local authorities and central government.*

The Orders then went on to specify cases of high-spirited misdemeanours occurring in the Brigade's theatre of war, such as:

*The acquiring by means other than legal the requisitioning of private property.*
*The obstruction of free circulation after sunset of uniformed carabinieri by unit guards.*
*The drinking of wines and spirits after closing hours.*
*The deliberate acts of assaulting carabinieri, particularly when on mixed patrols with British troops.*

And finally, in Serial No. 9, an order that *a soldier suffering from venereal disease must report sick without delay, as concealment delays treatment, with a resultant loss of manpower. This serious offence would be dealt with by court martial.*

The diversity of the Orders is confirmation that Brigade HQ was determined that their Jewish fighting force would emerge with enhanced performance in the field of battle, and a reputation that would reflect credit on the Jewish people. HQ ran a very tight ship, as the following two nuggets demonstrate:

*Paragraph 105: When returning beer bottles of the hinged stopper variety, units will ensure that stoppers are left open. It is necessary to preserve the life of rubber washers which are in short supply.*

*Paragraph 106: Cases still occur of Other Ranks cutting trees for fuel purposes. Such trees in many cases constitute the sole income of the owners. Disciplinary action will be taken against the culprits.*

Routine Orders could be regarded as the military equivalent of the house magazine of a large retail store chain, containing a mixture of admonitory head-office views, and in-house tidings. In February 1945 examples of the latter included:

*His Majesty the King takes pleasure in approving the Mention in Dispatches of Sergeant S V Jones of the 140 Field Ambulance of the Jewish Brigade.*

Three others, all belonging to Major Aron's 178 Company, were Mentioned in Dispatches: Sergeant S Ginsburg, Private Hirschburg, and Driver M Tobias.

The Orders were analogous to the tightening of the nuts and bolts that ensured the Brigade ran smoothly and efficiently. For example, Paragraph 116 read:

*A. The War Office has notified a worldwide shortage of greatcoats. There is no improvement of this situation in sight.*
*B. There is a vital necessity for all ranks to take care in usage.*
*C. The loss by neglect will be liable to punishment.*
*D. No troops, in groups or individuals, will be sent to forward positions without one.*

Italy could be surprisingly cold in winter. If Hitler and the *Wehrmacht* High Command had planned things so that every German soldier fighting on the Eastern Front was equipped with suitably warm clothing, the war might have taken a different turn – in Germany's favour.

The Brigade's War Diaries complemented Routine Orders. The former were terse, and listed the daily happenings of the fighting with a minimum of words – the bare bones of the patrols, Brigade casualties, and such like. They totally omitted emotionally driven incidents, a very blurred area, where Brigaders did not treat German prisoners according to the provisions of the Geneva Convention. Ex-Brigaders I spoke to skirted round certain questions, and would merely say something bland, such as, 'Well, things did happen, of course.' One or two would expand on this with, 'Certainly when they captured the SS.'

At the heart of this particular issue was the fact that, by the time the Brigade entered the line, every man knew about the genocide of his people in Europe. And, while they were in the line for that short period, they knew it was still going on. This knowledge sickened and angered them, especially the Polish, German, Austrian, Hungarian and other European Jews among them. The more they discussed and visualised the appalling suffering and humiliation of their kith and kin, the greater their burning desire for revenge against the perpetrators. As the enormity of the crime sank in, one young corporal, who had escaped from Dusseldorf to Palestine in the mid-1930s, put into words what others could not bear to utter:

Gassed them. My two sisters and parents. Just like a pest controller exterminates rats and cockroaches. I can't sleep for thinking of them fighting for their last breath in the chambers . . . God, then into the ovens. No graves, no head-stones, no prayers, no remembrance. Nothing.

Now, the doers of those terrible deeds were to hand, just across the Senio river. The fury of that young soldier, and of others like him, was palpable. Sometimes it expressed itself when prisoners were taken, they displaying the fearful apprehension of men facing summary execution. Seeing the Jewish shoulder flashes, the prisoners tended to plead innocence, and ignorance of what had gone on in the concentration camps, all of which served to infuriate their captors even further.

On 6 March 1945 Brigadier Benjamin addressed his troops in Routine Orders:

A. I want to impress the supreme importance of capturing alive German prisoners and sending them back quickly for interrogation.
B. I realise that there are a large number of men who have every personal justification for revenge themselves, and wish to kill every German they come across. Our object is to hasten the defeat of the enemy. It has been proved that by taking prisoners and extracting information from them more is to be gained.
C. However great the crimes committed by the German, I am determined that the Jewish Brigade Group shall act correctly in accordance with recognised convention.

Taking Benjamin's admonitory Routine Orders of 6 March with the cautious admission by ex-Brigaders that 'things did happen', together with the undisputed fact that when the war ended members fanned out across Europe in revenge squads to execute high-ranking Nazis guilty of terrible crimes against humanity, it is impossible to escape the conclusion that some young Jewish soldiers did take the law into their own hands. Benjamin later admitted:

> I, for one, could not blame them. As a Canadian-born Jew, whose family resided in safety in London, apart from the danger from *Luftwaffe* raids, when I learned of the Holocaust and saw the first documentary films of the camps, given a gun I would cheerfully have shot those responsible for the evils inflicted on my people.

Nevertheless, Benjamin and his HQ staff, wearing their military caps, took great pains to run a tightly disciplined Brigade, and conform closely to British army conduct and convention. As a result, the spick-and-span turnout of its soldiers, and its performance and dependability impressed all who came into contact with it. And they could well understand the state of mind of the Brigade's men. Few Allied soldiers suffered the same feelings of emptiness and despair. When the war ended, they would have no homes to go back to, no loved ones waiting to fall into their arms. They could not envisage a normal future life. The darkest moments came with the arrival of the mail. Other Brigaders would pile in to grab their letters, then lose themselves in them. But for the ones who had escaped from Europe there was nothing, and it was then they felt the full enormity of their loss. Benjamin and his staff understood. Not a single Brigade soldier was put on a charge of ill-treating or killing an enemy soldier illegally.

On 3 March 1945 Brigade HQ issued a summary of the enemy it faced:

> The overall strategy of the German High Command points to their holding on to as much of Italy as they can for as long as possible. The number of defence lines indicates a defence of no ordinary tenacity. It appears that Field Marshal Kesselring will not withdraw unless pushed very hard.

For the first three weeks in the line from the Adriatic up to Alfonsino, the Brigade faced the 42nd Jaeger Regiment and the attached 362 Infantry Division. This in turn was attached to the 98th Infantry Division, which took the line up to Cartignola. Also in the area was the Fascist Lupo Battalion comprising four companies. It was made up of Italian naval personnel formed into an infantry battalion. The companies were named after naval ships which had been sunk or captured. The Lupo Battalion had a reputation for fighting well, and for not deserting.

General Walter Jost was the commander of the 42nd Jaeger. He was born in Baden, and saw infantry service in the First World War. In April 1941 he was wounded on the Russian Front, and received the Knights Cross. In September 1944 he became CO of the Jaegers. He had no links with the Nazi Party but, whatever his personal views, he was a professional to his fingertips, and he would do his duty.

The commander of 362 Infantry Division was Colonel Reinhart. He had taken over from General Grainer, an ardent Nazi, who was renowned for having thrown away a division in Russia. 362 Division had been engaged in heavy action in Russia, then in Italy. During the Allied breakout at Anzio, it had suffered severe losses, and endured further heavy casualties when it defended the Gothic Line. There was a strong infiltration of Party members, who kept a stringent eye on the morale of the battle-weary soldiers. When a Gestapo officer named Heimann declared to a group of soldiers, 'Even if the company is whittled down to one man, and he wants to desert, I will shoot him', he was enraged when a soldier commented aloud, 'You are not the only one who can shoot.' The soldier was placed under arrest, pending court martial. With a little comradely help, he deserted to the Allies.

But what of those first enemy troops to bloody, and be bloodied by, the Brigaders? Opinions tended to vary among those who fought against them. The Jaegers ranged from mediocre to tough. The German 362 Infantry were categorised by all as aggressive and a hard bunch to encounter. Did the enemy know they were facing all-Jewish soldiers? Answers from ex-Brigaders to this question range from 'They must have done' to 'I don't think so'. The German press cottoned on to the story and made a meal of it. They ridiculed the Brigade, sneeringly accusing the British of unleashing barbaric savages from Asia on the continent of Europe.

So it was that the end of February and early March 1945 saw the first Jewish soldiers as such kill, and be killed by, the enemies of their people since the revolt of Bar Kochba against Roman oppression in Judea. The Germans had planted mines over a wide area on both sides of the Senio river. These took their toll, certainly of the careless. Intermittent but intensive spells of German artillery and mortar fire inflicted more casualties, but most resulted from the fire-fights between the probing patrols sent out by both sides.

The Jeagers 1st Battalion had an assault platoon well versed in mounting raids. Their weapons included T mines, bangalore torpedos, and flame throwers. The Brigade soon discovered that non-Germans were not used in raiding parties and forward outpost duties. The infantrymen of 362 Division used T mines with five-second fuses as powerful grenades. They also laid them with concealed wires tripped when Brigaders got close to their positions. The Brigade was getting the taste of war the only way, by waging it. Its War Diaries usefully pinpoint dates and incidents, and, paradoxically, despite the spare wording, breathe life into the events described:

*1st March. Brigade recce parties visited Armoured Brigade area.*
*2nd March. Patrols out on recce.*
*3rd March. 0600 hours. Brigade attaches to and comes under command of the 8th Indian Division.* [ASM Len Sanitt had served with this division through the Western Desert, Sicily and Italy. He paid it visits and renewed old acquaintances.] *1200 hours. Brigade infantry in counter attack supported by 12 tanks of the Royal Irish Horse. Successful. Prisoners taken petrified by being abused in their own language and even dialect. Softened by fear they gave valuable information when interrogated.*
*6th March. Brigadier T S Dobree DSO MC Commander of 8th Indian Division visited 2nd Battalion Palestine Regiment. Commanders conferred. Enemy shelled and mortared forward positions. No casualties.*
*7th March. One officer 2nd Battalion Pal Regiment wounded. Two privates 1st Battalion Pal Regiment wounded.*
*8th March. Quiet day. One other rank wounded. Decrease in enemy mortar and artillery fire.*
*10th March. Forward locations mortared and shelled.*
*11th March. 3rd Battalion Pal Regiment relieves 2nd Battalion. One other rank wounded. Claire Booth Luce, US Congress-woman, visits Brigade HQ.*
*12th March. Mortaring and shelling of forward locations.*
*13th March. Enemy working parties active in front of sector.*
*14th March. 1st Battalion Pal Regiment patrol in fire fight with enemy. One officer and two other ranks wounded.*
*15th March. 3rd Battalion Pal Regiment successfully ambush enemy patrol. Enemy casualties estimated at 8. Own casualties nil.*
*16th March. Daylight patrol made in assault boat along Fosso Vetro. No casualties.*
*17th March. 2 Bn Pal Regt relieves 1 Bn Pal Regt*
*18th March. Quiet day.*
*19th March. In morning forays two Pal Regt patrols made no contact with enemy. Instructions by Division to probe until contact is established. In subsequent fire fights and patrol clashes 11 prisoners taken and 30 casualties inflicted on enemy. Own casualties 2 killed and 19 wounded. 2nd Bn remaining on Fosso Vetro. Prisoners taken belong to the 1st Bn 40 Jaeger Regt 42 Jaeger Division.*
*20th March. Operation completed according to plan. Own casualties 3 killed 6 wounded. Evening shelling and mortaring of our positions. 3 Bn Pal Regt repelled attack by strong enemy patrol. Own casualties 1 Officer 2 Other Ranks wounded.*
*21st March. Enemy spandau and mortar fire. Reverend Israel Brodie, senior*

*Chaplain to HM Forces, visited Brigade HQ.*
*22nd March. 3 enemy escapees recaptured nr Mezzano.*
*25th March. Jewish Infantry Brigade under the command of 10 Corps is ordered to relieve the 43 Gurkha Lorried Infantry Brigade between the 25th and 28th March. Captain Nabarro reported for duty as acting ACMO JB Group.*
*27th March. 3 Bn Pal Regt relieves 2/8 Gurkhas without incident.*
*28th March. Evening patrol. 1 Bn Pal Regt clashed with enemy. One Other Rank killed.*
*29th March. Enemy mortaring caused 1st Bn Pal Regt casualties. 2 killed 15 wounded. 1st Bn Pal Regt sends patrol to Plicotto. Clash with enemy. Enemy casualties 6. Own casualties 1 killed 2 wounded.*
*30th March. 1 Bn Pal Regt patrol made contact with enemy. Casualties inflicted on enemy. Own 1 Other Rank killed, 2 wounded.*
*31st March. 1 Bn Pal Regt patrols have sharp clashes with enemy. Own casualties 4 killed 13 wounded 1 missing. Outpost established at position M2277243.*

The terse entries in the War Diary barely do justice to the performance of the men in the actions, but Brigade HQ did receive from General Mark Clark, commander of the 5th Army Group, the following message:

We are delighted to have the Jewish brigade operating with our forces on the Italian Front. I wish the Brigade all the luck and success. I am greatly satisfied that the Jewish people who suffered so terribly at the hands of the Nazis should now be represented by this front line fighting force.

That warm, idyllic spring, soldiers on both sides of the last main German defensive line realised the war was nearing its close. They all had the same ambition – to stay alive and go home. Brigaders fortunate enough not to have been born in continental Europe shared the same desire. But the Brigade was burdened with new responsibilities. Even while it was under the military command of the British Eighth Army, the hearts of most of its men lay with the future of the Yishuv. Its political master was the Jewish Agency, and it was from Tel Aviv that the low-key but urgent instructions came to step up the rescue of Jewish refugees and move them south on to the Palestine-bound boats. Yishuv leaders like Ben-Gurion and Shertok laboured under no illusions. They knew that when the war ended political expediency would prevail again. The worldwide sympathy for the victims of the Holocaust would fade, and a million rootless European Jews would become a problem for their erstwhile allies. Even after all that had happened, surviving Jews would find themselves between a rock and a hard place, and only other Jews would give a damn.

The rock was the impossibility of going home. Their homes, if they still

1. Recruiting poster for the British Army, Tel Aviv, November 1941.

2. British Army volunteers parading in the streets of Tel Aviv, 1940.

**3.** German soldiers leaving the Synagogue in Genoa after cleaning it under the supervision of Jewish Brigade soldiers.

**4.** Brigaders of the Royal Army Service Corps dancing a *horah* with refugees adopted by the unit, Giovinazzo, Italy, 1944.

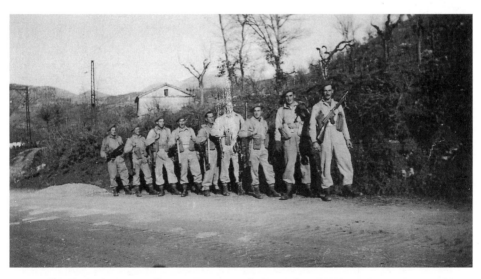

**5.** The front line in Italy, 1945. A Jewish Brigade patrol prepares to go out.

6. Brigade staff, Italy, 1945. Left to right: Captain David Spector G3, Major Jackson G1, Brigadier Benjamin GOC, Captain Goodman IO.

7. Open-air speech given before the attack on the Senio front, April 1945. Captain Norman Cohen RAMC is in the foreground.

8. Commonwealth War Graves Commission cemetery at Ravenna, Italy, containing the graves of Jewish Brigaders of the Palestine Regiment.

9. 'A' Company, 1st Battalion Palestine Regiment's victory parade, Faenza, Italy, 1945.

10. Guard duty, Tarvisio, Italy, 1945.

11. Announcement of a football game between the Brigade and Belgian Maccabi, Brussels, 14 October 1945.

| Association Sportive Maccabi-Belgique | Sportclub Maccabi België |
|---|---|
| **Dimanche 14 octobre 1945** | **op Zondag 14 October 1945** |
| à 15 heures | te 15 uur |
| au Terrain de la R.U.S. Laeken, rue Steyls, à Bruxelles | op het Terrein van R.U.S. LAEKEN, rue Steyls, Brussel |
| (Trams : 11-46-49-81) | (Trams : 11-46-49-81) |
| **MATCH de FOOTBALL** | **GROOTE VOETBAL WEDSTRIJD** |
| entre | tusschen |
| Jewish brigade Group et | Jewish brigade Group en |
| (Champion du Moyen-Orient) | (Kampioen Midden-Oosten) |
| Selection A.S. Maccabi-Belgique | Selection A.S. Maccabi-Belgique |
| à 19 h. 30 réception suivie de Soirée Dansante à l' " ELBERG BOURSE " Rue Marché-aux-Poulets, 35 | te 19 u. 30 ontvangst gevolgd door Dansavond in de " ELBERG-BOURSE " Rue Marché-aux-Poulets 35 |
| Jazz Jean DELHEZ             ATTRACTIONS | Jazz Jean DELHEZ             ATTRACTIES |

**12.** Brigader M Goldblum with his truck, May 1946. Note the Brigade insignia on the mudguard.

**13**. Foreign Representative of the Jewish Agency, Moshe Shertok, presenting the Jewish Brigade standard at Fiuggi, northern Italy.

**14**. The Jewish Brigade at Tarvisio after the war. The soldiers are being addressed by the Jewish Agency on the task of finding and rescuing Jewish survivors.

stood, would have been taken over, and what the new owners had they would not give up. It was not uncommon for solitary Jews, trying to regain their property, to be run out of town, even murdered. But, even if they could go home, they would be living in their families' graveyards, where once they had played happily. And they would be living among the hostility aroused by an endemic, poisonous anti-semitism.

And the hard place? As before the war, no country wanted them, or would take no more than a token handful of refugees. In short, Jews in numbers were unwelcome. The Jewish Agency's tentative requests for visas fell on deaf ears.

So where could they go? Was there any alternative to ending their relentless misery in suicide, the fate of so many? The actual figure will never be known. There was only one answer – Palestine, where they would be welcomed and absorbed into normal life. Irreversible changes were being created by the pressure of events. The Jews of Palestine were no longer simply Jews who worked on the land and in the towns, and asked only to be left alone to get on with life. They had been propelled by war into a new state of national consciousness. Party politics and internal feuds dissolved in a new unity of purpose. These Jews now regarded themselves as a nation reborn. They looked towards Europe and saw their surviving brethren in dire straits. An overwhelming spirit of cooperation built up between the two bodies of Jews – the refugees in Europe would reach Palestine or die in the attempt, and the Palestine Jews would pull out all the stops, legal or illegal, to bring them home to the Promised Land.

The Brigade found itself in a strange situation. Because of events utterly outside its control, its allegiance began to shift. Its soldiers would fight like tigers as part of the British Eighth Army, and do all that was asked of them until the last day of the war. But after that, all their energy would go into saving as many Jews as they could, and getting them on their way to the Land of Israel. Their Allies would no longer be the British, the Americans, Indians, and Gurkhas, but only other Palestine Jewish units scattered throughout Italy and north Africa, and Jewry elsewhere in the world. This would be the second Exodus in the history of the Jews to the same Holy Land. Only this time the enemy would not be the pharoahs, but the cabals of Arabists entrenched in the higher echelons of the British Foreign Office and the Palestine government.

The Brigade, with its Refugee Committee linked to the Net, found itself playing a unique 'Salvation Army-type' role while engaged in close combat with a redoutable enemy. Apart from its links with other Palestine Jewish units, it received calls for help from Jewish soldiers and airmen serving with other Allied units, who had come across desperate, starving Jews all over Italy. Appalled by what these refugees had to resort to simply to survive, they wanted to know where they should be sending them for rehabilitation. The consciousness of belonging to a nation reborn was affecting Jews other than just those in Palestine and Europe. Chanan Greenwald, an ex-Brigader, said later:

> When we came across them, we cried with anger at their pitiable condition, physical and mental. We did anything for them. We stole milk, food, blankets, clothing, and gave it to them. They were dead and we brought them to life and promised they would get to Palestine.

Even in these last days of the war, even knowing that it was lost, the corrupted Waffen SS and Gestapo searched for Jews to murder in the rapidly diminishing territory still under German control. There were thousands of serial killers on the loose. The Brigaders discussed this problem. One, Pavel Moses, said afterwards that feelings of revenge were very very strong, in fact uncontrollable. Yet, in the liberated areas of Europe, a great trek was under way, as Jews – men, women and children – in small groups, twos and threes, walked south towards where they had been told the Jewish Brigade would take care of them and get them to Palestine. Where the Brigade was camped, the indomitable Senior Chaplain, Bernard Caspar, organised religious services. For the first time in years, the refugees could don prayer shawls and yarmulkas, and pray with tears streaming down their cheeks. They had come home.

As they looked around at the mainly khaki congregation, and saw the tough, spick-and-span Jewish Fighting Force soldiers praying alongside them, they experienced a sense they had all but forgotten – they felt safe and protected. Those who had blasphemed in their despair now prayed with awesome fervour. A young man from the German town of Halle, who had escaped from the Sobibor concentration camp, and had reached the Brigade after a hazardous journey, said:

> In Halle for years we lived with the fear that one day the Gestapo would burst into our home and take us away. Day after day after day we waited for that dreaded early-morning pounding at our street door. It was almost a relief when it finally happened. The Gestapo took me away with my parents, my sister and younger brother. They must be dead . . .

He paused to watch two soldiers opening the Holy Ark, and two more taking out the sacred scrolls, and said:

> When I get to Palestine I want to join the Jewish army. Somewhere, some time, I have scores to settle.

In one sense the Brigade was the Jewish equivalent of the French Foreign Legion. It comprised Jews from so many different countries that, in some units, more than twenty different languages were spoken. Some men could speak three or more quite fluently, though neither English nor Hebrew. In the early days this led to bad feeling between the British NCO instructors, who spoke no Hebrew, and their recruits who spoke only Hebrew. There was anger and contempt, and also a falling away of initial eagerness, to be replaced by bitterness and a loss of interest. Prompt disciplinary action by the frustrated instructors turned potentially good, but aggrieved soldiers into recalcitrants. The ever perceptive Aron spotted the problem early on, and his solution was a demand that the lingua franca in all Palestine Jewish units was to be Hebrew. It would be the living symbol of unity and nationalism, of rebirth, a rallying point.

Every privilege and freedom a new recruit enjoys depends upon the understanding of his officers and NCOs. Imagine, then, the newly enlisted Palestine Jew. He speaks no English, and perhaps just a little Hebrew. He has already suffered the tyranny of Nazi rule, and the nightmare of the concentration camp. He belongs to a country that is not yet a country. He has been persecuted, and has been forced to become a wanderer. He lacks the stability of knowing what traditions in the, to him, alien British military culture he can cling to. He wonders what he has to look forward to. He is intelligent, but out of his depth. He will do what is asked of him. But what he needs is good leadership and understanding, and to feel an important cog in the machinery of his unit. With the passage of time, Palestine Jews had taken the place of nearly all the non-Jewish NCOs when they went into battle. A few were commissioned and made first-class officers. They suffered their share of casualties, and won a gallery of medals for gallantry in the field.

By the end of March 1945 the Brigade had matured into a highly dependable British-trained fighting force. As General Orde Wingate had predicted when he led the first night squads of settlers into battle against marauding Arabs in the 1930s, the motivated Jewish soldier was the equal of any in the world.

So they waited, south of the Senio river, for the signal to attack. At last, after nearly 2,000 years, a Jewish fighting force, armed to the teeth, and in the peak of physical condition, strained at the leash to get at the murderers of their defenceless race. At this point their primary motivation was revenge. How deep this feeling ran was expressed by an infantryman, Hanoch Bartov, in his book, *The Brigade*:

The Jews are coming to avenge their slaughtered brothers. No deeds before had ever cried out for such bloody vengeance. It burned in us all. Just once to be like the Tartars. Like the Germans. Like the Ukrainians. All of us spoiled, sensitive farmers, workers, students – all of us will move in on one city and burn it street by street, house by house,German by German. Why should we be the only ones to remember Auschwitz?

Let them remember the one city we shall raze.

Norman Lourie was the war correspondent attached to the Brigade. He reported that this was a time of activity and casualties. He wrote about Lieutenant Tony van Gelder, a young Jew from Finchley, north London. He was known as Mickey Rooney because of his striking resemblance to the film actor. At his own request he had transferred from the Sherwood Foresters to the Brigade. He led a fighting patrol across the Senio, accompanied by Private Moshe Wadel, aged 20. Wadel had been born in Vienna, had managed to escape, and slipped into Palestine in 1941. He had volunteered immediately to serve with the British forces.

It was a daylight reconnaissance, yet they managed completely to surprise a group of Nazis well dug in with spandau machine-guns. The patrol captured twelve Germans. Lance-Corporal Joram Lewy of kibbutz Maabarot searched and interrogated the prisoners. The half-mile return journey to their company was made through continuous spandau fire, during which one German was killed by his own side. The Germans displayed obvious signs of fear when they realised they had been captured by Jewish soldiers. One admitted that they expected to be shot. But after interrogation at Brigade HQ, they were sent on to prisoner-of-war camps without incident.

During Passover five Brigaders were killed in action, three died from wounds, and fifty-two more were wounded. British and South African Jewish soldiers planted trees in their memory in the Wingate Forest.

In London Lord Strabolgi, president of a committee for a Jewish army, was notified by Sir James Grigg, Secretary of State for War, that the Jewish brigade was now fighting in the Allied line.

The Jewish community in the Argentine collected £100,000 for the British war effort, and allocated £8,000 of it to the families of Brigaders killed in action.

Hanna Rovina, the celebrated actress fom the Hebrew Theatre, arrived at a forward position to entertain the Brigade. She enjoyed a rousing welcome. Not everyone did – the Brigade had become 'flavour of the month' and anyone with a sufficiently inflated sense of his own importance found a pretext to visit it.

# Chapter Nine

During the preparatory softening up and acclimatising period across the banks of the Senio river, Brigade staff continued to monitor the welfare and conduct of the troops by circulating Routine Orders to be read by all. These were usually drawn up by Brigade Major David Spector. From Routine Orders of 19 March, Serial No. 17:

*Paragraph 126: Prevention of water-borne diseases.*
*A. Only authorised water points to be used for drinking.*
*B. Adequate personnel are trained for water duties.*
*C. All men in all units to be protected by TAB inoculation.*

*Paragraph 127:*
*A. It has been reported that military personnel have been using explosives for fishing.*
*B. Use of explosives for fishing is strictly prohibited. Offenders will be punished.*

*Paragraph 130:*
*A. Equipment to be returned to German prisoners is as follows: blankets, water bottles, mess tins, knife, fork and spoon. Deficiencies will not be made up from stores.*

*Paragraph 131: Petrol containers.*
*A. Petrol cans are being returned with petrol in them due to fear of sediment.*
*B. Every can is thoroughly washed before being refilled, eliminating dirt entering until the can is opened by users.*
*C. Petrol units will not accept cans unless empty and with caps firmly shut.*

The Routine Orders were as efficient as a fine-tooth comb. They missed very little. It is intriguing, therefore, to note the complete absence of references to illegal or unmilitary conduct. There is no mention of Brigade vehicles missing from their parks for hours, even days, on end. No other organisation had the drivers and vehicles available and willing to go to the rescue of Jews. It was thus that the Brigade came to be regarded as the keystone at the centre of the Net. Both Jewish and non-Jewish Allied soldiers contacted the Brigade with information whenever they stumbled across destitute and desperate refugees. Mechanics and workshop fitters worked all hours to minimise the likelihood of breakdowns. And there was never any shortage of drivers volunteering to make the long and hazardous journeys. Routine Orders never referred to the frequent occasions when the consumption of petrol and diesel shot up. Nor were any of the extra-curricular journeys logged. Len Sanitt told me about the false documents and passes issued to drivers to get them through checkpoints with their human cargoes. He joked that he had the best forgers and printers not behind bars.

In the *Jewish Chronicle* of 9 November 1984, David Spector had a letter published:

> The other problems faced by Brigadier Benjamin and myself were how to reconcile our military duties and responsibilities with the political objectives of the Yishuv. They expected our priority to be in helping the victims in Europe by giving them to understand that the Jews in Palestine had not forgotten them and wanted them.

So there it was. The Holocaust had forced the promulgation of a supranational law for Jews, and for Jews only. It was to save and improve the conditions of the remnants of European Jewry above all else, except the waging of war against the Nazis. The 5,500 Brigaders at all levels dedicated themselves to both tasks. Perforce the Brigade had been pushed into a Messianic role, as was illustrated by a report on the Eichmann case published in the *Jerusalem Post*:

> The 111th and final witness for the prosecution was Mr Aharon Hoter-Yishai, a wartime officer in the Brigade and now a Haifa attorney. He said, 'The dimensions of the Holocaust threw the whole Brigade into relief work. I went from camp to camp. Hundreds of creatures, you could not call them anything else, fought among themselves with all their feeble strength to touch the shoulders carrying the flash. They kissed the Jewish flag on our vehicle. They crawled on stomachs to hug the feet of Jewish soldiers and kiss their boots. In Bergen-Belsen some 27,000 of the 52,000 liberated did not have the will to live or respond to efforts to restore them to health. They died.
>
> 'In June 1945 I visited Theresienstadt camp. 4,000 Jews there were disappointed that only one truck had been sent to fetch them. Survivors and Jewish soldiers wept together. Children clambered on to the military truck and begged to leave right away. I don't know of any paragraph in the King's Regulations or the Standing Orders of the Eighth Army which could have gotten an officer to tell those children to climb down.'

In common with other Palestine units and the relief bodies being set up, the Brigade registered the names, addresses, and relevant details of every transient refugee. Copies were circulated to all units. New lists were eagerly scrutinised by the men from continental Europe hoping to see a name they knew. Disappointed, they would shrug and walk away. One Romanian lance-corporal commented wryly, 'Miracles are for fairies, not for Jews.'

But on one occasion, a Polish cook uttered a cry of joy as he pored over a recent list. He recognised the name of someone he had known when he lived in Krakow. He rushed to the canteen, where the latest batch of rescued refugees were being fed, and greeted his long-lost neighbour. They embraced and wept, then the cook put the question he had been afraid to ask, 'My family . . . what news?' The newcomer put his arm round his old friend's shoulder and sighed. 'I'm sorry. They were taken away.'

'My two sisters . . . my parents?'

'The four of them . . .'

The cook clutched at straws. 'Are you certain?'

'Certain. I saw them being forced into a German truck.'

In April activity increased on both banks of the Senio. There were more clashes and casualties mounted. Right along the line, the Allied infantrymen were tense with strain as they waited for their approaching 'D-Day'. As primed as highly trained boxers waiting to be unleashed by the first-round bell, they oiled and checked their weapons over and over again. They were avid listeners to the news bulletins put out by the BBC in London, and by radio stations in liberated Europe. They played chess and card games, and argued about every topic, except one – the Holocaust. It was an open sore, whose ramifications so overwhelmed them many could not bear to talk about it. They fervently prayed that there would be no armistice before they could get into action.

Two small but vital units finally moved up to their forward positions. Brigade Ordnance Field Park was commanded by Captain Erdman RAOC. His trucks were loaded with necessities such as new tyres, especially for jeeps, spare batteries and engine parts. They were ordered to take up position by crossroads on the Faenza road. This turned out to be in direct line of German artillery fire. Fortunately there were no direct hits during the first two bombardments. Erdman quickly ordered his trucks to disperse to safer hiding places each night. They would drive off before dusk, and return every morning at 0700 hours, the drivers and storemen sleeping in their vehicles overnight.

The Brigade's Provost Unit settled in and took charge of enemy prisoners and deserters, who were locked in cages before being handed over for interrogation to Captain Goodman, the Brigade's Intelligence Officer. The unit was commanded by Captain Lipschitz, and comprised one sergeant, four corporals, nine lance-corporals, and thirteen privates. They set up checkpoints and traffic posts. and erected direction and place name signs in both Hebrew and English. They policed the passage of convoys, paying particular attention to the maintenance of the correct distance between vehicles, and delays and accidents were kept to a minimum. Their brief was to enforce Routine Orders and, like policemen everywhere, they developed a sharp nose for miscreant behaviour. But strangely, they did not seem to notice when military personnel and vehicles were used illegally on missions of mercy. Perhaps when instincts clash, the strongest prevails. Several NCOs in the Provost Unit were Haganah men, and instructions from the Jewish Agency to give priority to saving Jewish refugees overrode other priorities. Ex-Brigader Mark Hyatt recalled:

It was strange. We were aware that never before had Jews been in a situation like us, in the Brigade, where we had the power and the means and the ability to save our less fortunate co-religionists. There were so many odd things about that time. The non-Jewish personnel knew what was happening and they were one hundred percent with us. Even British and other nationalities in other units in our area were sympathetic towards what we were doing. It was of course the horror stories of the Holocaust that knocked everyone for six. The half-expected reprimand from on high never came.

In retrospect, it seems very likely that Eighth Army High Command knew what was going on. Apart from the Brigade, there were quite a number of Palestine Jewish units in Italy and, by the beginning of 1945, they had already set up comfort and rehabilitation shelters for refugees. The camps were established in areas inhabited by Italians, a tolerant and basically decent people, who were so appalled by Nazi atrocities against Jews that they never failed to offer food, clothing, and sympathy to the rescued wretches.

It is possible too that High Command had become aware of the remarkable change of attitude among Jews, especially the young and combatant. No Jewish soldier was going to be prevented from pulling out all the stops to help his distressed fellow Jews. The Jewish people were sloughing off their survival skin of servility, humility, and caution. Now they would fight for what they wanted, nay needed. Small boats, overloaded with rescued Jews, continued to sneak out of Italian ports bound for Palestine.

There was another factor. The final 'Great Offensive' was about to be made in Italy. Every front line Allied unit was in place, ready and eager to go. Among them was the Jewish Brigade. Politically, it was high profile, not something that Brigadier Benjamin and his staff wanted, but there was nothing they could do about it. They concentrated on the immediate matter in hand – winning the war. An English Jew, Major A C Jackson, recorded in the customarily terse style of the War Diary:

> *April 1st. 1st Bn Pal Regiment in sharp patrol clashes. Our casualties 4 killed 1 missing 13 wounded. Outpost of 13 other ranks established. Enemy casualties seen being removed by ambulance at 0900 hours.*
> *April 2nd. Quiet day.*
> *April 3rd. Quiet day. One prisoner captured at 2100 hours. Enemy loudspeakers broadcast music during the night from the Cuffiano area.*
> *April 4th. Deserter from 2nd platoon 2nd Company 1st Bn 12th Para Sturm Regiment 4th Para division.*
> *April 6th. Quiet day. Intermittent mortar and spandau fire.*
> *April 7th. 1st Bn Pal Regiment in patrol clashes. Our casualties 1 killed 8 wounded.*
> *April 8th. Prisoner taken from 4th Company 11th Para Regiment 4th Para division.*
> *April 9th. Isolated fire fights.*
> *April 10th. 8th Army General Offensive starts. 2nd Bn Pal Regiment crossed the Senio River and very quickly seized and occupied the objective of Fantaguzzi M233231 by 0145 hours. No casualties.*

The attack was launched on schedule to the minute. It was preceded by air support and artillery which pounded the enemy positions. The Brigade took the two positions allocated to it, and established a firm bridgehead on the north side of the Senio. The Polish Corps on the Brigade's right flank were equally successful in establishing their designated bridgehead. The Italian Folgore Regiment flanking their left failed. The Brigade was assigned to capture its target, which it did.

In the last fifty years, many of the Brigaders who took part in the attack have died. But in interviews and written notes, I have come across references to an initial attack with fixed bayonets. Meir Zorea, interviewed for a television documentary, said:

> It was a fantastic feeling. You did not feel afraid. You were pumped up with exaltation . . .

Another Brigader in that attack was Yohanan Pelz. He recalled:

> We waited on the start line 300 metres from the objective and the Germans. The order was given to fix bayonets. We did. At full pelt we rose and charged. We could not stop. We lost all fear. We hit them so hard they seemed to melt away. We showed the world that we could fight and win.

The Hebrew newspaper, *Davar*, published a letter from a captain in the Brigade, describing a series of patrol clashes in which they took a number of German prisoners. He wrote of one skirmish in which Lance-Corporal Levy, who was born in Germany, approached a strong point, kicked open a door, and shouted, 'Swine! Come out. The Jews have come.' Four trembling Germans emerged from their dugout with hands raised. One, whose face was white as chalk, repeatedly pleaded in a shaking voice, 'I am not a Nazi. I am a Social Democrat.'

On the morning of their major action, this captain's platoon was waiting at the jumping-off point during the preliminary barrage, when at zero hour he shouted in Hebrew, 'Advance! Attack!' To his astonishment, they jumped up and, in his own words, 'raced forward with fixed bayonets like a pack of wolves'. Quickly reaching the German positions, they began lobbing grenades, and the captain heard German voices cry, 'Mum, Mum. God Almighty. Help.'

The Brigade set fire to all the strong points, and one daring private went from house to house, firing his sub machine-gun, until he himself was killed by a burst of fire. The infantrymen wiped out all of the enemy positions within fifteen minutes. Then, as ordered, they withdrew, leaving behind destruction, fire, and dead Germans. A whole German redoubt was ablaze, and no further firing was heard from the enemy lines. The Brigade's own dead were buried in a nearby military cemetery.

On their return journey, the Brigaders passed some British tanks. One man jumped out of his tank and shouted, 'Three cheers for the Palestinians!' The other British troops joined in enthusiastically.

Further entries were recorded in the War Diary:

*April 11th. Intermittent mortar and spandau fire on forward defensive positions. Bridgehead across the Senio extended by 2nd Battalion Palestine Regiment. 3rd Battalion passed through the 2nd and commenced the ascent of Mt Ghebbio against enemy rearguard opposition.*

*April 12th. 10 Corps gave Brigade the task of capturing Mt Ghebbio 2024, Querzola 2025 and area Mazzalano. Contact maintained with enemy north of the Senio. The Battalions moved forward to occupy the features Col Ca Zanelli and Torre. 2nd Bn Pal Regt engaged by spandau and mortar fire from Padiano. 3rd Bn Pal Regt reached Serra. It lost 3 killed and 8 wounded on ascent of Mt Ghebbio.*

*April 13th. Contacted enemy in area of Torre. Own casualties 3 killed 7 wounded. 2nd Bn Pal Regt patrol advanced to La Torre hit by mortar fire. 3 wounded. No contact with enemy.*

*April 14th. 1st Bn Pal Regt mortared from area Sirolo. 2nd Bn Regt withdrawn and concentrated in area 25824 and 243187.*

*April 15th. 1st Battalion Pal Regt withdrawn and concentrated in area 2520. Headquarters Jewish Brigade Group ordered to take command of MAC Group in conformity with relief of 13 Corps by 10 Corps. Function of MAC Group is to hold vital pivotal position at Mt Grande.*

Major David Spector referred in his notes to the important hinge position of the established bridgehead. During this period, other units which came under Jewish command were the Lovat Scouts, 2nd Royals, 2nd Highland Light Infantry, 4/11 Sikhs, Jodhpur State Light Infantry, Nabha Akal Regiment, 57th Field Regiment, and the 11th Light AA Regiments of the Royal Artillery.

*April 16th. HQ Jewish Brigade Group settled at San Clemente and Brigade established command over MAC Group.*
*April 17th. Immediate award of Military Medal to Pal/15435 Moshe Zilberberg 2nd Bn Pal Regt approved by Field Marshal Alexander, Supreme Allied Commander Med Theatre. Nabha Akal Regt still maintains contact with enemy around Monte Calderraro and also to the west. Patrol reached Mt Castellaro and encountered spandau fire and withdrew after a fire fight.*
*April 18th. Some mortaring of MAC Group area. Contact still maintained with enemy. Patrols clash. Casualties 17 wounded 4 missing.*
*April 19th. Enemy patrols approached forward defence locations at positions 994334 and 983327. Increased enemy movements observed in our own sector and on both flanks. Our artillery fired 14 rounds of 7.2s on Mt Castellaro. Direct hits observed on dugouts.*
*April 20th. No contact with enemy.*

At this stage the demoralised German forces were crumbling into not quite a rout, leaving behind individuals and small groups of soldiers eager to be taken prisoner by the Allies, knowing this would ensure their survival. They had lost the war. For them the news was universally bad – the reducing of their towns and cities to rubble, and stories of the Red Army pouring into Germany. Initial, and sometimes stubborn, rearguard actions were giving way to sporadic, last-gasp fire fights.

*April 21st. Immediate award of Military Medal to Pal/38518*
*Private Aharon Ben Kimche of 1st Bn Pal Regt approved by Field Marshal Alexander.*
*April 22nd. Nabha Akal left for concentration area at Brisighelle.*
*April 23rd. Mr McKenzie attached to the Brigade with mobile canteen. 1300 hours 2nd Loyals left command for 13th Corps. Brigade placed on 72 hours notice. MAC Group dissolved.*
*April 28th. 1200 hours 643 Pal Field Company RE passed to command of HQ 10th Corps for employment on Po river crossings.*
*April 29th. Brigadier Benjamin lunched with Lt General Richard L McCreary KCB DSO MC MBE, Commander of the 8th Army.*

Shimon Behar, a platoon sergeant in the Brigade, and later a lieutenant-colonel in the Israeli Defence Forces, and later still General Secretary of the Israeli Veterans League, recalled that the conversation between Benjamin and McCreary was friendly. The British did not worry that the Brigade would be a weak link and fail to seize objectives. On the contrary, they were aware of the Brigaders' hatred for the Germans, and their eagerness to advance beyond the remits given to their patrols, seeking to clash with the enemy – an eagerness which could lead to carelessness and unnecessary casualties.

As with anything to do with Palestine, there were political overtones. The Yishuv had made it clear to the Palestine government that they had too many of their best young men in Italy. The word went down to Eighth Army Command that a high casualty count among Brigaders would inflame the always fragile relationship with the Jewish Agency. This unusual approach contrasted sharply with that adopted towards other front line units.

There was a logical explanation. Many infantrymen in other sectors were veterans who had had their fill of combat in various theatres. Now that the war was nearing its end, they wanted only to get home and resume a normal life with their nearest and dearest. On the other hand, too many Brigaders knew that they now had no homes to return to, no loved ones left to embrace. They faced a chillingly bleak future, one without purpose. Their overwhelming urge was to take revenge. With guns in hand, and the murderers of their kith and kin just across the river, they could not wait. And this feeling affected even those who did have homes and families to go back to. The lust to spill Nazi blood was felt by all. How to dampen this down was one topic earnestly discussed by Benjamin and McCreary.

An incident on 19 March reinforced the British belief that the Brigade would acquit itself well against the best the Germans could field. There were unconfirmed rumours of a German withdrawal. Scouts were sent into no man's land to check. The Germans had not withdrawn – far from it. They were spoiling for a fight, and the one that ensued embroiled reinforcements sent into battle by both sides. It was the Germans who broke off first. They left nineteen dead, eleven were taken prisoner, and an unknown number were wounded.

On 27 March the 3rd Battalion Palestine Regiment moved into a sector of the line to face one of the toughest German units on the entire front, the crack 4 Paratroop Division. The sector was at Faenza to the west of their previous position. Two battalions of the 4 Paratroop Division faced the Brigade. These elite *Wehrmacht* combat troops were specially selected men whose political loyalties as 'good Germans' were beyond question. They were, in short, diehard Nazis. Formed in 1943, the division had seen action in Russia and Italy. At Anzio in 1944, it had fought hard and stubbornly, and had staged an ordered and disciplined withdrawal across the

Appenines. It was armed with a deadly accurate automatic rifle that was only issued to elite combat troops. At Faenza it was under the command of Major-General Heinrich Trettner.

In places, the opposing lines were two close for comfort. The Germans were entrenched on rising land, and could look down on and across the Senio river. Daytime activity was perilous and limited. Between dusk and dawn both sides sent out probing patrols and, when they clashed, the fire fights were short and furious. Both sides pounded the enemy with intermittent artillery and mortar bombardment. Captured paratroopers crossed the river on rafts made of wooden boxes and by improvised bridges. For the first time in two thousand years, Jews would face an enemy on a level playing field.

The Brigade had become a high-profile fighting force. It neither sought nor wanted this celebrity, indeed many of the men were not even aware of it. But the Jewish community in Palestine was hungry for any scrap of news, and the Palestine government, with an eye to the future, took a close interest in how it performed. They knew that Palestine Jewish servicemen had smuggled weapons into Palestine, and had hidden them on farms and kibbutzim across the country. They feared that returning Brigaders, and the other 30,000 Palestine Jewish servicemen, would provide the Jewish community with a ready-made, well trained army – which is exactly what they did. Diaspora Jews everywhere prayed for the Brigade's success and, in the wake of the Holocaust, there was a great deal of sympathy and encouragement from the Allies.

It is unclear whether the bayonet charges during the initial attack resulted in hand-to-hand fighting. It is known that the Brigade infantry did fix bayonets and charge. There was some German resistance, before the enemy fell back, and the retreat gathered momentum. The Allies were taking prisoners and stragglers. The heroes of the Third Reich, who had jackbooted their way across Europe, were now only concerned in a frantic attempt to save their own necks. They were terrified of capture by Italian partisans, many of whom were ardent communists, and who tended to give fascists of any nationality short shrift, hanging them or, in the absence of a rope, shooting them. Relief among Germans captured by British Eighth Army units was palpable. However, even the battle-hardened paratroopers were visibly unhappy when they fell into the hands of Jewish soldiers. One young, Berlin-born Brigader remembered:

When the bastards saw our shoulder flashes and realised we were Jews, you could almost smell their funk. There was no doubt that they knew all about the camps and what had happened to the Jews. I did take great pleasure in making them kneel down and pointing my gun at them. I didn't fire. I wanted to, yes. They could see that. I made more than one member of the master race mess his pants with fright.

Fifty years on I dared to ask him, 'Did you shoot any Germans?. 'You mean Nazis,' this now prosperous Israeli garage owner corrected me courteously, with a slight edge to his voice. 'Well, yes.' And again that non-commital reply, 'Things did happen, certainly to the SS.' He paused for a long time, then he said, 'I'll answer your next question before you ask it. Yes, I did lose my family. All five of them.' That left no room for further questions. I thanked him and left, aware that even after all that time, and despite his new life and new family, the old grief would never free him.

What stripped away any remaining vestiges of arrogance among captured Germans was being railed at in their own language by Brigaders, expressing feelings that had been bottled up for years. The Brigaders were angered by protestations from their prisoners that they had never been Nazis, were rather Social Democrats and, in any case, had 'only been obeying orders'. They were especially enraged by denials of knowledge about the concentration camps and what had gone on there.

Continental-born Brigaders were just ordinary young men who had been plunged into purgatory by Nazis. The first nightmarish invasion of their homes by Jew-haters had destroyed forever their happy family lives, along with their families themselves. If emotions did spill over, and some were not able to observe strictly the provisions of the Geneva Convention, who could blame them? Hatred, particularly irrational hatred, has never been a Jewish trait. The Nazis changed all that. If officers happened to be around, some turned a blind eye. Others intervened. But no Brigader, regardless of rank, saw, heard or spoke of misbehaviour. Fifty years on, I was told with a wry smile, that memories tended to fade.

The Eighth Army forces advanced rapidly right along the line – Forli, Imola, Castel San Pietro, villages, hamlets all fell as the Germans hastily discarded their proud oaths to defend the Third Reich with their lives. The 'Big Offensive' had been planned in two phases – first the crossing of the Senio river, then the crossing of the Po. Because of the speed of the Allied advance, the two phases merged into one. The main Brigade forces lost contact with the Germans, with just a handful of units attached to other nationalities encountering rearguard German actions. Brigade engineering units raced ahead to assist with bridging the Po. Then the Brigade received orders to pull out of the chase and return as a reserve unit in the British 10th Corps. That was effectively the end of their wartime fighting. The British were unstinting in their recognition of the Brigade's performance in the field. The 10th Corps commander wrote:

> The Jewish Brigade fought well and its men were eager to make contact with the enemy by every means available to them. Their staff work, their commands and their assessments were good. If they get enough help they certainly deserve to be part of any field force whatsoever.

Even so, when the Brigade went into the line, there were units understaffed. Some companies went into action below officer strength, and platoons were led by sergeants. The pro-Arab obstructionists who had delayed the formation of the Brigade until the last phase of the war, had ensured that enthusiastic volunteers were given too little time to train, and provide Palestine Jewish officers and NCOs. In addition, by the time its formation was announced in September 1944, the Yishuv leaders' disapproval of more Jews leaving Palestine had reduced recruitment virtually to zero. Nevertheless, the Jewish Agency's determination to achieve its own fighting force had finally paid off. When its soldiers returned home to Palestine, their morale and confidence were sky-high. They had confronted the *Wehrmacht*'s best and had more than held their own.

They had been involved in day battles, night encounters, both offensive and defensive actions, ambushes and firing strategies. They had learned the meaning of true comradeship, the principle of never abandoning their wounded, and the requirement to do their utmost to avoid capture. Most potently of all, they had been transformed by an overwhelming consciousness of nationhood. They were the foundation stone of the new Jewish army that would protect the rebirth of the Jewish Homeland.

After 2,000 years in the wilderness, living with the stigma of being the unwanted alien, Jews sloughed of the role of victim, and regained pride in their identity. The Brigade's message proclaimed to Jews everywhere a new, uncompromising call to arms:

The centuries of always being rootless victims are behind us. There will be a country we can call our own, and where we can live among our own people without threat of pogroms and prejudice. And if the need arises, not only will we defend it, but we will be able to defend it and win.

# Chapter Ten

A letter sent to the Committee for a Jewish Army by a Brigade infantryman crystallised what motivated the Brigaders:

> After years of hope, constantly disappointed, our dream is at last realised. I am writing this letter to the accompaniment of a great orchestra of guns firing. I am in the trenches and taking part in the symphony. I call it a symphony and its name is War Against Nazism. We have been here now for three weeks and I have never been so happy. I am doing what I want to do, and not only I alone, but all of us here. Imagine how a Jew feels who holds a machine-gun and sees Germans ahead of him. We want to answer for our brothers and sisters who were killed and tortured by the Nazis. The only thing we are waiting for is the word to advance and fight. Then, leave the rest to us.
>
> I would like all members and supporters of the Committee for a Jewish Army to know that my comrades and I are grateful for what they have done. If the Committee had not existed we would still be somwhere in Egypt peeling potatoes and doing guard duties, fit only for those, not fit for battle.
>
> The official hoisting of the flag was performed by Lieutenant Berman. When he was a sergeant he lost his stripes for leading a demonstration demanding the Jewish flag. When Brigadier Benjamin ordered us to attention for the first time, we saw before our eyes the legions of our dead in Treblinka, Auschwitz, Maidanek. When our banner of retribution was unfurled the strains of Hatikvah burst from our breasts and we heard the strains of hope, justice and rebirth.

Two weeks after the offensive against the Gothic Line began, Mark Clark declared that Bologna had been captured. Now the American Fifth Army and the British Eighth Army were inside the gateway leading to the flat Po basin, poised to destroy the last of the German army in Italy. In the final days before the fall of Bologna, the military situation was fluid in the face of patchy German resistance and counter attacks. It changed by the hour. Suddenly the Brigade was ordered to take under its command the pivotal sector at the junction of the Fifth and Eighth Armies in the vital Monte Grande area north of San Clemente, the dominant feature overlooking

Bologna. Brigade HQ now had under its command six well known British and Indian battalions, and the only British mountain artillery in Italy. Their task was to hold the Monte Grande area while Bologna was besieged from both sides.

Norman Lourie, the BBC war correspondent, witnessed a preceding action, when the Jewish infantry stormed Monte Ghebbio in the face of crack Nazi paratroopers' spandau fire, and sniping from hilltop positions. Sniper fire was particularly heavy around the church at Ossano, during an attack led by Major Maxie Kahan from Haifa. Fanning out in all directions on the mountains above Imola, the infantry moved at great speed and in great spirit, and undeterred by continuous enemy fire, they took their objective. Although the Brigade was a small cog in a large military wheel, it proved that it had matured into a confident, well coordinated fighting force. Given its objectives, it went out and accomplished them all.

One of the luckiest men was Shlomo Levins, a member of the Mizrachi kibbutz of Tirat Zvi. He was in the forefront of the attack on Monte Ghebbio when a sniper's bullet tore open the front of his helmet, ripping the lining. Miraculously, although shocked, he was unhurt. The next day Levins was still wearing his lucky helmet as his company rested on a hilltop. He was very cheerful.

Lourie recalled that arguably the greatest danger the men faced were the many types of mine that appeared to have been laid everywhere. The schu-mine caused many casualties, needing a pressure of less than three pounds to detonate it. No man died more bravely than Private Zelig Zankelis who was caught by one of these. Mortally wounded, he would not allow his comrades to rescue him. He kept shouting, 'SOS. Mines. Don't come closer. Throw me a rope and I'll tie myself to it.' Treading carefully his comrades got him out. Before dying six hours later at the casualty clearing station at Piedora, Zankelis warned, 'Look, boys. I have had my lesson. See that you are more careful.'

The end of hostilities saw the end of the chase. Germans who had not been taken prisoner were trying to surrender to the Allied forces, or make their way north in an attempt to reach home. They had become a frightened rabble. The Italians, who had been ground down by the heel of rampant Nazism, spat at them, beat them up and, especially when they found SS men, murdered them. For the SS, chickens had finally come home to roost. They desperately tried to dispose of their giveaway uniforms, and to hide. In Tarvisio, Brigaders found some hiding in the hospital among *Wehrmacht* wounded, who despised them and blamed them for Germany's misfortune. But then, no captured German confessed to having been a Nazi supporter.

At 0100 hours on 2 May the Brigade passed from the command of the 10th Corps to that of the Eighth Army. On 5 May it was ordered to reconnoitre the Teramo-Ascoli area, and to prepare to move south.

Advance parties had already moved north; then the order to move south was rescinded, and the Brigade drove north to Udine with orders to pacify the area, where there had been a build-up of tension between Tito and his partisans and the Allies.

Moving north on 19 and 20 May the Brigade reached Tarvisio, and the Palestine Regiment relieved the Irish Brigade. Tarvisio was a small, picturesque Alpine town, a fulcrum where the borders of Italy, Austria and Yugoslavia met. A river flowed through it, and here the Brigade set up its headquarters. The 3rd Battalion Palestine Regiment uncovered a massive munitions dump, and set guard over it, a duty later taken over by an American mountain regiment. HQ was informed that Field Marshal Alexander had approved the immediate award of the Military Medal to Pal/38333 Company Sergeant-Major Elijahu Hershkovitz.

Allied High Command gave the Brigade the job of securing and maintaining total military control of the area, while fostering good relations with the Yugoslavs, and preventing groups of their partisans from entering the zone. Tarvisio was in a bewildering state of turmoil, a microcosm of post-war Europe. It had a large German hospital, and a military supplies complex which had to be guarded. Hundreds of rootless, displaced Europeans were wandering about, concerned only to find the basic necessities of food, drink and shelter.

There were also many disarmed, disoriented *Wehrmacht* soldiers milling about. Some were not German nationals but had fought on the German side. And, from across the Austrian border, came the Jewish refugees, emaciated and desperate to grab the lifeline offered by the Brigade. They would seek out the soldiers with the blue and white shoulder flashes, who would take them to the large shelter which the Brigaders had built in only five days. There, they were deloused, showered and medically checked by the Brigade's field ambulance unit. Their old clothes were burned, and they would be given completely new garments, even down to the underwear.

The children were given Hebrew lessons by the Palestinian soldiers, while others would instruct them in a range of basic subjects. The soldiers took the refugees under their wing totally, and when they clambered on to Brigade vehicles to begin the journey south to the Palestine-bound boats, they well and truly left the hell of Europe behind. Their accounts of what they had suffered stoked the embers of the Brigaders' hatred for the Germans. They sought out members of the SS, even those in hospital. Major David Spector recalled to me later:

You must bear in mind that some 1,500 soldiers in the Brigade were European-born and when we were in Tarvisio they had heard enough to convince them that their families had been murdered. Not only that. There was this irresistable symbiosis among all of us, refugees, the

Palestinian-born sabras, Jews in all the Allied services, all of us, that we were now one nation. Our kith and kin had been slaughtered and revenge was very much in the air. It was the SS the men wanted to get their hands on. The higher the rank the better. The SS covered their indelible identification with plaster and bandages, but they were found. Our fellows stopped Germans and made them lift up their shirts and then . . .

David stopped talking. I prodded, 'And then?' He shrugged, and his answer lacked the question mark, 'And then . . .'

How was it that the Brigade, still under the military command of the British Eighth Army, switched its allegiance so openly, yet escaped punitive reprimand? That it had performed its military tasks in an exemplary fashion could have been a factor, but every other colonial force serving with the Eighth Army had done well. Without doubt it was the Holocaust that threw a protective shield around the Brigade. The almost daily, shocking revelations about the genocide of the Jewish people aroused such massive sympathy around the world that it prevented even the thought of physically hostile action being taken against Jews outside Palestine. This reaction was as evident in the media and among the public in Britain as anywhere else. It is true that eruptions of anti-semitic sentiment were experienced in Britain as a reaction to the killing by Jews of British soldiers in retaliation for the sometimes wanton killing by the British of Jews. But the anger always simmered down as, by and large, the British saw both sides of the Palestinian equation. Military action against the Brigade on Italian soil was not on.

With the Holocaust and the troubles in Palestine in mind, many Brigaders would have fought back. The idea of military confrontation was unthinkable, and wisely the British Foreign Office confined its actions to trying to stop illegal immigration into Palestine. So it was that many Jews in their teens, who had lost their families, found themselves incarcerated behind barbed wire, and under heavy guard, in yet another camp in Cyprus. This time the guards' uniforms were not grey or black, but khaki. The detainees switched their hatred to their new jailers, and it was not surprising that, when they eventually reached Palestine, many joined extremist groups. The Irgun Zvi Leumi and the Stern Gang had no shortage of willing recruits.

The importance of the Jewish Brigade lay not in its numbers, nor even in what it accomplished in battle, but rather in its very existence. It became a rallying point for Jews worldwide. It inspired. Most importantly, it gave hope to thousands of fellow Jews dangerously adrift in a still hostile Europe. The casual lack of humanity shown towards the victims of man's worst ever example of genocide reinforced the realisation that Jews could only trust other Jews. Put every able-bodied Jew you can on to the boats, the Yishuv instructed the Brigade. They will be needed as soldiers in the coming war for survival.

On 14 December 1941 the SS *Struma* left Constanza bound for the Mediterranean. It was an unseaworthy vessel with many open seams. All the pumps had to work flat out just to keep her afloat. She was packed with 769 Jews, many women and children among them. About 150 miles off the Turkish coast, the *Struma's* engines failed. For nine nightmarish weeks, the ship wallowed in the Bosphorus until the Turks relented and towed her to a berth. But they would not let the passengers come ashore. Jews in Ankara donated food to keep them alive. The Turks agreed to let them land if they could then make their way overland into Palestine. But Britain rejected this proposal, and the Turks towed the *Struma* back out to sea and left it there. There was a violent explosion. The cause was never established. The ship sank six miles offshore. There was one survivor. Other rust buckets sailed from northern Mediterranean ports for Palestine. Some, including the *Milas*, the *Alsine*, the *Atlantic Pancho*, the *Patria* and the *Salvador*, went down, and their passengers perished.

But many of the most inhumane actions were political. As early as February 1942, the Jewish Agency informed Lord Cranbourne of the Foreign Office that it could offer irrefutable evidence that death trains were transporting Jews to mass extermination camps. Cranbourne's response was, 'In pursuance of existing policy of taking all practicable steps to discourage illegal immigrants into Palestine, nothing whatsoever will be done to facilitate the arrival of Jewish refugees into Palestine.' The death trains continued to roll.

In April 1943 the Swedish government offered to admit 20,000 children from Germany, on condition that Britain and the United States take responsibility for them after the war. That guarantee was not forthcoming until December 1943, by which time relations between Sweden and Germany had deteriorated and it was too late. So 20,000 children perished.

On 12 March 1943 Premier Antonescu of Romania and SS Colonel Richter had offered to release 70,000 Jewish children in return for a 'ransom' of $500,000. American Treasury Secretary Morgenthau called in Stephen Wise, President of the American Jewish Congress, who raised the money in five days. The Treasury approved its transfer to Switzerland, and their adviser, Dr Stephen Feis, brought the agreement of the State Department for the transfer of funds during wartime. But for two months things were inexplicably held up. On 25 May the State Department cabled Berne for information, and two months later it vetoed the project. After a further two months Wise brought the matter to the attention of President Roosevelt, who ordered the State Department to proceed. Then it was decided that it was necessary to seek the opinion of the British government, which of course had to study the whole matter afresh. This took four vital months, at the end of which, in December, the British stated their opposition. They were concerned about the dispersal from enemy territory of so many Jews – how would it be managed? And where would they go? There was no obvious safe haven in the free world for 70,000 children. The decision was a death sentence, and the children perished in the camps.

In May 1944 Eichmann, Chief of the Gestapo's Bureau for Jewish Affairs, offered for ransom the lives of several hundred thousand Hungarian Jews. One of them, Joel Brandt, conveyed the offer to the British in Palestine, and was promptly imprisoned in Cairo. The American War Refugees Committee stated that it could not countenance ransom transactions. The Hungarian Jews went to their deaths. Years later, before he was hanged, Eichmann accurately summed it up when he said, 'The heart of the matter is that no place on earth was willing to accept Jews.'

By the autumn of 1944 there was a growing consciousness of Jews shedding the nationalities of their birth to fight purely as Jews. From the Baltic to the Romanian border, thousands of Jewish partisans were fighting as individuals in Polish and Russian units, or in the all-Jewish units which had been springing up. They operated in the rear areas of the German lines in forests, swamps and hills. News about the Jewish Brigade had reached their ears, and many of them began to think seriously of trying to get to the Brigade, and then to Palestine. Very few wanted to stay in Poland, the Soviet Union or the Baltic States when the war ended. Motivated by a new sense of self-esteem, delegates from forty Jewish groups met, and drew up a resolution that partisan groups should be permitted to fight as a Jewish national army under their own officers under overall Red Army command. This was a daring request – they were of course unaware that the formation of dissident, national splinter groups ran directly counter to post-war Soviet plans. Their request was turned down.

Reaction was swift and severe. The Red Army ordered all Jewish groups to disband, and disperse their men among other Russian formations. One third obeyed the order; the remainder refused. Their minds were made up. They would continue to fight the Germans, but as soon as the war ended, they would make their way south to meet up with the Brigade. Ex-partisans recalled later that learning of the existence of the Brigade had been a shot in the arm and gave rise to great excitement. It also gave them something to aim towards.

Poles outnumbered Russians among the partisans. They had many scores to settle. Two, Benno Feld and Hanna Baum, both in their late teens, had survived the Lublin massacre. Word got round that SS Lieutenant Georg Mussfeld had boasted to SS Judge Konrad Morgen that the ashes of Jews he had roasted had floated like a cloud over Lublin. In 1958 two tourists, with the help of information supplied, track Mussfeld down to his inn at Oberammergau. He was now fat and prosperous. The tourists hanged him in his kitchen – they were Benno Feld and Hanna Baum.

Hard as it was to believe, in the light of everything that had happened, anti-semitism in Europe, far from abating, had actually got worse. In some cases, it was prompted by simple greed. When Jewish families had been taken away, their comfortable homes, with their furnishings and fittings, lay empty. A covetous non-Jewish family moved in. Then sometimes, out of the blue, the Jewish owner returned, wanting to move back into his rightful property. On occasions this wish cost him his life. For the family 'in possession' murder solved an awkward problem. Allied occupation could not cover every corner, and killing Jews had become an ingrained habit.

But the Jews, particularly the young, had changed. The elderly had had no chance of escape, but the young had witnessed death, had escaped it, and were not afraid of it. Now they lived only for the chance to kill Germans. It was all they thought about until they got to know about the Brigade, and how impressively it had acquitted itself in action. Hard facts and rumours spread like wildfire. It became the goal of Jewish fighters not only to reach the Brigade but to take with them every surviving Jew they could find. The partisans would corral their charges. Money as such did not exist. What they needed – trucks, fuel, food, drink, clothing, blankets, medical supplies, cooking utensils – they took by force.

Their trek south towards Italy gathered momentum. They crossed Poland, followed the Czech border until they found a weak, unguarded spot, moved into Hungary and through Austria – ever southwards drawn by an irresistible force towards the Jewish Brigade. On the way they encountered *Wehrmacht* troops under guard of Russia's peasant soldiers. Neither side took any notice of the other. But Russian-speaking partisans engaged the Red Army guards in friendly conversation, especially when they spotted the black SS uniform on prisoners who had not had time to find civilian garb. The partisans plied the guards with wine, vodka and schnapps, all purloined along the way. When the guards awoke from their deep stupor, they found the partisans gone and their SS prisoners dead. Post-war, killing was no longer a one-way exercise.

Obernau was a peaceful, picturesque village in Saxony, just north of the Czech border. For the most part the war had passed it by, except for the Stolhaus, a slave labour complex where Jews worked in a Krupps von Bohlen munitions factory. After a long, hard day's work, on the most meagre rations, the Jews would be marched back to the specially built kennels where they slept. These were three feet high, nine feet long, and six feet wide. Five Jews slept to a kennel. They became emaciated, living skeletons with a covering of skin. They began to die of malnutrition and exhaustion. Some committed suicide. They were guarded by an SS garrison which on Sundays gave the robust, well-fed villagers conducted tours of the camp. Survivors described Sundays as carnival days when the

SS guards roistered with the village girls. No spark of compassion was ever shown by guard or villager. When occasionally a worker escaped and tried to hide in the surrounding wheatfields, the male villagers joined the SS and their dogs in the hunt for the quarry. For them it was good, healthy fun. And the local farmers and merchants grew rich selling their wares to the sizeable SS garrison.

This way of life came to an end when orders from Berlin closed the factory. The machinery was dismantled, and the Jews moved out. The war was over, the deserting SS men crept back into Obernau. They discarded their uniforms, and several married the compliant farmers' daughters they had been sleeping with. They felt safe from discovery and having to pay the price for war crimes, and settled down to enjoy the good life.

Then, one frosty morning, the Jews returned to Obernau. There were three hundred of them. They had been led by Malachi Wald and Avraham Becker out of Lublin, across Poland, German Silesia and Saxony, and were on their way to Italy and the Brigade. They were cold, hungry and very tired. The two veteran partisans decided to give their charges three days' rest.

Wald sent ten men into Obernau in a truck. They took no weapons, and went in to ask for food, water and milk for the babies and children. They had no money – in those days who did? Certainly not partisans and camp survivors. The truck stopped in the centre of the village near the town hall. It was soon surrounded by the Obermeister, two policemen, some farmers, ex-soldiers and about ten SS men some of whom, with heavy Teutonic humour, donned their black uniforms to frighten the Jews. When the Jews asked for food and water they were jeered at and then attacked. Six were pulled from the truck and killed. The other four managed to fend off their attackers, turn the truck round and escape.

Two hours later on that crisp, sunny day, Wald and Becker led three trucks and twenty partisans back into Obernau. This time they were armed with grenades, automatic rifles and machine pistols. They pulled up outside the town hall. An hour earlier, the Obermeister had called a meeting in a large, ground-floor room. It was attended by prominent citizens, merchants and some of the returned SS men, in all about three dozen. They were debating whether they should chase out the Jews, or hang six of them and leave them hanging from trees to frighten away the others.

The partisans quietly took up position by the doors and windows of the meeting room. At a signal they flung open the doors and smashed the windows. They hurled in grenades, and opened fire, raking backwards and forwards. All those present died where they sat. When the partisans left Obernau their trucks were loaded with food – cheese, milk, bread, meat, butter, eggs, vegetables – and wine.

They took basic cooking utensils, crockery, cutlery, salt and pepper.

They took blankets and clothing, especially for the children, sleeping bags and every other comfort. They stayed at Obernau for three days, maintaining an armed guard on their trucks and tents day and night. For three days they took everything they wanted from the stunned and cowed village. Then they went on their way south again through Europe to find the Brigade.

The incident at Obernau was not unique. Other groups moving south, starving and exhausted, met with little charity when they begged for food and drink. Without money or any other means to pay, they simply took what they needed. In places off the main route, with no sympathetic occupying troops to help them, they had to fight for what they got. There were fatalities at Glachau, Limbach, Auerbach, Hildburghausen, and several other places.

The Allies were setting up displaced persons camps where refugees could find food and shelter. The camps were intended for all refugees, but inevitably Jews outnumbered the rest. Because of the attitude of their erstwhile neighbours, they had no homes to go back to. The nomadic groups would not enter the camps, or even go near them. They pressed on, picking up groups or individual stray Jews and took them with them. They got hold of all the weapons they needed. Sympathetic Red Army units gave them food and equipment, and even vehicles to carry the children, the old and the sick. The one thing they all had in common was a hatred of the Nazis.

Mostly, any anti-semitic sentiment was dampened down when Germans and Austrians found themselves confronting well-armed, trigger-happy young men with hatred and loathing in their eyes. The days when defenceless Jews were an easy target were over. No one will ever know how many Jews were killed during their exodus from Europe, nor how many anti-semites were put to death by vengeful partisans as they passed through.

At the end of the war, world Jewry split into those who needed help and those who were able and anxious to give it. At the heart of the matter were the mental and physical wrecks to be found in the displaced persons camps. Meir Zorea said that the Brigade had an enormous map of Europe on the wall, on which pins marked the exact locations of the camps. As the refugees trickled in they brought information about new camps, as well as the approximate numbers of men, women and children in them, which occupying army was mounting guard over them, and what help, especially medical and educational, was needed.

Individuals, unable to face being behind barbed wire for a moment longer, would escape and take their chance on finding a group headed for Italy. Penniless and alone, they were regarded as brave or crazy, or both. God alone knows how many made it and how many fell by the wayside. With the British armed forces increasing their blockade on Palestine, the only Allied solution to this pressing problem was to build more camps.

So, many found themselves inside yet another camp, depressing places in bleak areas such as Feldafing, Allach, and Bad Reichenhal. At least here no one tried to kill them. They were fed, had washing facilities and medical care. They could even marry and have children. And in these places they could quietly rot away. But the inmates had had their fill of man's inhumanity, and one day they decided to rise up and help themselves.

Forty-one delegates, men and women, representing hundreds of thousands of stranded people, attended a landmark conference at Feldafing. And there they witnessed a miracle. For the first time they saw with their own eyes a man in the uniform of the Jewish Brigade. They stared at the blue and white shoulder flash, and the Star of David emblems and badges, and they wept. The man in the uniform was Major Zvi Caspi, and he brought a message of hope and support from the National Council of the Palestine Jewish Community. He cut an impressive figure, spick and span and a soldier to his fingertips. He spoke clearly and strongly when he declared, 'You are bone of our bone, flesh of our flesh. We in Palestine wait to welcome you with open arms and it will be done. Be strong. Be united. Be organised and be disciplined.'

Afterwards the delegates could not resist the temptation to touch and even kiss the evocative shoulder flash. Caspi was embarrassed but he understood the depth of feeling. He waited until every delegate had shaken his hand and kissed his shoulder flash. His presence had been enough to give a tremendous uplift to morale.

That same day the delegates formed a new Jewish resistance, which they called The Surviving Remnant (She'erit Hapleetah). It had one aim – to force open the gates of Palestine to Jewish immigrants. Together with the many Haganah leaders and members who had joined the Brigade, and who were visiting the DP camps, they formed an active strategy which they called Escape (Bricha).

From that day, they published papers, sent delegations to different countries, held meetings, went on hunger strikes, and gave the issue of Jewish immigration into Palestine a much higher profile. They aroused enormous sympathy internationally, especially and embarrassingly in the United States. Because Britain held the mandate, history had conspired to throw the Jewish and British peoples into a conflict which neither wanted. Generally, Britain had a history of tolerance, and the British army, when given the green light by the politicians, did set up and train the members of the Jewish Brigade into a first-class fighting force.

But the refugees were there, and the situation could only be resolved by allowing them to go to the only country in the world that would willingly take them. They could not be left to rot indefinitely in the camps. It is arguable that no people had ever suffered as much as they had. Years later

Malachi Wald spoke to Michael Elkins, the BBC correspondent in Jerusalem. These are his exact words:

> I want you to think of a man coming out of the camps or the forests in 1945, and all he wants is to get out of Europe where everyone he loves is dead, his whole people murdered, and they will not let him go. He comes out of camps and they put him back into camps; no country wants him, only his people in Palestine want him and they will not let him go. Those who do this to him, who do it after all his years of pain, are not the enemy who killed him, but those others from whom he has the right to expect kindness and mercy and justice.
>
> The man looks at the world and what does he see? The eyes that were closed to his suffering are closed still. The hands that were not lifted to help him are not lifted now. The Germans who killed the Jews are free and they have their jobs and their families. They are the mayors and the policemen and the Jews are homeless vermin. The Germans are free and the Jews are back in their camps and no one wants them. What we learned in 1945 brought a pain that never ends. We learned at last in 1945 what we had not until then really believed. We learned in 1945 that only the Jew cares about the Jew. In all the world there is no justice for the Jew, but only the justice that the Jew can take for himself. That is what we did. We stood at the crossroads, then we turned our backs on Palestine and started to take our own justice and vengeance.

After bringing his charges to the Brigade, Malachi Wald turned away from going on to the boats. Around April 1945 he and fifty others, including Avraham Becker, Judah Klein, Benno the Messenger, and Hanna Baum, headed back into Europe. They formed a secret organisation with a fighting slogan going back to Biblical times: Dahm Yisroel Nokeam, which translates as 'the blood of Israel will take revenge'. The first letters of each word together spell out the Hebrew word *DIN*, which means 'judgement'.

DIN wreaked its vengeance, and many Germans and Austrians paid the price. In 1948 its surviving members, Wald among them, returned to fight for Israel in her War of Independence.

# Chapter Eleven

The Senior Chaplain to the Brigade, Bernard Caspar, vividly recalled the waiting and watching, and the nightly patrolling with infantrymen chafing at the bit, raring to go. Then came the thrill of the advance, and the elation of taking hundreds of prisoners from the much vaunted 'master race'.

The first large city to be freed during this final advance was Bologna. And it was here that the Brigade swung into action in its secondary, but for many more important role, the rescue and rehabilitation of Jewish refugees, and transporting them to the waiting boats in the southern Italian ports. Every man who was not on duty threw himself into this task. With Brigadier Benjamin's approval, a Brigade Refugee Committee had been set up to store food, clothing and other basic necessities exclusively for the refugees' use. Nearly every Brigader was contributing funds from his own pay. This initiative had come from Wellesley Aron and his 178 Company RASC, and , with no questions asked, the men saw to it that the special quartermaster's stores were always well stocked. It should not go unrecorded that Italian farmers and entrepreneurs, appalled by the Holocaust and the plight of the refugees, gave generously and refused payment.

Caspar was impatient to get into Bologna and to find out what had happened to the Jewish community which had numbered some 1,200 before the war. He was driven by a Londoner, Mordechai Gast. The military police were allowing only essential military traffic into the city, but Caspar turned on his considerable charm and the MP sergeant on duty waved him through. In a lilting Welsh accent, he said: 'I can't keep God out of Bologna, can I, Padre!'

There was a wild carnival atmosphere in the streets as the people celebrated their liberation. Gast was reduced alternately to crawling and coming to a complete standstill, as joyful civilians mobbed his vehicle. He clearly enjoyed the kisses and embraces offered by the young *signorinas*, and wholeheartedly entered into the spirit of the occasion. Caspar fended them off good-humouredly but, as Gast later reported, without much conviction. But the chaplain had other things on his mind. He kept asking where the synagogue was, and eventually an Italian policeman jumped onto the truck and offered to take them to it. He guided them to where the

107

synagogue had been – but, now there were only two walls standing.

'Those terible Germans,' the policeman commiserated, as a crowd of curious onlookers gathered, drawn by the blue and white Brigade flashes and emblems. Caspar asked them if they knew of the whereabouts of any Jews. The crowd shrugged, and simply muttered, 'Those terrible Germans'. Caspar went on foot, asking in shops and in the streets, but with no success.Despondently, he walked back to his truck to find Gast deep in conversation with a wizened old man. They were talking animatedly in Yiddish. The old man was a Jew, born in Turkey, named Alexander Hakim. He did not know where to find any other Jews, but he was positive that there were some. Caspar thought quickly. He told Hakim to spread the word that the Jewish Brigade would be holding a service at the synagogue at sundown on Friday. All Jews would be welcome.

Gast sped back to base and Caspar buttonholed Aron. As a result, the next day Caspar returned to Bologna with two trucks sporting large posters written in Italian and Hebrew, inviting all Jews to attend the reconsecration service at the synagogue. The six soldiers with him helped to stick the posters up all around the city centre. At the same time two American loudspeaker vans toured the streets broadcasting the announcement.

The soldiers then searched the ruins of the synagogue in an attempt to find the Sifrei Torah, the handwritten scrolls of law of the five Books of Moses, and the holiest articles in any synagogue. When they found them, the Nazis tended to burn them. Their search was in vain, but the next day a young Italian visited the Brigade. He was a Catholic and a scholar, and he knew the importance of the Sifrei Torah. When the Germans had occupied Bologna, he had taken the scrolls, and had hidden them, carefully wrapped, in the attic of his house. For their safe return he refused payment, but requested permission to attend the Friday service.

Restrictions were easing. The Brigade was given the go-ahead to take two 3-tonners into Bologna. On the Friday over thirty officers, NCOs and privates attended the service. Caspar was flabbergasted when the congregation swelled to 300. These people had been hidden by friends and neighbours, or had survived by scurrying from one bolthole to another, constantly keeping on the move to avoid detection. There were partisans among them, a few still carrying their weapons. And there were refugees who had trekked across Europe to reach Italy, and who had hidden themselves away in the mountain forests and caves. Their emaciated bodies and darting, hunted eyes bore witness to the suffering they had endured. They stared open-mouthed at the immaculate Brigaders, with their polished boots, trousers pressed to a knife-edge, oozing the confidence of the victors. Here surely was confirmation that the Germans were gone, and that they were safe at last. Inevitably emotions spilled over, and the Brigaders stoically put up with the kisses, embraces and endless questions. Tears flowed on both sides, and the ruined synagogue made a dramatic backdrop to another almost medieval scene.

Two months later Caspar had occasion to return to Bologna. Now he found a thriving Jewish community, smaller than before, and sadder, but rebuilding itself well enough to have been able to establish aid facilities for less fortunate survivors struggling in from central and eastern Europe. Returning Italian Jews, unlike their counterparts elsewhere, did not experience danger or difficulty when they came to reclaim their homes.

One by one Modena, Ferrara, Milan and Venice fell to the advancing Allies. In each Brigaders found Jewish refugees from every European country. They reconsecrated the defiled synagogues, and provided those in their care with rest, food and new clothes, before giving them safe conduct to the receiving centres for the boats to Palestine. Under armed guard, they forced German prisoners to clean and repair the synagogues and, sensing the hostile mood of their captors, the prisoners worked very hard.

The Brigade entered Milan to find it under the total control of the Resistance. They were everywhere, sporting their distinctive berets and armbands, and searching out fascists and collaborators. The Brigaders witnessed many ugly scenes as the Resistance meted out their own form of justice. An air raid had destroyed the main synagogue, but here Caspar and Aron were delighted to meet a most remarkable man. He was the leader of the Milan Jewish community, a prominent local citizen, an idealist, a Zionist, and a man of tremendous energy and efficiency. Dr Raphael Cantoni drew on all of his talents and connections to work with the Brigade in the revival of all aspects of Jewish life in Milan. And both worked closely with the American Joint Committee, quickly drafted in after the city had fallen, to dispense relief and emergency funds from an office they opened there.

With refugees crossing the Alps into Italy in increasing numbers, the problem of providing for them became overwhelming. They had no money, they needed food and shelter, and worst of all they had nothing to occupy their hands and minds. Synagogues, schools, sequestered buildings, and small communities were quickly swamped. For example, in Padua only 300 local Jews had survived, and they were trying to cater for the needs of some 800 refugees. In Milan, a favourite destination for the destitute, religious services held in communal buildings could scarcely be heard for the chatter of all the refugees in the adjoining courtyards. This was a heartbreaking crisis. In July and August 1945 Dr Cecil Roth gave a lecture tour in Britain to report on his fact-finding visit to Italy. He reported:

The tragedy of the refugees in Italy would have been even more appalling but for one thing: the assistance poured out unselfishly by the Jewish soldiers from Palestine who have shown a self-sacrificing devotion that is beyond praise. To place after place it was they who brought the message of liberation and hope. The refugees found in these bronzed, self-dependent youngsters a living testimony to the eternity and vitality of the Jewish nation.

Brigaders opened the synagogues and cleared them of debris. They opened their hearts and pockets to the undernourished remnants. They set up an educational system for the children. When given leave, instead of visiting tourist attractions, they went to the nearest refugee camp to help out. They have introduced order where there was chaos, hope where there was darkness, and life where there was only the stench of death. They and they alone have been responsible for the moral regeneration of these outcasts. The Jewish people owe the Brigade a debt of gratitude which must never be forgotten, and which can never be discharged.

In the second week of May 1945, Brigadier Benjamin passed down word that there was a wealth of goodwill and sympathy coming into Brigade HQ from British and other national Eighth Army units. They had all been shocked and angered by revelations about the Holocaust and the condition of the refugees they had come across. Individually, rather than as units, they had delivered blankets, clothes, tinned food, confectionary and other goods to the Brigade for distribution to the needy. One day Field Marshal Lord Alexander, GOC, visited the Brigade. After inspecting several units, and expressing satisfaction with their turnout, he had a long tête-à-tête with Benjamin. He intimated that, in the current circumstances, the Brigade had a free hand to act as it saw fit, with the proviso that, if it ever came unstuck, it could not plead that it was acting under orders.

Before the war, a number of Palestinians in 178 Company had been trade unionists, members of a cooperative, farmers and kibbutz leaders. They were socialists to a man. They appealed to Major Aron to allow a celebration of May Day. Thinking this would amount to little more than a canter round a maypole, Aron agreed. But 200 officers, NCOs and other ranks held a large, noisy jamboree. Next day Benjamin asked Aron why his consent to such an event had not been sought. Aron apologised, and said it had not occurred to him to seek permission from Benjamin.

'Or perhaps,' Benjamin suggested thoughtfully,' you felt I would refuse permission?'

'I suppose that was a possibility,' Aron admitted. Both men smiled, an expression of the strong bond of mutual respect between them.

With the war over and Hitler dead, Aron relinquished his command of 178 Company. He had served four roller-coaster, historic years. In a low-key ceremony, he handed over command to Captain Israel Adiv, who in turn was later replaced by Major Igad Caspi. Present to see Aron off were Captains Adiv, Beretz, Mazo, Shalit and Silberstein, as well as several platoon subalterns, among them a young English Jew, 2nd Lieutenant Harris. At the same time, *The London Gazette* announced the award of the MBE (Military) to four Brigade officers – Wellesley Aron RASC, Major E A Aronoff RE, Major Z Beretz RE, and Major Y Rappaport RE.

Armoury Sergeant Major Len Sanitt watched the arrival in Tarvisio of the Jewish refugees making their last-gasp escape into Italy. He spoke to them, listened to them, and smelled the incipient grime of a once civilised, educated people who had forgotten the luxury of being able to lather their skeletal frames with soap and hot water. Sanitt knew that, from then on, his overriding priority was to help such people. He was not a political man, not a Zionist, and he did not know of the Jewish Agency's plans to get as many able-bodied Jews as possible into Palestine to swell the ranks of the Haganah. But if the only way the wretched creatures he encountered could once again live a normal life was by getting to Palestine, he would do his damnedest to help them. Like many British and western Jews, he had no thoughts of living anywhere but in the country where he had been born and bred. But the contagious consciousness of Jewish nationalism affected him deeply.

Because of its geographical position Tarvisio became the refugees' target. For Jews, and not all the rootless wanderers were Jewish, reaching the Brigade became synonymous with going home. Many of the exhausted wretches collapsed completely when the Brigaders found them. It was as if they had used up every last ounce of strength to get that far, and having achieved it, they could not take a further step. Many of the less seriously wounded German soldiers were made to give up their beds to the most dehydrated and enfeebled refugees. Some of the most heartbreaking survivors were those whose minds had become unhinged by the terrible tortures and humiliations they had been subjected to. One macabre group comprised those who had undergone medical experiments without anaesthetic at the hands of German doctors. These were souls who would take a long time to heal, but nobody was going to leave them behind.

Three main camps and the smaller shelters built by the Brigade and other Palestine units stretched south towards the ports like beads on a necklace. The Brigade's 3-tonners made the perfect vehicles for transporting purposes. Sanitt and his LAD workshops ensured that every vehicle was checked down to the smallest detail – brand new tyres replaced any that showed the slightest signs of wear and tear. In the event no vehicle broke down, and there was no shortage of willing drivers, mainly NCOs, with two to every vehicle to accomplish a non-stop journey out and back.

Journeys to ports such as Naples and Bari took several days. All of the

Brigade's transport got sucked into the escape organisation (Bricha), and formed the backbone of the movement of people to the boats. The LAD organised the printing of false papers and documents to be shown at military police checkpoints. The drivers were taught to be polite and maintain a low profile whenever stopped. Their papers showed that they were on their way to collect stores from the ordnance depots at Naples and other ports.

In all this the fuel unit played a vital part. These unofficial journeys used many gallons of petrol, but this was disguised and the drivers ensured that stocks always tallied with the paperwork. Milometers on the trucks were adjusted downwards. Figures differ, but it is estimated that the Brigade made it possible for some 20,000 men, women and children to board the boats for Palestine. Sanitt declared that every journey was a 'fingers crossed' operation and, ironically, he was the first to fall foul of the military police.

An hour after he had overseen the departure for Bari of a 3-tonner packed with rested and fed refugees from Valbrunna on the Italy-Yugoslavia border, a woman and her daughter appeared. They were in great distress, made worse by the realisation that they had narrowly missed transport out. Sanitt decided to take them himself in a faster, 8-cwt truck with the aim of catching up with the recently departed 3-tonner. En route, probably because he was travelling at a good speed, Sanitt was stopped by British military police. By this time, High Command had become fully aware of the Brigade's clandestine activities, and had issued strict orders that civilians were not to be carried in military vehicles.

The MPs saw Sanitt's passengers, read the riot act, booked him for an offence, and warned him that he would face a charge. Soon after that, Sanitt caught up with the 3-tonner, transferred the two women to it, and sped back to base. He said nothing about his encounter with the military police, but a few weeks later Mark Hyatt, the Chief Clerk, told Sanitt that his charge sheet had turned up, but that he had extracted the document and had destroyed it.

'With a bit of luck,' said Hyatt, 'it will be lost in the army bureaucratic machine and no more will be heard about it.'

He was wrong. Four weeks later another communication arrived from the military police enquiring about the charge against one Len Sanitt. Hyatt again destroyed the incriminating document. A few more weeks after that, Sanitt and his LAD left the Eighth Army and drove into Holland. No more was ever heard of the matter.

After Major Aron handed over command of 178 Company he was restless. He was a man of tremendous energy with nothing to do. Benjamin called him into his office for a friendly drink and a chat, and told Aron that he was free to take extended leave in Palestine. Benjamin said, 'The war's over. You've done more than your bit. Go home to your wife and family and concentrate on your future. In your case, Wellesley, extended means . . . extended. Good luck.'

Before he left, Aron was approached by a group of worried Palestinian Brigaders, who said to him, 'Could you approach the Mandatory Government of Palestine and endeavour to obtain help for those of us who wish to build homes after demobilisation? Most of us have been in the army for several years and few, if any, have the means to buy land or a home. Our pay has just covered personal and family expenses. We feel we have acquired the right to a basic need for a home.'

When Aron got back to Palestine he plunged into this mission with his customary forcefulness, and he succeeded in securing twenty-five dunams of land from the Custodian of Enemy Property. This land had been owned by German Nazis who had been deported to Australia. Ninety Brigade officers and NCOs built their homes there, just on the outskirts of Tel Aviv. Later they named the area Neveh David after Colonel David Marcus of the US army, who was killed in the Israeli War of Independence.

On VE Day, 8 May 1945, reactions among the Brigaders were mixed. In the mess the whisky flowed among the officers transferred from British and Empire units. The Palestinian officers were more subdued, their state of mind somewhat anticlimactic. The NCOs and other ranks eschewed celebration altogether. They were silent. Some went to bed early, others sat alone smoking, their minds filled with thoughts of their families. The deadweight of reality smothered any flickers of hope that tried to surface. Hitler's war had been overwhelmingly disastrous. Now these men knew that they would have to journey home to find out if any of their relatives were still alive. They dreaded the prospect. Deep down they feared the worst. What was there to celebrate? Not many European-born Brigaders slept that night.

Ten days after the victory, the Brigade, after pushing north by way of Mestre, Venice and Udine, settled in at Tarvisio. As if at the flick of a switch, the Brigade appeared to have turned from a formidable fighting machine into what one British officer whimsically called 'the Salvation Army'. The Brigaders remained disciplined and observed the obligations of their uniforms, but now their first loyalty lay elsewhere. Here at Tarvisio, for the first time, they came face to face with their skeletal brethren trudging across the bridge from the Russian zone, and they were appalled. They had never before seen so many in such a pitiable state. From liberated concentration camps, and from hills and forests where they had been forced to live like animals, they came in pairs, small groups, and sometimes in large crowds, all shepherded by well organised, armed young men. The Brigaders turned away to hide their tears when these wretched people gave vent to their joy and relief. But they soon set to with a will, and for the first time in years the new arrivals had hot meals twice a day, could sleep in proper beds without fear of sudden death, received medical attention for their sores and ailments, and wore new clothes. Some enjoyed the showers so much they had to be forcibly removed from them to make way for others.

Stores left behind by the Germans in Tarvisio were appropriated by the Brigaders, but nothing proved so valuable as the huge stacks of cut timber. Working flat-out, the Brigaders built a shelter capable of accommodating 800 refugees. They built twenty sturdy huts with raised wooden floors and insulated walls, each with room to sleep forty. They put up separate latrines for men and women, installing hygienic drainage, washrooms, large canteen and cooking areas, a medical centre, a dental surgery, and two large recreation rooms for the children. Education was not neglected. The Brigade did not lack teachers and professors in its ranks, and they concentrated on teaching the youngsters Hebrew, and the history and geography of Palestine.

Every evening the chaplains conducted religious services, which were always well attended by soldiers and refugees alike. As they joined in the beautiful, age-old liturgical songs, the congregation felt a fusion. They were one people. Hardship and fighting lay behind them. Although they knew that in a largely indifferent world the same lay ahead, so too did their Holy Grail, a National Home for the Jewish people. They would endure. They would fight. Once again they would topple the walls of Jericho.

The soldiers had commandeered a large hall for concerts. These were held most evenings and were always well attended. They were moving occasions, especially when refugees played parts in the makeshift orchestras. Where had the musical instruments and that magnificent Bechstein grand piano come from? Well, they were just 'found'. After one concert of the works of Mahler, a tough young infantry sergeant said to a frail, middle-aged Polish survivor who had been playing the cello:

'Well, sir, you certainly look much better in the few days you have been with us. It must be the food and the rest . . .'

'No, no,' the cello player interrupted, 'you are wrong. The real tonic for us is seeing you young Jewish soldiers so smart, so disciplined and so self-assured. Now, I know that Israel will survive and become one again a nation.' He gripped the sergeant's arm and said, 'When we get to Palestine I'll throw away the cello and you'll teach me how to use a gun, yes?'

The Palestine-born soldier sighed and then nodded in agreement. He had grown up during the troubled '30s and had served four years in the war. He would be going home to face further trouble, with British and Arab hostility unresolved by Hitler's war. He had no illusions. His fighting was not yet at an end.

The Brigade was notified that a German radio station had been located in the area under its command, and it was ordered to seize it. Months later it turned up in Palestine where it was being used by the Haganah. 178 Company was now being used to transport Allied troops on leave through Europe to the Channel ports. And so another rescue chain of communication was established.

Many Brigaders itched to get across the border into Austria. They were curious to set foot in the enemy's home territory, as well as to use their vehicles to pick up more desperate refugees. But the border was firmly closed and watched over by military police. The reason given was that Austria was politically and in every other way in a state of turmoil, and the Soviets would not have taken kindly to incursions by Allied troops, for whatever reason. Suspicion reigned. Through an accommodation reached with their Red Army counterparts, only military police vehicles were allowed to cross the border.

Then fate played a part. Early one morning two military policemen drove up to the Brigade and asked for help. One of their trucks had broken down in Austria. Could the Brigade provide somebody to get it going again, and so avoid the need for a towing vehicle? Sanitt jumped at the opportunity. He and a corporal, who had a way with recalcitrant engines, followed the MPs in their jeep. The policemen were impressed by Sanitt's rank, and by the fact that he came from London. They became friendly. Once they were across the border, the few civilians in this sparsely populated area stared in astonishment at the Jewish insignia on the Brigade jeep. While Sanitt and his corporal were having a look under the broken down truck's bonnet, they heard one of the MPs call out, 'Hold it!' They were startled to see two young men in *Wehrmacht* uniform, clean and freshly pressed but without flashes or badges. The policemen had drawn their revolvers. The two young men frantically started shouting, 'Shalom, Shalom . . .' Sanitt replied in kind and told the MPs to put away their guns. These two were Jews. They rushed up to the Brigade jeep and stroked the emblems in disbelief. Then they gabbled away to the Brigade corporal in Yiddish. For the bemused MPs' benefit, Sanitt translated the men's story.

Two weeks earlier they had been in a camp guarded by the SS. They had been slave labour. A week before that the SS guards had selected some of the healthiest men and women and had shot them, gloating that they were Jews who would not live to enjoy liberation. Here was Nazi blood lust at its worst. The two men were forced to help dig a hole into which the dead were thrown and buried. Then the SS drove away. The gates were open, and ninety-eight men and two women walked out of the camp, these two among them. They stumbled across a deserted German army store, where they found and put on the freshly laundered uniforms. They tore off all the flashes and badges in order to make the uniforms as unremarkable as possible. They also found stale bread and cheese, and tins of meat which they devoured. The two young men then reported that the others were in a large old house on the Italian side of Villach, not far away.

The MPs thanked Sanitt and the corporal for repairing their truck and asked if there was anything they could offer to show their gratitude. Sanitt said, 'Yes. I want to take these two back to the house and have a look at the others. It's not far. Come with us, if you like.'

The two young men jumped into the Brigade jeep, and they were all soon driving into a cobbled courtyard fronting a large stately mansion which had seen better days. The two military policeman looked in some discomfort at the emaciated wrecks with their hollow eyes and sunken cheeks, incongruously dressed in fresh *Wehrmacht* uniforms. Their noses wrinkled discreetly at the sweetish odour of decay of those close to death.

Meanwhile Sanitt and his corporal hurried inside, and quickly found themselves surrounded by the fitter of the ex-slaves. Others were too frail or exhausted to move. Sanitt and the corporal gently freed themselves from the survivors' grasps, and went back outside. The MPs had lit cigarettes and were quickly joined by silent, hungry men greedily sniffing the smoke. They passed over their remaining cigarettes and matches, and watched as those yearning for a smoke patiently queued to be given a single cigarette each. Len Sanitt said to the shocked policemen, 'Half of them will never make it to Tarvisio. You must allow us to come back and pick them up.'

One of the MPs said, 'We'll put in the word for you. You should be able to go through on the nod on a purely humanitarian basis.'

And so it was. With Rabbi Bernard Caspar in charge, a convoy of three 3-tonners was waved through into Austria. It carried two doctors, two sergeant clerks and three soldiers to give general assistance. The convoy was headed by the jeep containing Sanitt and his corporal. They took sustenance in the form of sandwiches, still drinks, and fruit. It was in the early hours of the next day when they trundled back across the border to Tarvisio. Their charges turned out to be mainly Hungarian Jews. Their names, addresses and other details were recorded and circulated to the appropriate organisations in the hope that some families and friends might find themselves reunited.

Later Sanitt learned that of the hundred they had rescued six went back to Hungary, thirty-three stayed in Italy, and the rest had made it to Palestine.

# Chapter Twelve

It had been a lucky throw of the military dice that had positioned the Brigade on the Italy-Austria border. It could not have been better placed to offer assistance to the stragglers making their way south through Europe. On the whole, the Russians were easy-going and friendly towards those who were unmistakably victims of Nazi persecution. If they wanted to cross into Italy, they were free to do so. But on the other side of that border, the British military police were not nearly so accommodating.

When Sanitt and his corporal repaired that truck, it was the first breach in the dyke. The MPs' sergeant major visited the Brigade, and formally asked that the skilled fitters and mechanics in its REME unit look after their vehicles, a lot of which, through wear and tear, were giving trouble. Sanitt agreed, and he and other NCOs were entertained in the MPs' mess. Friendships developed. The MPs were in turn shown round the Brigade, and were greatly impressed by the way the Brigaders were looking after the refugees, and by their attempts to return them to the human race. The Brigade mechanics made a point of overhauling the British military vehicles to perfection.

During this period, Brigadier Benjamin and his staff were coming under intense pressure through circumstances not of their making, and outside their control. They knew that only the Brigade could rescue, rehabilitate, protect and transport the survivors in comfort and safety to the waiting boats. This was an obligation to the Net, the Jewish Agency and the Jewish people which they felt bound to fulfil. But they could not go against express orders and drive without permission into what had been enemy territory. That would have been asking for trouble.

Meanwhile frustration was building up among men anxious to be off in search of their families. Some had already gone in Brigade vehicles through Yugoslavia and up into Hungary, Czechoslovakia, and elsewhere. It only now needed a few hotheads to try to drive through the military police posts into Austria for the fur to fly. The situation was made worse by the Brigaders' awareness of Nazi atrocities – there was no shortage of stories to fuel their anger.

In Genoa, a squad from the SS *Totenkopf* (death's head) had burst into the office of Rabbi Ricardo Pacifici. They beat and tortured him until he telephoned members of his congregation asking them to come to see him on a matter of urgency. When the congregants arrived, they were grabbed and thrown into trucks concealed in side streets. They were never seen again. Similar incidents occurred in Modena and other Italian towns. In Pisa, the SS squads swiftly rounded up leading Jews and their families, and took them away to an unknown fate. In Florence, Livorno and elsewhere, architectural gems of Sephardi synagogues were pointlessly wrecked. The SS compounded their evil actions by urinating and defecating in the holy places.

Top Nazi leaders had met at Wannsee to plan the 'Final Solution', the cold-blooded extermination of a people. Their principal weapon was Himmler's SS, which trained its recruits to staff and run concentration and slave-labour camps with ruthless efficiency. When the *Wehrmacht* captured a town or city, the SS were not far behind. In league with the ubiquitous Gestapo, they wasted no time in rounding up Jewish families. They herded the victims, men, women, children and babies, to quiet spots in nearby woods, made them dig their own burial pits, then machine-gunned them to death. The *Wehrmacht* did not always emerge with clean hands, but it was the SS that vengeful members of the Brigade and the DIN had firmly in their sights.

In late summer 1996, I drove down to Brighton on the south coast of England. It was an idyllic day, the sparkling green waters of the Channel dotted with small, white, triangular sails. I entered the semi-gloom of a nursing home and again interviewed David Spector, once the wartime major of the Jewish Brigade. He was now crippled by arthritis and was deaf. To communicate I showed him cards on which I had written my questions. His mind was as sharp as ever.

Spector confirmed that, when the war ended, there was a flood of requests from members of the Brigade to be allowed to find out if their families in Europe had survived, and to search for them. They were expressing an almost physical need. David remembered:

Their emotions worried us. They were over the red line of danger. Crossing into Austria was forbidden by High Command. We issued instructions accordingly. Then we learned that our lads were bypassing Austria, and going through Yugoslavia and up into Hungary, Romania, Poland, everywhere. They were seen driving every type of vehicle from water-carriers to transporters. So, we had no option but to issue fourteen-day leave passes to those who wanted to go. We even managed to arrange with the British Military Mission in Bucharest that at the expiry of their leave time, the lads could report to it and avoid being classified as absentees or deserters. It was a nerve-wracking time for us.

There were so many bizarre incidents. We crossed fingers that they would not run into trouble with the Red Army. It turned out that seeing the Jewish pennant on the vehicles and the Brigade's blue and white insignias, the Russians proved to be friendly, even helpful. During this time, reports of our men came in of having been seen in the farthest reaches of Europe. I recall Lord Mancroft calling in to see us. He was serving at Headquarters in Brussels, and was instrumental in getting permission for our men to cross borders. When he saw me, he said that he was driving to Czechoslovakia with a general who was to receive a Czech decoration. He asked me to congratulate three Brigade sergeants whom they encountered at the Czech border. The general was impressed with their smart turnout and crisp salutes, and their clean and polished truck. Lord Mancroft was delighted to have found Major Spector's signature on the passes they showed him. They were false and certainly not signed by me. Yet it was my signature, all right. They must have been a Jewish Agency party on special business. There were some very competent printers and forgers in the Brigade, and they could create any document required for any situation. They were certainly on a job for the Net.

David tired quickly. As I bade him farewell, I showed him my last card. Its question was, 'Did any Brigaders find their families when they got to their homes?'

'Not to my knowledge,' sighed David. 'They would certainly have brought them back to the Brigade. No. They had no luck.'

Revelations about the Holocaust, and the growing rapport between Brigaders and the British MPs opened doors that would otherwise have remained firmly shut. Jewish refugees were now allowed to walk over the bridge from Villach into Italy. Help was even given when needed. One day the military police brought a Hungarian on his last legs into the canteen for a hot meal. He refused to eat. He was starving, but would not take a morsel until he had spoken to an officer on urgent business. He was taken to see Bernard Caspar. The Hungarian told Caspar that there were about 150 Jewish men and women, freed from a labour camp, living in squalid conditions in railway wagons at Klagenfurt. No Austrian would go near them, let alone help them.

This was enough for Caspar. The ordnance unit provided him with a top-priority pass for the journey. Soldiers loaded an 8-cwt truck with food, drink and cigarettes, and Caspar and his Palestinian driver set off. The MPs at the border knew him well. They opened the back of the truck, saw the supplies, and waved him through. In railway sidings at Klagenfurt Station, they found the wagons and, unexpectedly, found a British sergeant in charge.

His relief at seeing Caspar was immense. He told him that the Austrians were hostile to the Jews, and were the opposite of helpful. It had been a struggle. Only through the threat of *force majeure* had he been able to secure the use of the station toilets and water standpipes for his charges. He helped the two Brigaders unload and distribute the supplies among the refugees. The resourceful Caspar had even brought openers for the tins of meat, fish and soup taken from Brigade stores. Caspar and his driver stoically endured the expressions of gratitude and exhilaration, as the refugees embraced them, and stroked the emblems on their uniforms and on the truck. Before he left, Caspar told the British sergeant that he would be back to collect all these people. Would the man get into trouble?

The sergeant shook his head. 'It seems I'm forgotten, sir. So are these poor sods. You take them. If they stay here they'll just rot and die.'

'What will you do if we collect them?'

'I'll report to the British Military Mission and explain that one morning I found them all gone. They won't care. They'll probably be relieved. Another small problem solved.'

'And you? What will happen to you?'

'Well, sir, I'm banking on being shipped back to Blighty and being demobbed.'

The very next day, Caspar and his driver led a convoy of three 3-tonners to Klagenfurt, collected the refugees, and headed back home. On the outward journey, on the instructions of the border MPs, they pulled down the canvas screens that hid what was inside the trucks. On the way back, the MPs walked round the vehicles, tapped the screens, and asked what was inside. Caspar nudged his driver and said, 'You tell them. A rabbi must not tell a lie.' The driver grinned. 'They're empty,' he called. They were waved through.

After this, Brigade vehicles could cross into Austria more or less at will, provided of course that their papers were in order – and they always were. Brigade HQ followed set procedures. They listed the names, addresses and next of kin of every rescued refugee, and sent copies to the search bureaux that had been set up in Jerusalem, New York, Rome and London, as well as to the British Military Mission in Budapest. They experienced one real miracle. A whole family had survived – both parents, two daughters, and a son-in-law. For three years they had hidden separately. Within two weeks they were on their way to Palestine.

One Sunday, four young Jews in their late teens/early twenties walked into the Brigade. They had travelled the last leg from Klagenfurt non-stop. They were not in the same desperate state as the other refugees – they were thin, certainly, but wiry, strong, and displaying the arrogance of the untamed. They told the Brigaders their galvanising story.

There were an estimated 50,000 Jews still stranded in Poland. Many had been organised into groups of several hundred, each group protected by disciplined and armed young men and women, survivors of ghetto battles and breakouts from camps, as well as by partisans. They were all on the move south towards Italy, and determined to get to Palestine.

Conditions and attitudes in Poland had not changed. Anti-semitism was rife. Those who had gone back to their homes encountered nothing but hostility. If they asked for news of their families, the Poles laughed and jerked their thumbs skywards. During a House of Commons debate around this time, the British prime minister suggested that the Jews should go home and help to rebuild Europe. In his defence, he was clearly as remote as it was possible to be from the Polish hell on earth for Jews. To the victors, European Jews had swiftly metamorphosed from victims to a damned nuisance. No country would take them except the Jewish community in Palestine, and the might of Britain's armed forces was doing everything in its power to keep them out of there. But there was no carpet under which this barrier to a quiet life could be swept.

The four young Jews explained that what the Nazis had started the Poles appeared to be intent on finishing. No Polish Jew should be made to remain in that mass graveyard. So how were these groups living? They lived off the land. They took what they needed, especially motor vehicles, and horses and carts in which they carried the elderly, the infirm, and the young children. As they travelled south they tried to avoid the towns and cities, following minor roads and tracks. Poles had never before encountered Jews like the strong, young protectors, and they tended to give them what they wanted to hasten them on their way.

Three weeks earlier, the four had set out with the intention of meeting up with the Brigade, and of telling its members of the Jews stranded in Poland. They also wanted to alert the Brigade to the numbers making their way towards it. Whenever possible, they had travelled by train; they hitched lifts in refugee transport vehicles. Or they walked, night and day, resting only when absolutely necessary. They lived off the land, learned how to cross frontiers undetected and how to move from one Allied zone to another without attracting suspicious attention. They were thrilled to see, in Klagenfurt, their first military vehicle bearing the Star of David pennant, and with the Jewish emblems painted on the bodywork. They walked on through Villach, across the river bridge, and were over-whelmed by the welcome that greeted them. They felt they had come home. Two of them went back to Poland to reassure the refugees that the Brigade was indeed a powerful Jewish force that had the men and the means to help them get to Palestine. The other two stayed to work with the Net.

It was by now widely accepted that the brigade was engaged in rescuing Jewish refugees, and helping them along the underground routes to the ports. Officers, landed with the onerous task of running displaced-persons camps, contacted Brigade HQ and suggested transferring their charges to the Brigade. Brigadier Benjamin received a short letter from the British commander of a camp at Micheldorf:

I have in this camp a number of Jewesses. Their story is too long and too tragic to write about. I have done my best to give them their new optimism, but as yet without success. None wishes to remain in Europe. I would appreciate a visit from you and so would my charges.

Caspar and his driver made their way to the camp, where they distributed food and drinks. A Brigade doctor made a medical check of those pointed out to him by the sympathetic camp commander. Two days later they led a convoy of those invaluable 3-tonners back to Micheldorf, and took all the inmates on board. Before they left, Caspar shared a bottle of wine with the British officer and asked:

'I'm curious. How will you explain all this to your peers?'

'I'll write out a report stating that they all broke out of the camp and headed for their homes. Correct paperwork covers every movement of goods and people and a multitude of sins,' the captain replied.

'Will you get away with that?' Caspar asked.

'Rabbi,' explained the captain, 'the war is over. Every Jew still alive represents a problem to the Allied authorities. The more that go back to their homes the better. My paperwork won't be queried. By whom anyway? I have never taken kindly to being the jailer in this Godforsaken place to those poor devils.'

The two men shook hands, and then the British officer said, 'I hope they make Palestine, Rabbi, I really do. They deserve a crack at making a new life for themselves.'

On 26 June three Polish Jews arrived at the Brigade. They had come from a large camp at Ebensee, near Salzburg, in the American zone. They came with a letter of introduction, dated 22 June, from the MGO, G5 Office, HQ of the 11th United States Armoured Division. The camp contained 10,000 refugees, and the Americans wanted to close it down and send the inmates back to their countries of origin. But 1,600 Polish Jews refused to go back to Poland. Many made it clear they would rather kill themselves. They were determined to go to Palestine. The Americans appealed to the Brigade for help. They offered to transport these 1,600 to Villach. They also asked the Brigade to introduce the three delegates to the American Joint Distribution Committee.

The numbers involved came as a shock to Brigade staff. They had handled a seemingly endless flow of groups, but nothing on this scale. However, they could not be forced to return to Poland, a country they hated and feared, nor left to rot in the camp. Caspar approached the military government HQ, but ran into a brick wall. The officers appeared only able to tackle the problem with red tape, regulations and procedures. Bypass them? Impossible! The camp inmates had to be returned to their homes in Poland. Caspar's eloquent pleas fell on stony ground. Orders were orders, and that was that.

After casting around frantically, Caspar did a detour round the military mind-set, and approached the UNRRA (United Nations Relief and Rehabilitation Administration) Italian mission to Rome. There he found a sympathetic and humanitarian response. After some negotiating, the UNRRA agreed to accept the 1,600 refugees at two of their bigger camps near Bari, at Ferramonte and Santa Maria. The Americans delivered the refugees to the Brigade in batches, and the Brigade passed them on to the UNRRA.

May, June and July were extraordinary months for the Brigaders. They had never imagined, when they volunteered to fight, that they would end up so deeply involved in saving souls. They toiled as if for a sacred cause, which in truth to them it was. The Germans seemed to have had a mania for cutting down trees, and piling up large stacks of timber. The Brigaders worked from dawn to dusk, and sometimes longer, building shelters and schoolrooms for the refugees. Nothing was too much trouble. They especially cossetted the children, who appeared to have insatiable appetites, passing on their rations to them. They gave them clothes to wear – many of the soldiers, when they eventually left Italy, had nothing but the uniforms they stood up in.

Estimates of the number of refugees who passed through the Brigade's hands vary considerably, from the lowest at around 9,000 to the highest at up to 20,000. Whatever the true figure, the Brigade's conduct was exemplary, and there is little doubt that its reputation encouraged countless desperate Jews to make that last effort to survive and to reach the Land of Israel. Pride took the place of humiliation. By the time, in the summer of 1946, when the Brigade was sent home at the rate of 500 a week, it left behind a string of camps well-managed and equipped to handle the coninuing stream of refugees making for the boats to Palestine.

The great majority of Brigaders were Palestine Jews, most of them sabras (Jews born in Palestine). Their families, homes and future were all in that troubled land. Every time Palestine sneezed, they felt the draught. This state of affairs created a sharp dichotomy. A strong mutual respect had grown up between the British units and the members of the Brigade who had fought side by side in the Western Desert and north Africa campaigns. But in Palestine itself, relations between the British and the Yishuv soured with every violent incident. It was ironic that the year which had brought peace to the world should end with the first bitter clashes between the British Foreign Office and the embryonic State of Israel. Why should this have been, when by and large the Jews had admired and respected the British over all other Europeans?

The root cause began to emerge when documents were not released in 1976 under the thirty-year rule as was the norm. In fact, they were only made public in 1997. The delay was evidence of official embarrassment over the content. These documents showed beyond question that Foreign Office and MI5 officials had an ingrained dislike and suspicion of the Jewish people. They considered Jews untrustworthy, and they had scant sympathy for the victims of the Holocaust. In a letter, Sir Christopher Steele, senior Foreign Office official in Germany, referred to a Colonel Soloman, a Jew on his staff: 'It is a pity that a Jew was ever appointed. Any honest Jew will admit that no Jew could be objective on Jewish affairs, and anyone who is not objective cannot advise His Majesty's Government reliably.'

Steele was displaying doubts about whether any Jew would support British policy against the founders of what would become the State of Israel. His letter continued in similar vein: 'I have nothing against Soloman personally. He is a likeable man trying to do a good job. The trouble is he serves more than one master. He recently put forward plans for the appointment of four Jewish liaison officers in Germany. All have been unmitigated nuisances for a long time.'

Another document related to a Whitehall meeting chaired by two senior MI5 officers, 'Tar' Robertson and a Mr Kelly. The meeting was told that, by playing on the sympathy of relief organisations in Europe, the Jewish Agency and the Zionists had built up an organisation that hardly left a country in Europe untouched. These details were published by the *Daily Mail* on 3 January 1997.

If it was the British Establishment's miscalculation that appeasing the Arabs would make them love the British and want them to stay on as the Mandatory Power, it was the problem of immigration that remorselessly propelled Palestine towards a state of near war. The situation was becoming more explosive by the day. The spark that lit the flame was 'The Rescue of the 100,000'.

The situation of Jews incarcerated in displaced-person camps had become intolerable. True, they were fed after a fashion, and they were no longer at the mercy of murderous Nazis. But they had reached a dead end in desolate, dreary locations among hostile people. If anything anti-semitism had got worse. The future looked bleak, and the suicide rate remained high. A solution had to be found, and soon. On 18 June 1945 the Jewish Agency applied to the Palestine government for 100,000 immigration permits for surviving Jews to enter Palestine. There was no reply to this request.

In July that year the Labour Party won the British General Election. The Jewish Agency felt a flicker of hope. Socialist members of parliament had been among the most vociferous urging Jewish immigration into Palestine. But now they remained silent and, when approached on the matter, eva-sive. On 24 September Dr Weizmann informed the Jewish Agency that the Colonial Office had offered him just 1,500 immigration permits, and that these would be the last under the provisions of the white paper.

In the same month the US President wrote to the British Prime Minister, urging him to let the 100,000 into Palestine. That request also remained unanswered. Criticism of Britain now blew up worldwide, some of it, it must be said, from nations that would not themselves admit Jewish refugees, even on humanitarian grounds. Indignation was at its greatest in the United States, where cancellation of a massive loan to Britain was seriously considered.

In Palestine the Haganah, which had hitherto restricted its activities to defending settlements, fighting terrorist groups, and smuggling in refugees, took its first offensive action against British forces. It attacked the Athlit detention camp, and released 170 illegal oriental immigrants destined to be returned to prison and worse in their Arab countries of birth. A British police constable was killed during this action, the first Briton to be killed by the Haganah since the beginning of the mandate. On 31 October the Haganah paralysed the entire Palestine railway system by blowing up over a hundred bridges and junctions. It sank police patrol vessels in the ports of Haifa and Jaffa, and set off explosions in the Haifa oil refinery.

On 13 November the British Foreign Secretary, Ernest Bevin, made his first official statement on the Palestine question at a press conference. This included his refusal to admit 100,000 Jewish displaced persons into Palestine, implicitly condemning them to an indefinite stay in the camps. He also made a deadly crack to the effect that Jews should not push to the head of the queue. The tone of this statement gave rise to resentment and anger which has never been forgotten by Jews. The members of the Brigade smouldered. If they now had to go to war against the British in order to rescue their wretched co-religionists, so be it.

Following Bevin's statement, the Jewish National Council called for a general strike throughout Palestine. There were widespread outbreaks of violence. Nine Jews were killed, and thirty-seven British soldiers hurt. Government offices were blown up, and the authorities retaliated. 15,000 troops, including the Brigade of Guards and 6th Airborne Division, carried out arms searches in kibbutzim in Samaria and the plain of Sharon. There was a brutal edge to these searches. Eight settlers were killed. In return, the Haganah demolished British police headquarters and electricity power stations. The Brigaders stayed glued to their radios, listening to every scrap of news coming out of Palestine.

However, they were now focussing on other developments. Picking out the strongest and fittest of the refugees, they gave them weapons and fieldcraft training. There have seldom been such enthusiastic students, all with scores to settle with the murderers of their families. Meanwhile the revenge squads were also busy. Finding information about them, however, proved as difficult as getting water out of a stone. Then I was fortunate enough to see a documentary in BBC Television's 'Everyman' series. It was primarily about the renowned young Jewish hero, Abba Kovner, a poet born in Vilna, where he grew up to witness Nazi occupation. He was the first and only Jew to appreciate that the Nazis meant to exterminate his race.

He went round telling all the Jews in Vilna that the Nazis planned a genocide, and that they would surely be murdered. Even his family thought him a little mad. He unsuccessfully tried to persuade the Jews to escape to the safety of the forests. The Nazis were behaving well, lulling the Jews into a false sense of security. The desperate Kovner slipped out of town to start a resistance movement. He never saw his family again.

All the Jews in Vilna were taken out into the woods, machine-gunned, and buried in mass graves. Kovner became the leader of a sizeable partisan group, operating behind the German lines throughout the war. Later they concentrated on retribution, culminating in a scheme to poison reservoirs supplying German cities (which failed), and poisoning bread supplied to 3,000 SS prisoners in a camp near Nuremberg (partially successful).

The film switched its attention to the Brigade's revenge squads. They spoke openly. Israel Carmi was an infantry officer, who finished up at Tarvisio. He recalled:

> We had a tip-off. We had many, but this one was about a house in Austria. I and two others got into a car and drove to the house. We found a man and his wife. We were amazed at the large amount of clothes, jewellery and other things that we found. It was a treasure trove. The woman was brazen. She said it had all belonged to Jews. We told them that we would execute them there and then for crimes against humanity. The man said: 'Gentlemen, I will cooperate if you don't kill me. I know many people and I can give you a list . . .'

Carmi asked when they could have the list. The man said they could have it the next morning.

> We returned the next morning. And to our amazement found that the man had stayed up all night typing out the lists of SS NCOs and officers. We could not believe that it was all true. The man gave us several pages of names, home addresses, dates of birth, their work assignments and what they had done, and their rankings in the SS and Nazi parties. We could not believe that the list was a true one, so we extracted a lot of the names on it, and passed them over to Brigade staff and British Intelligence. We kept back the highest ranking SS because we wanted to deal with them ourselves. We were informed that the lists were accurate. The Nazi Judas had bought the lives of his wife and himself for a list.

Each squad selected its targets. We would set off in our cars for the journeys. When we arrived at the home of our suspect we would put on military police helmets with the white band and the police armlets. Then we would enter the home and take the suspect with us, saying we wanted him for interrogation. Usually they came without a struggle. Once in the car we told the prisoner who we were and why we took him. Some admitted guilt. Others kept silent. We did the job.

Another avenger was Zeer Keren, who later became a member of Mossad. He said:

We were quite happy to do to the Nazis what they did to Jews. Our goal was to execute them. I strangled them myself once we got in the forest. It took three to four minutes. We weighted the bodies with heavy chains, and threw them into lakes, rivers, streams. They were remote places. We left no trace of our activities.

Another avenger, Shmuel Givon, said:

During a trip to the Austrian Alps, we came across two SS men. In conversation we quickly concluded they had been high-ranking *Totenkopf* officers. They admitted they had done terrible things to Jews. We took them to the edge of a high, ice-covered cliff with a sheer drop. We told them they were being executed for crimes against Jews. We pushed them over the edge. They fell, and must still be there.

At Tarvisio, Abba Kovner reached the Brigade. Reports of his exploits had gone before him. Some 300 Brigaders sat in a huge circle while he told them about his experiences. He spoke with passion and anger, and they were spellbound. He told them that it was his duty, and that of those like him, to exact payment in kind, and that he was going back to do just that. It was a very emotional gathering. The Brigaders did not entirely approve of his plan to mass-murder German civilians, but the rapport was there. When Kovner left to undertake his task, the Brigade gave him provisions, weapons, ammunition, and two very serviceable trucks.

# Chapter Thirteen

The Brigade had become the cynosure of Jews worldwide, the thread that pulled them together in unprecedented unity. For the moment there were no factions, only Jews waking up to the possibility that the Jewish nation could be born again in its own land. Enemies seeking the demise of the Palestine Jewish communities would have to be confronted. But, for the first time, the world's traditional victims would not be led like lambs to the slaughter. On paper, the Yishuv would face overwhelming odds. But Jewry had the vision of nationhood. It was a prize they could not afford to lose. And, incredibly, flying in the face of world opinion, they were confident that, with the British gone from Palestine, they would win.

Several factors explained their confidence. The events of the Holocaust had provoked such intense anger that it could only be assuaged by the creation of a National Home for the Jews. The six million who had perished could not be allowed to have died for nothing. The war had created a substantial reservoir of battle-experienced ex-servicemen, both in Palestine and the countries of the diaspora. In the prevailing climate there would be no shortage of volunteers to come to the defence of another Jewish community threatened with extinction, and this is how it turned out in the 1948 War of Independence.

They had to win to survive. There was no alternative, a fact which inspired extraordinary feats of bravery and fortitude among otherwise ordinary men and women. And then there was the 'Brigade effect'. Its importance greatly outweighed its relatively small size of only 5,500. It acted like a magnet, attracting Jews fighting with other national units in Italy. Many more than ever could wanted to join the Brigade. But for some it did happen. One such was a Canadian squadron leader, David Goldberg DFC, who had 234 fighter sweeps over France, Italy and Germany under his belt. He escaped to England after being shot down over France.

Goldberg was in command of the 'City of Windsor' squadron in Italy during the offensive against the Gothic Line. He was requested to attack German mortar positions in support of the Jewish Brigade's advance, and led his formation of Spitfires in several effective, low-level attacks. He was later honoured by his home town of Hamilton, Ontario.

The *Jewish Chronicle* of 12 June 1945 reported that 3,000 German-born

Jews in France had refused to join the French Foreign Legion. To a man, they wanted to serve with the regular French army or, preferably, with the Jewish Brigade. In Stockholm, 200 Danish Jews, who had escaped the Nazi round-up in Denmark, applied for visas for England, where they would be able to sign up to the Brigade. In London, the first batch of volunteers accepted by the Brigade were entertained by the Jewish Agency before leaving for their training centre. Many of these had been born in continental Europe, and the genial registration officer, Maurice Rosette had the dispiriting job of marking against their next of kin 'whereabouts unknown'.

There were several Brigade registration offices in Britain. The central London office was in Bloomsbury Square, and there were branch offices in Manchester, Leeds, Birmingham, Liverpool and Glasgow. They dealt with a steady flow of requests to join up. Volunteers came from North and South America, South Africa and the Antipodes, inspired by reading accounts of the Brigade's war service, as well as by seeing photographs and documentary film reports. It was, of course, too late for most of them to be accepted.

A major problem among fighting units once a conflict is ended is boredom. The adrenalin rush brought on by victory dissipates, the reins of discipline slacken. Troubles increase among soldiers leading an apparently pointless existence. The military response is to try to keep such men occupied, something which did not apply in the case of the Brigade. True, the members found life after victory something of an anti-climax, and they tended to carry out their less than arduous military duties on auto-pilot. But as they continuously discussed the situation in Palestine, they were not idle, far from it. As David Spector put it to me:

We on the Staff had to emulate the three wise monkeys. We saw nothing, heard nothing, and said nothing. However, we were buoyed by the fact that other British units in Italy knew what was going on, and were indeed quite understanding about it. Their minds were focussed on getting home and getting demobbed. As I have told you, the Jewish Agency had planted quite a number of their leading lights in the NCO and other ranks of the Brigade. They had of course been planted with a definite purpose. The fighting to them was not their main task. Mark you, they fought well and were bloody good soldiers, and in fact quite a number eventually became colonels and generals in the Israeli Defence Forces.

Nothing we could have done would have stopped them taking spontaneous revenge and going AWOL with Brigade vehicles and rescuing Jewish refugees from all over Europe and bringing them back to the shelters we had built for them. I know for a fact that some Brigaders loaded their trucks with arms and ammunition, which they handed over to the young ex-partisans who were wreaking their revenge on those who had murdered their families. To be honest, we knew we couldn't stop them, and being Jewish ourselves, we didn't want to. But it was tricky at times, and we sweated quite a bit I can tell you.

All Brigade units were now providing men to help with Bricha, which rescued camp survivors from Europe and rehabilitated them mentally and physically, before transporting them to the Palestine-bound bucket ships. Acting on instructions from the Yishuv, the active Brigaders were selecting the fitter among the refugees and, apart from training them in weaponry and fieldcraft, they fitted them out with Brigade uniforms, complete with the distinctive blue and white shoulder flashes and badges. One of the Palestine infantry sergeants explained:

When they put on the Brigade uniforms, they became immediately transformed. Their shoulders snapped back. Their chests came out, and they rushed to look at themselves in the nearest mirror. Watching their elated disbelief gave us all a tremendous thrill. They needed no instructions to keep their boots highly polished, and their trousers creased to knife edges, and their hair cut to short back and sides. They were determined not to let the Brigade down in any respect.

'Why the uniforms?' I wondered. 'You had already provided them with adequate clothing.' 'Well,' said the sergeant, 'during the training we were taking them out into the mountains and open fields . . .'

Brigaders training civilians would have attracted the attention of passing military police and other units, although at that stage no one really cared. But we wanted to avoid having to deal with unanswerable questions by the curious. They learned quickly. The ex-partisans among them needed no teaching, and in fact helped us to train others. They were especially skillful at killing in unarmed combat.

It was very touching when we put them into the trucks for departure for the ports. They all wanted to keep their uniforms. They were so proud to wear them. We decided to let them keep them, but first the shoulder flash and every badge had to be taken off so that they were completely plain. Could you imagine the Royal Navy boarding a blockade runner, and finding soldiers of the Jewish Brigade among the steerage? My God, we would have woken up and found half the British Eighth Army surrounding us. And they would not have been the friendly types.

There are varying estimates of the number of refugees trained to a degree of proficiency by the Brigade. There were certainly several hundred. No time was wasted in square bashing; there was just intense concentration on weapons use and fieldcraft. When the time came, they would all count, the brightest of them used to train others.

While all this had been going on, Bernard Caspar was busy attending to the needs of the refugees. They were still coming, or in some cases were being brought in, to the Brigade. In this sterling, endless task, he was well supported by the other Brigade chaplain, the Palestine-born Reverend Doctor Jacob Gil Lipschitz. The latter spent a lot of time in forward positions with the Brigaders. He also officiated at religious services, and helped to organise classes for the children, conducted by the trained teachers among the Brigaders. To prepare the children, now mostly orphans, for their future life, they were taught Jewish history, the geography of Palestine, and written and spoken Hebrew.

The rumour mills now switched their attention to the Brigade's impending move from Italy to north-west Europe. Wise heads in British High Command recognised that, with trouble in Palestine multiplying by the day, a confrontation with the Brigade in Italy was out of the question. Britain's sledgehammer tactics, aimed at stopping Jewish immigration into Palestine, were turning into a public relations disaster, even castigated by sections of the British press and members of parliament. They reached the only practicable decision – move the Brigade from its prime strategic position at Tarvisio, and as quickly as possible.

Chaplain Caspar knew that the plight of the displaced persons in camps in Italy would worsen without the protection and support offered by the Brigade. He sensed that the Brigade would shortly receive the order to move, and decided he would inform all interested parties accordingly. He sent the same handwritten, and therefore more personal, letter to all the bodies involved in the refugee question. It went to the American Joint Distribution Committee, UNRRA HQ in Rome, the Inter-governmental Committee for Refugees, the Jewish Agency, and the senior chaplain in Rome. This is a summary of what he said:

We have been contacted by large numbers of Jewish refugees scattered in groups in various parts of Italy. They are stateless and want to get to Palestine as quickly as possible. Their number could be close to 12,000. I have knowledge of four groups. They number 3,000 in Modena, 2,000 in Santa Maria, 1,000 in Ferramonte, and 1,000 in Cine Città outside Rome.

These people need a great deal of attention and care. Conditions in camps are far from good. Our Brigade will be moving and no longer able to help them. We hope that in conjunction with other organisations you will press for the urgency of their homelessness so as to obtain for them certificates of immigration to Palestine. I can see no other solution to their plight. They will never consent to return to their countries of origin where they have suffered so much. The sooner they get to Palestine the sooner they will begin to heal mentally and physically.

One factor remained constant – the Brigaders' hatred of Nazis and their need for vengeance. It was generally accepted that thousands of SS, guilty of crimes against humanity, would escape punishment in the post-war chaos. The Brigade's barracks at Tarvisio had housed an SS garrison, some of whose members had belonged to the *Totenkopf* regiments, which had hunted down Jewish families in captured towns, and which had run the death camps. When the Brigade arrived, the boot was on the other foot.

Much as they wanted to escape the Jewish soldiers in Tarvisio, the *Totenkopf* were afraid to cross into Austria. Capture by Soviet troops would have meant a bullet in the head, or the prospect of years slaving in the salt mines of the Urals and Siberia. So they opted for going to ground in Italy, and trying to make contact with one or other of the networks set up to smuggle Nazis to safety in other parts of the world.

The German- and Austrian-born Brigaders seemed to have an unnerring instinct for sniffing out Nazis. No matter how fluently an SS officer spoke Italian or English, a Brigader could detect the underlying, guttural, German accent. Any Nazi caught would be given short shrift. Brigaders questioned about the fate of such captives tended to develop sudden amnesia.

Len Sanitt recalled one particularly effective form of treatment that would be meted out to high-ranking *Totenkopf* officers. While they waited in the small Brigade prison for the British military police to come for them, the members of an NCOs' mess would set up a fictitious court martial. German-speaking Brigaders would officiate as judge, prosecutor and defence counsel. Under relentless questioning, the SS officer on trial would usually confess to being guilty as charged. In response to questions from 'defence counsel', he would protest that he had acted under orders, had never been a Nazi, and was in fact a Social Democrat. Sentenced to death for crimes against humanity, he was told that he would be executed immediately by firing squad.

He would be led or dragged out into a courtyard surrounded by high brick walls, blindfolded with his wrists tied behind his back. He would be placed with his back to the wall, and have a marker pinned to his chest over his heart. He would hear the 'firing squad' march in and take up position in front of him. He would recognise the Hebrew commands as meaning 'Ready' and 'Take aim'. Just as he heard the click of the rifle bolts, a motorbike would roar up, there was shouting and arguing, and if he hadn't slumped to the ground in sheer terror, his blindfold was removed and he was told that he had been granted a last-minute reprieve. He was not told that he had been subjected to a mock court martial.

I asked Sanitt, 'Were the rifles loaded?' He shook his head. 'That really would have been tempting fate.'

'Did these courts martial happen often?'

'Well . . . a few times, certainly.' Sanitt added the familiar words, 'All sorts of things did happen. You must take into account our feelings at the time. The Holocaust had changed everything.'

The Yishuv leaders were making it clear to the Brigaders that revenge and the settling of scores would become peripheral to their next important role, preparing for the war that Israel was going to have to fight in order to survive. That same year the Arab League was formed, its members pledging to drive 650,000 Palestine Jews into the sea.

Having finished with one war, the Brigade's officers, NCOs and other ranks began to prepare themselves for the next one. However, they continued their humanitarian work of rescuing Jews and getting as many of them as were fit to travel on to the boats. They also continued to smuggle military supplies into Palestine. Their techniques were ingenious and varied, and they were often helped by sympathetic French and Italian officials. Cash bribes were effective, and were often available in return for arms, ammunition, grenades, light artillery, and vehicles of all types. The money often came from American and Canadian Jews.

But the Brigade's most important contribution was to give Israel the foundation of what was to become the most powerful and professional defence force in the Middle East.

On 29 July 1945 the Jewish Brigade finally left Tarvisio, and headed through Germany for Belgium. The period leading up to their departure was hectic. Refugees who volunteered to carry on the rescue mission were handed over to young members of the Haganah who had come specially from Palestine. Their express task was to increase the flow into Palestine of what the British mandatory power referred to as 'illegals'. Some Brigaders, swapping their uniforms for civilian clothes, stayed on in Italy to continue the Bricha movement; their places were taken by fit, able-bodied, young male refugees who assumed the uniforms and took the papers and pay books of those who stayed behind.

All of this was, of course, strictly against the rules. Like Jews throughout the world, the Brigaders were becoming increasingly angered by the pro-Arab bias of the British in Palestine. From newspapers, radio broadcasts and letters from home, they learned of the heavy-handed searches conducted by the British in kibbutzim, farms and rural settlements, and of the wanton destruction of buildings, and injuries sustained by settlers. Ex-blackshirts, members of Oswald Mosley's pre-war British Union of Fascists and now in uniform in Palestine, made no secret of their hatred of Jews and their rabid anti-semitism.

Benjamin and his staff were quietly relieved to be on the move.

Appreciating the volatility of the men's state of mind, they had nevertheless imposed strict discipline. The men knew that Benjamin knew what had been going on, and that in his own low-profile way, he had shielded them from justified military punishment. Many hundreds of cases of AWOL were just a part of it. Benjamin did not let them down and they, in turn, maintained a smart turnout, and performed their military duties in exemplary fashion.

It took several days to work out and implement the logistics of the move. Some 600 assorted vehicles made up the convoy. The Brigade's Provost corps briefed all the drivers on route, speed, distance between sections, and the required gap between vehicles. The move itself was spread over two days. A unit set off at two-hourly intervals, each carrying selected spare parts for their vehicles. Sanitt positioned his ROAC workshop unit at the end of the convoy, and his jeep was the very last vehicle in it. From here he could cover every Brigade vehicle in case of breakdown.

As they rolled through the Brenner pass, the soldiers were captivated by the gloriously panoramic view towards Innsbruck. They could not help wondering how such evil could spring from such beauty. There were to be no unscheduled stops en route. Good maintenance meant there were very few breakdowns. As the convoy entered Germany, Caspar was aware of an increasing tension among the European-born Brigaders. Everything German was anathema to them. Who could not think of the millions of Jews, including members of their own families, who had been slaughtered in this benighted land? Perhaps they derived some comfort and satisfaction from the sight of German refugees trudging along with handcarts and scruffy packages.

When they passed through Bavaria, Caspar learned of two small displaced-person camps. As they were not far away he visited them. Here he found the same sad sight, mainly Jewish women and children, with very few men. Nearly all of the children were orphans. They had had no contact with the outside world, least of all with any organisation that could help them. Despair was rife and the suicide rate high. The inmates were overjoyed to see Caspar, who told them that the Brigade was nearby, but could not stop. He reassured them that he would contact the Bricha and UNRRA on their behalf, and that they would soon be on their way to Palestine.

The convoy trundled on northwards through Germany. They used the main routes and *autobahns*, some of which had been used as runways by the *Luftwaffe*. This was an almost surreal experience for the members of the Brigade. Local civilians stared at them in disbelief. 'The bastards can't believe there are any Jews left and now they see us,' one Polish-born corporal remarked wryly.

Benjamin had issued strict orders that, while they were passing through

Germany, the Brigaders were not to allow their feelings to get the better of them, and that they were to behave as civilised, disciplined troops. At night they pulled off the highway to sleep in their vehicles or in the fields. All-night armed guards were mounted – they could never quite shake off the feeling of being in hostile territory.

Fifty years later, in July 1995, Londoner Gerald Smith faxed Mark Hyatt, who was collecting material for the museum of the Association of Jewish Ex-Servicemen:

> I saw action in Cyrenaica and Tunisia with the 7th Rifle Brigade, and later in Italy through to the battle of Cassino. I transferred to the Jewish Brigade and time spent in the Brigade was a rollercoaster. During the fighting across the Senio I was sent forward as a stretcher bearer. Then I became a driver. I'll never forget driving through Austria and Germany. The deeper into Germany the more silent we all became. There was utter devastation everywhere. People stared at our Jewish flags with incredulity. We pitied the people of ruined Cologne until we encountered that indescribable smell and realised that we were close to the Bergen-Belsen concentration camp.
>
> Our remaining months were taken up by guard duties at POW camps for Germans. Several Germans were killed while clearing minefields under our supervision. They were in the charge of Palestine Jewish soldiers and stories did filter through. Brigaders given extended leave to find their families were coming back desolated. They were resigned to the worst. We British and Empire Brigaders could only console them in any way we could.

From time to time, one of the Brigade chaplains would leave the convoy to follow up a report of a displaced-persons camp. Caspar visited one near a town called Landsberg-am-Lecht, and was astonished to find 4,000 Jewish refugees, who greeted him in the now familiar, ecstatic manner, clambering over his vehicle. Caspar and his driver extricated themselves, promising to return with the entire Jewish Brigade. As they approached the camp for a second time, they found that the inmates had lined both sides of the road. A large Jewish flag flew above the wide, metal gate, and a banner bore in Hebrew the words 'Blessed be they who come'. Inside a choir sang Hebrew songs. A young girl handed the convoy commander a bunch of flowers as it processed through cheering crowds. The refugees mobbed the Brigade's vehicles and hugs were exchanged all round. As one Brigader observed, it was a bit like like a family reunion. Lisa Berman, who later became an American citizen, said, 'I jumped on them, hugged them, embraced them. I couldn't believe that Jewish soldiers had come. It was better than the coming of the Messiah.' Galili Penn said, 'You saw them, touched them. kissed them, embraced them. You begged to be taken to Palestine. The soldiers promised that they would see to it. Definitely.' Over and over the Brigaders were asked the same two questions: 'How much longer do we have to stay in the camp? When can we go to Palestine?'

The camp CO was an American Jewish captain. He had achieved miracles in providing food, beds and bedding, sanitary facilities and much else for those in his charge. He admitted that he had called upon the local American garrison to lean a little heavily now and then on the local citizens. But he was worn out by the weight of responsibility on him. The refugees were desperate to know about the fates of their families, but the camp had no postal facilities. There was no contact with other camps, and the news famine caused enormous stress.

The Brigaders found one beacon in that camp. There was a sizeable number of Lithuanian Jews, intelligent, steeped in Zionism, and fluent in Hebrew. They had organised themselves into a strong Zionist movement, gave lessons to the children, helped those weaker than themselves, and generally raised morale and promoted enthusiasm about getting to Palestine. While imprisoned in Dachau, they had produced seven issues of a handwritten Zionist magazine in Hebrew and Yiddish – a hazardous operation. They would have been hanged if caught.

The displaced persons in the Landsberg camp could only leave if they were issued with special passes. The gates were guarded twenty-four hours a day by American soldiers. Why? Because the CO had his orders: if the inmates were allowed to roam at will, there would have been mayhem with the people of the surrounding area. When the Brigaders told the CO that the Lithuanians would make it out, he shrugged, 'If they do I won't stand in their way. The goddam war is over anyway.'

Years later, in a coffee house in Tel Aviv, there was a flicker of recognition between two customers. One was an ex-Brigader, the other one of the Lithuanians he had spoken to in the Landsberg camp. The latter, now an Israeli citizen, reported that five weeks after the Brigade had left the camp, forty-two young, Lithuanian Zionists cut their way through the perimeter wire and slipped out. It had all been carefully planned, They had maps, torches, and knapsacks filled with stolen provisions and toiletries. And they had weapons.

'Weapons?' queried the ex-Brigader.

'Our CO was a Jew, was he not?'

'Of course.'

The day before the breakout, two of the escapees had obtained special passes and went into the town of Landsberg. They walked around quietly, attracting nothing more than dirty looks. They found what they were looking for in a large area cleared of rubble, which the locals used as a public car park. Once they had got through the perimeter fence, the forty-two Lithuanians made their way back to the car park in small groups, and helped themselves to three serviceable ex-*Wehrmacht* Mercedes trucks. Two who had some knowledge of mechanics got the engines started, when a pair of angry German policemen rushed up and demanded to know what they were doing. Silently the Lithuanians surrounded the policemen, and showed them their concentration camp numbers. The policemen froze in terror. They knew that Germany at that time was full of lawless bands, and life was cheap. They were greatly relieved to be allowed to scuttle away with their tails between their legs.

The Lithuanians headed south through Germany, taking what they needed on the way. They siphoned fuel from parked lorries and vans. Civilians gave them a wide berth, and other armed groups left them alone, as did the Allied troops they encountered from time to time. No one, having made it through the war, wanted to get themselves killed now. The band passed quickly through Austria and reached the Italian border, where they voluntarily surrendered their weapons to customs officials.

They showed the Italian border guards their concentration camp numbers, and asked to be allowed to enter Italy on their way to Palestine. The Italians waved them through and wished them luck. It was the first time in years that these young men had met a friendly gentile face. They reached a camp run by members of the Haganah, and reported on the Landsberg camp. After a few days' rest, they were driven to the Adriatic port of Manfredonia and were put onto a small Greek coaster. Foul weather and seasickness made for an unpleasant voyage. They lived in constant fear of being sighted by a British navy vessel or an RAF scout plane.

In the early hours of one dark morning, they reached the coast of Palestine. Small boats came out to meet them. The less patient waded ashore. They were bundled into trucks and taken to various settlements and farms, where they quickly blended in, hidden whenever British troops came searching for 'illegals' and concealed weapons. The forty-two Lithuanian Jews played a full part in the War of Independence.

The Brigade was now on its last lap in Germany, and was passing through the French zone. An armoured truck broke down. As Sanitt and his best mechanic jumped down to repair it, a jeep pulled up. Out leapt a French army captain, who said he had been instructed to investigate an outrage committed not far from where the Brigade had rested for the night. A farm had been set alight, and as a result a German family of four had perished. Much as he might regret it, the Frenchman said, suspicion had fallen on the Brigade.

'Not us,' said Sanitt. 'I can understand suspicion falling on us if Germans get killed, but we are a highly disciplined body of men. Look for someone else.'

The French captain nodded reflectively and said, 'Well, I'll report the cause of the fire as unknown, perpetrated by criminals who are also unknown. Where are you heading for?'

'Demobilisation and then home to Palestine.'

'Ah, Palestine. Bon voyage and good luck when you get there. No peace for the Jews anywhere.'

They shook hands.

At last the Brigade left behind the uneasy atmosphere of Germany and crossed into France, where they found that their fame had gone before them. At Valenciennes, wildly enthusiastic crowds besieged their vehicles and brought them to a halt. The forty Jewish families left in the town were especially pleased to see the Brigade. It took the convoy two hours to make its way through Valenciennes, and roll on towards Belgium.

# Chapter Fourteen

By the end of August, the Brigade had settled down in the Low Countries. HQ was established in the Brussels area, with units detailed for duties in the surrounding towns. Others were engaged in Holland, guarding German POWs, supervising the clearance of mines and repairing damage. The 2nd and 3rd Palestine infantry battalions were given the task of overseeing the labouring prisoners. Some guarded the Pluto pipelines and oil depots, no sinecure as the Belgians, trained in resistance during the war, would tunnel their way into the dumps, and siphon petrol from the pipes. To outwit them, the authorities turned off the petrol and diesel in the most vulnerable lines, to pump water into them, and watch which cars stalled in the days that followed.

Wherever a Brigade unit was stationed, Jewish organisations, bodies, communities, individuals and refugees would make their way towards it. The very presence of the Brigade gave every Jew renewed optimism and a feeling of being looked after by their own people. The Brigaders were made welcome in Jewish homes, and were invited to many moving occasions. Brigade staff gave a Chanukah party for the children from the camps. No child left without a going-away present.

There was complete agreement that the most unforgettable event was the concert given by Bronislaw Huberman, internationally renowned violinist and founder of the Palestine Symphony Orchestra. The concert was staged in the large assembly hall of a school on the outskirts of Brussels. As Huberman came in, the entirely khaki audience rose spontaneously and sang the Hatikvah ('the Hope'), the Jewish National Anthem. Huberman stopped in his tracks and stood like a statue until the end. This was a tremendous gesture of faith, and the famous violinist was visibly moved. Deep down, it was a gesture of defiance, aimed at Jewry's two new enemies, the British Foreign Office, headed by Bevin, who made no bones about his determination to crush Zion, and the Arab League nations, sharpening their swords for the planned annihilation of the Jews in Palestine.

Britain supported the Arabs for two reasons: for oil, oil and more oil; and because Palestine lay at the heart of the strategically important Middle East. But its position proved only counter-productive. The opprobrium it attracted, particularly in the United States, lost Britain

139

much of the admiration won by her lone stand against the Axis powers for one vital year during the war. And it secured international support for the Jews. In Europe, this manifested itself in the help given to the Brigade moving refugees across frontiers with a minumum of formality and interference. Right up until the end of August 1946, when the last 500 Brigaders embarked at Marseilles for Palestine and demobilisation, that help and support was always there.

Two examples of British crassness reached the ears of Brigaders in the Low Countries, and fuelled their growing disenchantment with the famous British sense of fair play. On 27 July 1945 Christopher Holme wrote in the current issue of *Hagalgol*, the Hebrew weekly published by the British Ministry of Information: 'No better victory could have been expected by Jews than victory over Hitler.' Tell that to a Brigader who had lost all his family and friends. It went down like a lead balloon with Palestine Jews. Naturally, Holme was highly praised by a new Arab weekly, *Al Widha*.

The second gem concerned the King's Birthday Parade, which took place in Jerusalem on 17 August and was also regarded as the <u>Palestine</u> Victory Parade. A Tel Aviv monthly published a list of awards won by the Brigade, along with Field Marshal Alexander's tribute to its conduct in action. It went on to describe the parade in roughly these words:

It seems regrettable that Jewish soldiers should have been so inconspicuous in the King's Birthday Parade which was also a Victory Parade. It gave the public a chance of cheering the men who had taken part in the fighting. There was no doubt that the colourful Camel Corps of the Arab Legion made a most attractive feature of the parade. But it was curious that the Arab Legion and Transjordan Frontier Force, whose war service was so minimal in scope, should be allowed to dominate the parade the way they did. The onlookers were left with the impression that only those brightly coloured soldiers made up Palestine's contribution to the war effort.

With the Brigade firmly ensconced in Belgium and Holland, it continued to cooperate with the Bricha to open new escape routes through the ports of Rotterdam, Antwerp and Marseilles. There were always seafarers and boat owners willing to risk running the British naval blockade in return for the substantial cash payments offered by representatives of the Jewish Agency. And there always was an element of risk. The Greek owner of a small island-hopping coaster in Antwerp agreed to transport 150 Jews to Palestine. He was paid half of a considerable sum in a nondescript hotel, then announced that he would have to make for Marseilles to discharge a cargo, would take the refugees on board there, and would sail for Palestine. Times, dates and all other relevant details were agreed between the Greek boat owner and the Agency's man.

Sanitt organised eight trucks for the long overland journey. He handed to a trusted driver the balance of payment due to the Greek, to be paid once the human cargo had been taken aboard. The refugees were put onto the trucks and Sanitt waved them off. The convoy eventually reached Marseilles on schedule – and there was no Greek skipper and no boat. The sergeant in charge of the convoy learned that the boat had berthed alongside the day before, but had quickly unloaded its small cargo, and had sailed straight away to collect another cargo at Messina in Sicily. The refugees were stunned by disappointment and the Brigaders had a harrowing journey back to Belgium. But these refugees were given priority, and were finally on their way to Palestine only three weeks later.

In Brussels close links were forged with the Maccabi sports organisation. One night a young lady told a Brigade staff officer that she knew where a unit of his RASC Company was at that moment. The security-conscious officer asked misleadingly. 'And whereabouts in Belgium do you think it is?'

The woman smiled and replied, 'At this moment it is in Poland heading back here with a group of survivors.'

She was right. The Brigade officer was not particularly surprised. So many Brigaders were working with the young Haganah boys and girls, and with helpers from the Jewish community that security had become something of a joke. The Brigade's movements tended to be common knowledge.

The Jewish Agency appointed a Palestinian NCO as the Brigade's liaison officer with the Net. His name was Mordechai Makleff, later to become Chief of Staff of the Israeli Defence Forces.

Generally speaking the Belgians exercised stricter border controls than the Dutch and the French, which meant that the movement of refugees south to Marseilles involved careful planning. All convoys had to be completely self sufficient in fuel, oil, spares, rations and relief drivers, as no help could be expected from elsewhere. On occasions the problem of fuel shortages was solved by drawing direct from the Pluto pipeline from England. Sometimes drivers siphoned off petrol from parked vehicles. Spare fuel cans were carried, smuggled by the drivers into their trucks. There was no shortage of individual initiative among Brigaders. The necessary official documents, authorising the movement of refugees across borders, were produced by those skilled in such things.

If the paperwork was missing, the Brigaders followed a set procedure. A very charming and friendly officer named Memie de Shalit would go ahead of the convoy and would strike up a conversation with the frontier officials. He would tell them that the trucks were carrying German POWs into France. He was sorry that the canvas blinds were pulled down at the rear . . . but orders were orders. It would be immensely troublesome to

141

have to raise them. The guards accepted this with sufficient irony to indicate that they knew perfectly well who was being carried by the convoy. And still they allowed it to pass. The same cooperative attitude was adopted by the French. No obstacle was ever put in the way of the convoy's progress. And when the trucks returned to Belgium at the end of a mission, they were overhauled by German prisoners under the supervision of Brigade mechanics.

From late summer, the Brigade was effectively operating under the direction of the Yishuv, coordinating efficiently with Reshet, Bricha and other organisations. They supplied the infantry or forward troops for this salvation force. Only the Brigaders, with their well maintained vehicles, experienced drivers and military clout, could have roamed back and forth across Europe in the way that they did. Whenever they could, they brought destitute Jews back to the Brigade. If the refugees were too numerous, or too ill or deranged by their experiences, they left them where they were, with the promise that others would come for them. Always they noted names, dates and places of birth, and any other details which could usefully be passed on to the various tracing organisations established in a number of countries.

It was mandatory that Brigaders were at all times well turned out, and their vehicles gleaming and flying the Brigade pennant. Being so readily identified often eased their passage off the beaten track, and drew the attention of the truly forgotten, those emaciated Jews who would appear waving their arms and shouting in Yiddish, unable to believe that their luck had changed.

Of all the Allies it was the Russians, with their staggering 20 million military and civilian dead, who truly appreciated the scale of what the Nazis had inflicted on the Jews. They were almost invariably friendly in their encounters with the Brigade, and at times Red Army officers would greet the Brigaders in Yiddish and talk wistfully of Palestine.

In October 1945 David Ben-Gurion visited DP camps in France and Germany, and then had discussions with the Brigade. Although small in stature, Ben-Gurion was dynamic and inspirational, and certainly one of the great figures of the Zionist movement. When he addressed Jewish audiences, his clarity of vision and purpose stiffened the sinews of doubters and waverers. Always his message was:

The Jewish people will have their National Home. It will be a struggle. It will be hard. We will confront the enemy intent on destroying us. But we will win. Have no doubt about that. The Jewish flag will fly over the Land of Israel, and no one will stop this from happening.

As a result of Ben-Gurion's visit, the Brigade stepped up its search for survivors, especially in Poland, Romania and Hungary. The drivers and workshops now set about the task non-stop, seven days a week. And the human river flowing south to the boats swept on. The Royal Navy did succeed in filling incarceration camps in Cyprus with some 12,000 'illegals', but many of the boats found the gaps and slipped through to be welcomed by youthful members of the Haganah on the beaches of Palestine.

Ben-Gurion's visit had had another purpose. He looked at the Brigade in detail, and decided that to survive Israel needed to bring its fractured fighting forces together into one disciplined army. Politics would not be allowed to create factions, and all units would obey orders from the top. The entire army would be in the service of the state. There would be no left wing or right wing, no terrorist extremists.

Ben-Gurion's party was Mapai, which enjoyed the support of workers and trade unions. The Palmach, the elite stormtroopers, belonged politically to the more conservative Mapam party. It was their exclusive preserve, and of its sixty-four commanders and officers, all but four were members of Mapam. These sabra officers tended to look down on the spit and polish Brigade. Ben-Gurion was determined to put an end to this factionalism, and his visit to the Brigade persuaded him that its structure of command and discipline was what Palestine Jews needed. It was the template for the future Israeli Defence Force, a united army of the people, accountable only to a democratically elected government. The weakness occasioned by division was to be eliminated. It speaks volumes for the genius and toughness of Ben-Gurion that he succeeded in bringing a nation of stubborn individualists to heel.

And what was the relationship between Brigade HQ and British Army of the Rhine (BAOR) HQ? In a word, it was confused. The Palestine 'troubles', as they were euphemistically called, and the overt anti-semitism of the British Foreign Secretary and his coterie had made the Brigade a hot potato. There were, it must be said, many seasoned British officers who were not at all happy with Bevin's attitude, and his foot-in-the-mouth remarks. The Royal Navy was uncomfortable with its blockading role – some British sailors commented later that being ordered to board a small caique or schooner crammed with desperate men, women and children was a filthy job. But orders were orders.

The refugees were not going to disappear. They were there, and they had to be helped. Because, to begin with, so many Brigaders were commandeering vehicles and going AWOL, Brigadier Benjamin applied to BAOR HQ for permission to send authorised teams into Europe instead. His request was turned down. But in October the Brigade was told that it could send a team to Czechoslovakia, and in December permission was given for a team to go to Poland. This latter set off, reached Warsaw, and was informed that consent had been withdrawn. Why? HQ of 21st British Army Group gave permission for five search and rescue teams, each comprising three men, to look for displaced persons in the British zone in Germany only. Four weeks later, the order was countermanded. Again, why?

Was there pressure from the mandarins? Ironically, Brigaders were out and about anyway, without permission, laying the Brigade open to serious and justifiable charges. However, this did not happen, no doubt because common sense and decency prevailed in BAOR HQ. Confrontation on Dutch or Belgian soil with simmering Brigaders was unthinkable. Unlike their political masters, and the government in Palestine, the British military never hesitated to give credit where it was due. In *The Soldier* of 2 March 1946, Staff Sergeant Robert (later Lord) Blake wrote a laudatory piece about the Jewish Brigade, entitled 'Star of Courage'.

But in Palestine, because of the British Foreign Secretary's determination not to compromise one jot with the Yishuv, the situation was going from bad to worse. The Yishuv lost any remnant of faith in British justice. Trust had been supplanted by pragmatism and enmity. The Haganah threw caution to the winds and expressed itself frankly and openly. It would go all out to facilitate the arrival of refugees, and would protect them from being forcibly returned to Europe. There was a new mood of anger on both sides. This resulted in action, which was followed by retaliation, leading to further action, and so on. In November 1945 Bevin's heavy hand pushed the compliant Palestine government into threatening to impose a 24-hour curfew on the entire Jewish community. If that happened, the Yishuv replied, the authorities would have to place the entire 600,000-strong community under arrest, as they would all break any such curfew. Such an act of civil disobedience could never have been contained.

Letters from home, received by Palestine Jews in the Brigade, made grim reading. Sadly, their content was diverting anger from the Nazis to the British, an uncomfortable factor for the British and Empire Brigaders. The *Jewish Chronicle* of 23 November 1945 reported that new British troops arriving in Palestine had been given to understand that their role there was to fight the Jews, a directive that some, too young to have fought in the war, interpreted literally.

In the settlement of Ramat Gan at Emek, it had been the custom for the settlers to sell fresh milk and vegetables at reduced prices to appreciative British soldiers. The new arrivals startled the settlers by roaring up in an armoured car, with two men manning machine-guns, and others with mortars. They remained silent and menacing, as if expecting to be set upon, until business was completed and the unit left.

The officially endorsed spirit of hostility affected the score of war correspondents present. The label they bore gave them the feeling that it was indeed a war they were reporting. This infuriated the Jewish community which had loyally stood by Britain in her darkest days, while the Arabs had been consistently hostile towards the Allies throughout the war. The atmosphere was summed up in a range of sour jokes such as 'A dirty Arab is picturesque, but a dirty Jew is a dirty Jew.'

A disapproving world looked on. On 15 February 1946 15,000 American servicemen in the Pacific signed a petition to President Truman, urging that the gates of Palestine be opened to Jewish immigration. Well over seventy per cent of the signatories were gentiles. On 1 March a letter was published in *The Palmers Green and Southgate Gazette*, a London local newspaper, from Flying Officer Hugh Middleton RAF, a gentile, arguing that Palestine should be open to the Jews and the Arabs alike.

In his notes, Major Spector recorded that there was a two-way traffic of personnel between Palestine Jews and the Brigade. The Palestinians were steeped in British army procedure and training, a knowledge they would pass on to others when they got home. Apart from many ingenious ruses for getting across borders, there were other loopholes that the British could not interfere with, such as the normal sea and air traffic of people going about their lawful business. Dutch, Italians, French and Americans would not have taken at all kindly to having their vessels and vehicles boarded and searched for 'illegals'. Not even the British Foreign Office would contemplate 'piracy' on the high seas.

Mandate or no mandate, the Jewish refugee problem was a high-profile, international issue. Countries criticising Britain for her heavy-handed approach were not falling over themselves to accept quotas of immigrants. As Eichmann was quick to point out, Jews were not wanted. The UK and US governments appointed a Committee of Enquiry, made up of an equal number of British and Americans, to visit the DP camps in Europe, and to consider what could be done to alleviate the suffering. After two weeks, they were aghast at what they found. One committee member reported:

During our visit my colleagues and I smelled the unforgettable smell of homeless humanity. It was an experience of human degradation. A nightmare had become our everyday life. Policies seemingly sane enough in the White House and Downing Street struck these people as sadistic brutality.

We discovered some 98,000 people, mainly Polish Jews, in assembly centres in Germany and Austria. If the war had gone on for another few weeks, none would have been alive. Many had walked hundreds of miles back to their homes to find themselves sole survivors, and anti-semitism rife. So they trudged back to the camps. Nine months have passed since the end of the war. They knew they were not wanted by the western democracies or by anywhere. They knew one thing. There was a National Home waiting to receive them, not as aliens in a foreign land, but as Jews in their own country. Palestine was their only hope to escape from hell. As far as they were concerned, it was better to die fighting as members of a Hebrew nation than rotting away in assembly centres run by British and American soldiers who talked of humanity but shut their doors to human suffering.

The summer of 1946 was a crucial time. It became evident that Jewish resistance in Palestine would not be broken unless Britain launched an all-out war. Tel Aviv could have been razed. The settlements could have been wiped out. And yet another Jewish community would have been made homeless. But the British government was reined in by the checks and balances of an ancient democracy, and could not enforce totalitarian measures. The anti-Zionists in Whitehall lost game, set and match. Bevin and his cronies finally failed to stop the creation of the Jewish State.

During April and May 1946 the world was aghast at news coming from Poland of pogroms against Jewish survivors. In Kielce it was particularly vicious. Jewish returnees were actually hunted down by killing mobs, and nearly sixty were murdered on the spot. Refugees declared that they would commit suicide sooner than go back to Poland. The Brigade responded. It helped to organise a freedom train which went from Egypt into Palestine, crammed with survivors and festooned with Jewish flags. The members of the Brigade now made no bones about its new and only raison d'être – the saving of the largest possible number of European Jews, and their safe passage to Palestine. There was even talk among the more hotheaded of driving an armed convoy into Kielce, and giving its citizens a day they would never forget. In that same month of May, the Brigade learned that it was to be disbanded forthwith, at a rate of 500 a week, which is exactly what happened.

The attention of the diminishing number of Brigaders now switched rapidly to the acquisition of surplus and 'unserviceable' arms. They were diverted to dumps in the Toulouse-Pau-Marseilles area, the larger pieces being broken down into their component parts, and put into Brigade trucks that carried them to Palestine. As usual, the French were sympathetic and turned a blind eye. There was just one hitch. At Villeneuve-sur-Lot the French police pounced on a large consignment which they suspected was intended for use by former collaborators attempting to set free fellow collaborators. Intense negotiations went all the way up to M. André Blumel, who had been chef de cabinet to French prime minister, Léon Blum. A compromise was reached. Half of the consignment was handed over to Palestine units still stationed in Italy; the other half was kept by the French army.

Disbandment and demobilisation were not without further incident in the Brigade's European adventure. On several occasions, Brigaders, who were about to embark on the repatriation ships for the journey back to

Palestine, gave their uniforms, papers and pay books to refugees who had been smuggled aboard. Fifty or sixty 'instant' Brigaders would enter Palestine with the rest. After landing they would, as prearranged, lose themselves in scattered kibbutzim and moshavim. The real Brigaders who had handed over their identity slipped ashore in civilian clothes, and made their way back to Italy and Austria to help the Bricha and Reshet escape organisations.

Like all demobilised soldiers, the Brigaders were glad to return to their homes and families. But for them, unlike their Allied counterparts, there was no normality. They were horrified by the atmosphere and anger and fear in a country in a state of turbulence. This could not be called a real war, but they found their erstwhile comrades in arms, with the British as the new enemy. And lurking in the background, watching and waiting, were the Arabs. The question was now when, not if, the British would quit Palestine. The leaders of Palestine's neighbours met and planned, and stealthily began to sharpen their swords.

Chaim Laskov had been an infantry officer in the Brigade. He had led attacks against German paratroops and the famous Jaeger division. On demobilisation he carried the rank of major. Conscious of the struggle going on around him, he could only worry about finding a job and earning enough to pay for a home. He approached one Mr Feldman about work. Feldman asked Laskov what he could do. Laskov stared out of the window at a sign for the prominent Palestine Electric Corporation, and snapped, 'I can write your name with a machine-gun on the Electric Corporation.'

He was given the job of security officer. Towards the end of 1947 Ben-Gurion started to organise a new, modern Jewish army. Laskov was one of the ex-Brigaders called on, and the model copied was the British army. The Irgun Zvi Leumi and the Stern Gang would have to dissolve themselves, and their members join the Haganah. If not, they would be crushed. There was to be no dissent, no factionalism. Ben-Gurion was determined; he would not countenance defeat. And his confidence rubbed off on others. So Laskov began his army career. He was later to become Chief of Staff of the Israeli Defence Forces, and later still became its highly respected ombudsman.

There was to be a last, grim test. In July 1947 the most famous refugee ship, the *Exodus*, reached Haifa crammed with 5,000 Polish Jews. The British refused to let them ashore. No other country would take them. The *Exodus* was forced to return to Hamburg and dump her horrified human cargo back onto the dreaded soil of Germany. Palestine Jews were goaded into an unstemmable rash of acts of sabotage and demonstrations, and Britain was on the receiving end of the most savage opprobrium from around the world. The *Exodus* incident tipped Ernest Bevin over the edge. He resolved that Britain would give up the Palestine mandate.

On 27 November 1947 the General Assembly of the United Nations recommended the partition of Palestine. The British declared they would not support this move and would withdraw their troops and their administration on 15 May 1948. The Palestine Jews were jubilant. The Arabs announced that they would drive the Jews into the sea. Action followed words. Violence by Arabs against Jews erupted nationwide. The British stood aside and watched. The Arabs ambushed buses, cars and trucks. They set light to the commercial quarter of Jerusalem. They attacked and murdered rural Jewish settlers. Still the British stood by. The Haganah realised that it alone stood between the Arab forces and another massacre of Jews, and it was transformed overnight into a highly disciplined army. The ex-Brigaders had found their true raison d'être, defending the very birth of their own nation.

On 14 May 1948 the Independent State of Israel was proclaimed with David Ben-Gurion as its first prime minister. At once five Arab countries rose up to destroy the new state. Their flag was a Star of David slashed through with a scimitar. They did not want talks or compromise. In overwhelming numbers, well armed and confident, their aim was the total obliteration of the new democracy in their midst. The outside world waited with bated breath. It expected the annihilation of the new state.

But with memories of the Holocaust embedded in their souls, the Jews fought back with a rage and tenacity that completely unhinged the Arabs. Not only did they regain lands lost in the initial Arab assaults, but they advanced into and captured land that had not been granted to them by the UN. The Jews won their War of Independence. They lost 6,000 in the effort. Perhaps the most poignant were those concentration camp survivors who came under fire as they landed on the beaches. They died on the soft, inviting sand. They had reached the Promised Land, but only just.

Among many tributes to the Jewish Brigade, it is possible to cite two – one practical, the other inspirational. Israel's first prime minister, David Ben-Gurion, wrote:

Without the officers and soldiers of the Jewish Brigade, it is doubtful whether we could have built the Israeli Defence Forces in such a short period, in such a stormy hour.

And Dr S Levenburg wrote in October 1984 in the *Zionist Review*:

The appearance of the Jews as a fighting force was evidence of a momentous change. In a world accustomed to the sight of the Jew – beaten, weak, a passive object of human savagery – the Jewish soldier came with fighting spirit in unrelieved revolt against five years of Jewish suffering, helplessness and unrelieved tragedy.

# Appendix I

## Roll of Honour

In 1950 Captain Dr Jacob Gil Lifschitz, who was a senior chaplain in the Jewish Brigade, compiled *The Book of the Jewish Brigade*. It was published by Josef Shimoni in Tel Aviv, and Martin Sugarman translated it from Hebrew into English. A member of the Association of Jewish Ex-Servicemen in Britain, he helps out with the museum and, together with the archivist, Henry Morris, produced the most accurate list of Brigade casualties. In this task they received unstinting assistance from the Commonwealth War Graves Commission, and from the staff of the Imperial War Museum Reading Room. Apart from the 734 Palestine Jews killed in action, the Brigade suffered 83 killed in action or died from wounds, and 200 wounded.

# Appendix II

Awards won by Brigaders

| | |
|---|---|
| MC | 4 |
| MM | 7 |
| MBE | 4 |
| CBE | 1 |
| OBE | 2 |
| US awards | 2 |
| Mentioned in Dispatches | 78 |

# *Appendix III*

[This piece is reproduced as it was published]

TO OUR FELLOW BRITISH SOLDIERS!

TODAY THE SOLDIERS OF THE JEWISH BRIGADE GROUP ARE ON A HUNGER STRIKE THOUGH SCRUPULOUSLY CARRYING OUT ALL DUTIES.

WE WANT YOU TO KNOW WHY WE WERE FORCED TO EXPRESS OUR FEELINGS IN SUCH A WAY. WE FOUGHT TOGETHER IN CRETE AND EGYPT. WE BURIED OUR DEAD TOGETHER IN ITALY BECAUSE WE WHERE TOLD THAT WE WERE FIGHTING FOR THE FREEDOM OF THE WORLD AND IT'S PEOPLES.

OUR BRETHREN THE JEWS IN BERGEN BELSEN AND BUCHENWALD AND EVERYWHERE ELSE IN LIBERATED EUROPE HAVE NO HOME TO GO BACK TO. SOME OF THEM ARE STILL BEHIND BARRED WIRE AS IN THE TIMES OF THE NAZIS. THEY HAVE NO HOME EXCEPT PALESTINE. THEY WANT NO HOME EXCEPT PALESTINE.

OUR BRETHREN IN THE CAMPS DECLARED A HUNGER STRIKE BECAUSE THE GATES OF PALESTINE HAVE BEEN LOCKED IN THEIR FACES AND THEIR LAST HOPE SHATTERRED.

WE ARE DOING LIKEWISE TO DAY SO AS TO EXPRESS OUR SYMPATHY AND SOLIDARITY WITH THEM.

WE EXCEPT THE FULFILMENT OF THE PLEDGES GIVEN US BY THE LEADERS OF THE BRITISH PEOPLE:

' . . . *THIS PLEDGE OF A HOME OR REFUGE, OF AN ASYLUM, WAS NOT MADE TO THE JEWS IN PALESTINE, BUT TO THE JEWS OUTSIDE PALESTINE, TO THAT VAST, UNHAPPY MASS OF SCATTERED, PERSECUTED, WANDERING JEWS, WHOSE INTENSE, UNCHANGING, UNCONQUERABLE DESIRE HAS BEEN FOR A NATIONAL HOME . . .*

(Winston Churchill)

*' . . . THE BRITISH LABOUR PARTY RECALLS WITH PRIDE THAT IN THE DARK DAYS OF THE GREAT WAR THEY ASSOCIATED THEMSELVES WITH THE IDEAL OF A NATIONAL HOME IN PALESTINE FOR THE JEWISH PEOPLE, AND THAT EVER SINCE, THE **ANNUAL** CONFERENCES OF THE PARTY HAVE REPEATEDLY AFFIRMED THEIR ENTHUSIASTIC SUPPORT OF THE EFFORT TOWARDS ITS REALISATION.'*

(C R Atlee)

# *Appendix IV*

JEWISH AGENCY FOR PALESTINE

## Registration for the Jewish Brigade Group

". . . the Government have decided to accede to the request of the Jewish Agency for Palestine that a Jewish Brigade Group should be formed to take part in active operations. There are vast numbers of Jews serving with our forces and the American forces throughout all the armies, but it seems to me indeed appropriate that a special unit of that race which has suffered indescribable treatment from the Nazis, should be represented in a distinct formation among the forces gathered for their final overthrow, and I have no doubt that they will not only take an active part in the struggle but in the occupation which will follow." —*Winston Churchill.*

### Categories of Persons Eligible for Enlistment

1. Palestinians
2. Stateless
3. Aliens (enemy)          (Age 18 - 40)
4. Allied Nationals

5. British Subjects          (Age 26 - 40)

### Qualifications for Infantry and Technical Units

Note:—Application for Ministry of Labour approval will be made, where necessary, after registration.

Age – Infantry: British 26 - 35
Others 18 - 35
Technical Units: British 26 - 40
Others 18 - 40

Minimum Height – 5 feet.
Minimum Weight – 7 stone 2 lbs.
Lowest Medical Category – B.II (a).

List of Jewish Agency Registration Offices for Jewish Brigade Group:

#### CENTRAL REGISTRATION OFFICE:

Jewish Agency Registration Office, 25, Bloomsbury Square, W.C.1. Tel. MUS 2522. Office Hours: 10-6 weekdays, except Saturdays, and 10-1 Sundays.

MANCHESTER.—Manchester Zionist Office, 139, Cheetham Hill Road, Manchester 8. Tel. Blackfriars 8435/6. Office Hours: 10-5 weekdays, except Saturdays, and 10-1 Sundays.

LEEDS.—Leeds Zionist Offices, 17, Brunswick Street, Leeds 2. Tel. Leeds 24745. Office Hours: 10-5 weekdays, except Saturdays, and 10-1 Sundays.

BIRMINGHAM.—Birmingham Zionist Office, 61, Station Street, Birmingham. Tel. Midland 3349. Office Hours: 10-5 weekdays, except Saturdayls, and 10-1 Sundays.

LIVERPOOL.—Liverpool Zionist Office, 8, Princes Road, Liverpool. Tel. Royal 2809. Office Hours: 10-5 weekdays, except Saturdays, and 10-1 Sundays.

GLASGOW.—South Portland Street Synagogue, 95, South Portland Street, Glasgow, C.5. Tel. South 1934. Office Hours: 10-12 a.m. and 7-9 p.m. (except Fridays and Saturdays) and Sundays 3-5.

# *Appendix V*

## HEBREW WORDS OF COMMAND.
### (FOR CEREMONIAL PURPOSES).

The following vocabulary has been worked out by a Special Commission. Its main feature is that the "executive" word is always the same—"hen" (הֵן), used in the same way as the word "move!" in Physical Training. A few exceptions—words of command used without special executive—are singled out under 2 (a).

The adopted pronunciation of Hebrew words of Command is Sephardic. The tonic accent is shown in the English transcription by a ⌃; it must be remembered that this accent is usually on the *last* syllable, except in the words yamîna, semôla, kadîma, achôra, sêder, hâla, hashêchem, âlef, ôref, tsâad and ârtsa.

### 1. NAMES OF UNITS.

| English. | Pronunciation. | Hebrew. |
|---|---|---|
| Battalion .... .... .... | Haggedûd .... .... .... ... ... ... ... | הַגְּדוּד |
| Company .... .... .... | Happelugâ .... .... .... ... ... ... | הַפְּלוּגָה |
| Platoon .... .... .... | Hatserôr .... .... .... ... ... ... ... | הַצְּרוֹר |
| Section .... .... .... | Hakkittâ.... .... .... ... ... ... ... | הַכִּתָּה |
| Squad .... .... .... .... | Hatserôr .... .... .... ... ... ... ... | הַצְּרוֹר |
| Front Rank .... .... .... | Tur âlef .... .... .... ... ... ... ... | טוּר אָלֶף ... |
| Rear Rank .... .... .... | Tur bet .... .... .... ... ... ... ... | טוּר בֵּית ... |

### 2. SQUAD DRILL.

#### (a) Without the executive word "hen."

| Fall in .... .... .... | Histaddêr .... .... .... .... ... | הִסְתַּדֵּר ... |
| Cover off .... .... .... | Panîm el ôref .... .... .... ... | פָּנִים אֶל עֹרֶף |
| Stand easy .... .... .... | Nûach .... .... .... .... ... ... | נוּחַ ... |
| As you were .... .... .... | Chazôr .... .... .... .... ... ... | הַחֲזוֹר ... |
| Mark time .... .... .... | Al Makôm .... .... .... ... ... | עַל מָקוֹם ... |
| Left—right (when marching) | Semôl—Yamîn .... .... .... ... | שְׂמֹאל—יָמִין |
| March to attention .... | Sêder .... .... .... .... ... ... | סֵדֶר ... |
| March at ease .... .... | Sêder kal .... .... .... .... ... ... | סֵדֶר קַל ... |

#### (b) With the executive word "hen."

| Attention .... .... .... | Hatserôr—hen .... .... .... ... ... | הַצְּרוֹר—הֵן |
| Halt .... .... .... .... | Hatserôr—hen .... .... .... ... ... | הַצְּרוֹר—הֵן |
| Stand at ease.... .... .... | Sêder kal—hen .... .... .... ... ... | סֵדֶר קַל—הֵן ... |
| Right dress .... .... .... | Hityashêr yamîna—hen .... ... ... | הִתְיַשֵׁר יָמִינָה—הֵן |

155

| English. | Pronunciation. | Hebrew. |
|---|---|---|
| Left dress | Hityashér semóla—hen | הִתְיַשֵׁר שְׂמֹאלָה–הֶן |
| Eyes front | Yashár—hen | יַשֵׁר–הֶן |
| Number (in twos *) | Âlef-bet—hen | אָלֶף־בֵּית–הֶן |
| Right turn | Yamina—hen | יָמִינָה–הֶן |
| Left turn | Semóla—hen | שְׂמֹאלָה–הֶן |
| About turn | Achóra—hen | אָחוֹרָה–הֶן |
| Right incline | Hatsi-yamina—hen | חֲצִי־יָמִינָה–הֶן |
| Left incline | Hatsi-semóla—hen | חֲצִי־שְׂמֹאלָה–הֶן |
| Form fours | Arbaót—hen | אַרְבָּעוֹת הֶן |
| Form two deep | Bitsmadim—hen | בִּצְמָדִים–הֶן |
| Quick march | Kadima—hen | קָדִימָה–הֶן |
| Right wheel | Sa panim yamina—hen | שָׂא פָּנִים יָמִינָה–הֶן |
| Left wheel | Sa panim semóla—hen | שָׂא פָּנִים שְׂמֹאלָה–הֶן |
| Right turn (marching in fours) | Bitsmadim yamina—hen | בִּצְמָדִים יָמִינָה–הֶן |
| Left turn (marching in fours) | Bitsmadim semóla—hen | בִּצְמָדִים שְׂמֹאלָה–הֶן |
| Right form | Bené tur yamina—hen | בְּנֵה טוּר יָמִינָה–הֶן |
| Left form | Bené tur semóla—hen | בְּנֵה טוּר שְׂמֹאלָה–הֶן |
| Forward | Hâla—hen | הָלְאָה–הֶן |
| On the right (or left) form squad | Histaddér yamina (semóla)—hen | הִסְתַּדֵּר יָמִינָה–הֶן |
| Eyes right (or left) | Habbét yamina (semóla)—hen | הַבֵּט יְמִינָה–הֶן |
| Right wheel, quick march | Sa panim yamina, kadima—hen | שָׂא פָּנִים יָמִינָה, קָדִימָה–הֶן |
| One pace | Tsáad echâd | צַעַד אֶחָד |
| Two paces | Shené tseadim | שְׁנֵי צְעָדִים |
| Three paces | Sheloshá tseadim | שְׁלֹשָׁה צְעָדִים |
| Four paces | Arbaá tseadim | אַרְבָּעָה צְעָדִים |
| Two paces forward—march | Shené tseadim kadima—hen | שְׁנֵי צְעָדִים קָדִימָה–הֶן |
| Two paces back—march | Shené tseadim leachôr—hen | שְׁנֵי צְעָדִים לְאָחוֹר–הֶן |
| Two paces right close—march | Shené tseadim leyamin—hen | שְׁנֵי צְעָדִים לְיָמִין–הֶן |
| Two paces left close—march | Shené tseadim lismôl—hen | שְׁנֵי צְעָדִים לִשְׂמֹאל–הֶן |

## 3. ARMS DRILL.

| | | |
|---|---|---|
| Take up arms | Harovim—hen | הָרוֹבִים הֶן |
| Order arms | Harovim—hen | הָרוֹבִים–הֶן |
| Slope arms | Al hashêchem—hen | עַל הַשֶּׁכֶם הֶן |
| Present arms | Lekavôd—hen | לְכָבוֹד–הֶן |
| Ground arms | Ârtsa—hen | אַרְצָה–הֶן |

* Upon which the men will shout out: "âlef—bet; âlef—bet" in the same way as "one—two, one—two."

# Index

**A**boy, Pte 53-4
Adiv, Cpn Israel 110, 111
Adler, Rabbi Michael 2
Albert, Dov 68
Alexander, Field Marshal
    Lord 98, 110, 140
Aliyah Bet 8, 11, 17
American Jewish Congress
    100
American Joint Distribution
    Committee 109, 122, 131
Antonescu, Ion 100
Aron, Wellesley 17, 18, 19,
    20-1, 23, 24, 25, 26, 27, 28,
    29, 30, 31-2, 35, 37, 38, 39,
    40, 41, 43, 44, 45, 46, 47, 48,
    56-7, 63, 83, 107, 108, 109,
    110-11, 112-13
Aronoff, Maj. E A 37, 111
Assor, Reuven 65-6
Australian 6th Division 18
Auxiliary Military Pioneer
    Corps 15
Avny, Moishe 68

**B**abi Yar [massacre] 25
Baden Powell, Robert 17
Balfour, James 7
    Balfour Declaration 7, 8,
    9, 11
Bankover, Sgt-Maj. 26, 32-3,
    35, 37-8
Bar-Kimche, Pte Aharon 66
Bar Kochba 1, 78
Bartov, Hanoch 83
Baum, Hanna 101-2, 106
Beal, Col. W A 56
Becker, Avraham 103, 106
Behar, Shimon 92
Belisha, Hore 17

Belk, Maj. 20, 23
Benevolent Fund 30
Ben-Artze, Col. 72
Ben-Gurion, David xiv, 4, 11,
    14, 18, 80, 142-3, 147, 148
Benjamin, Brig. E F 46, 54-5,
    56-7, 59, 64, 67, 70, 71, 72,
    76-7, 86, 88, 91-2, 96, 107,
    110, 112-13, 117, 121, 143
Benjamin, Frank 46, 47
Ben Kimche, Pte Aharon 91
Beretz, Major Z 37, 111
Bergen-Belsen 86
Berman, Lt 96
Berman, Lisa 135
Bevin, Ernest xiii, 125, 139,
    143, 144, 147
Birt, Maj. 56
Blake, Lord 144
Brandt, Joel 101
Bregner, Lt-Commander
    47-8
Bricha [Escape] 105, 112, 130,
    134, 142
Bridges, Sir Edward 51
*Brigade, The* 83
Britain, Battle of 15
British Expeditionary Force
    15
*British Jewry Book of Honour,
    The* 2
Brodie, Squadron Leader
    Israel 23, 79
Burg-el-Arab 43, 53, 54, 55,
    57

Cantoni, Dr Raphael 109
Carmi, Sgt Israel 27, 126
Caspar, Bernard M 54, 55, 58,
    62, 63, 64, 82, 107, 108, 109,

116, 119-20, 122, 131, 134,
    135
Caspe, Moshe 19
Caspi, Maj. Igad 111
Caspi, Maj. Zvi 105
Cassino, Battle of 63
Cazalet, Col. Victor 17, 42
Chadash, Motke 54
Chamberlain, Neville 10, 13
Chanoch, Ben 19
Chanukah 58, 139
Churchill, Winston xi, 13-14,
    16-17, 24, 42, 43, 48, 51, 54
Clack, Jack 71
Clark, Gen. Mark 59, 80, 96
Cohen, Sgt Eliahu 26, 27
Committee for a Jewish
    Army 96
Cooper, Gerry 68
Cranbourne, Lord 100
Cubitt, Lt-Col. F L 56
Cullen, Maj.-Gen. Paul 18

**D**achau 136
*Davar* 90
Dayan, Moshe 16
de Salis, Col. Count 46, 47
Dobree, Brig. T S 79
Dreyfus, Albert 3
*Dundrennon* [HMT] 5

**E**ast Kent Regiment [Buffs]
    24
Eichmann, Karl Adolf 86,
    101, 145
Eidelsberg, Staff Sgt 59
Eighth Army xi, 28, 38, 39,
    40, 57, 62, 81, 88, 92, 94, 97,
    99, 110
El Alamein 26, 28

157

Elkins, Michael 106
Erchkovitz, Sgt-Major 6
Esterhazy, Major Ferdinand 3
Evitza, Sgt 26
Ewen, Lt 29
*Exodus* 147-8

Feis, Dr Stephen 100
Feldafing 105
Feld, Benno 101, 106
*Festung Europa* 37
Feude, Zvi 68
Fifth Army 37, 38, 44
*Forgotten Ally, The* 14
Franklin, Maj. Y 44

Gash, Col. 72
Gast, Mordechai 107, 108
Gelder, Tony van 84
Geller, David 67
Giladi, Sgt 21
Gilbert, Joe 18
Ginsburg, Sgt S 75
Givon, Shmuel 127
Glover, Brigadier 29
Gobernick, Cpn I 37
Gofton-Salmond, Col. 72
Goldberg, David 128
Goodman, Cpn Cyril 71-2
Gordon, Joshua 25
Gothic Line, the 78, 96, 128
Grainer, Gen. 78
Greenwald, Chanan 82
Grigg, Sir James 84
Groushkowsky, Pte M 6
Growse, Lt-Col. P F A 72

Habonim [Movement] 17-18
*Ha-Chayal* 56
Hakim, Alexander
Hamilton, Bob 68
Hawes, Maj.-Gen. A 14
Heathcote-Smith, Sir Clifford 40-1, 48
Hebrew University 8
Henriques, Maj. 63
Hershkovitz, Sgt-Maj. Elijahu 98
Herzl, Theodore 3-4, 18, 68
Hildesheim, Corporal 6
Hirschburg, Pte 75
Histadrut, the 8
Hitler, Adolf 7, 10, 41
Hoffman, Dan 67
Holme, Christopher 140
Holocaust, the xi, xiv, 28, 37, 38, 61, 80, 86, 87, 88, 93, 99, 107, 110, 119, 128, 148
Hos, Dov 19
Hoter-Yishai, Aharon 86

Huberman, Bronislaw 139
Hyatt, Staff Sgt Mark 67, 68, 71, 88, 112, 135

Independence, 1948 War of 30, 62, 106, 113, 128, 137, 148
Irgun Zvi Leumi xiii, 9, 99, 147
*I Shall Live* 41
Israel Institute of Technology 8
Italian campaign xi, 63

Jabotinsky, Vladimir 5, 7, 9, 18, 69
Jackson, Maj. Cecil 47, 56, 89
Jaeger Division 78, 147
Jesus Christ 1
Jewish Joint Distribution Committee 41
Jewish National Fund 43
Joffe, Harry 18, 23, 25, 26
Jost, Gen. Walter 78

Kahan, Maj. Maxie 97
Kennedy, Col. Jack 44
Keren, Zeer 127
Klagenfurt 119-20
Klein, Judah 106
Klinghoffer, A 68
Kosciusko, General Tadeusz 2
Kovner, Abba 126-7
Kramer, Corporal 35
Krichefsky, Warrant Officer 'Tasch' 59
Laskov, Chaim 62, 147
Lazer, Sgt 66
Levenburg, Dr S 148
Levins, Shlomo 97
Lewy, Joram 84
Lipschitz, Danny 57, 88
Lipschitz, Dr Jacob Gil 131
Lourie, Norman 84, 97
Lucasz, Corporal 29
Luce, Claire Booth 79

Maccabi [sports organisation] 141
McCandish, Brigadier 31-2
McCreary, Lt-Gen. Richard L 91-2
McDonald, Malcolm 11
McMichael, Sir Harold 17, 24
Makleff, Mordechai 141
Mancroft, Lord 119
Mapai 143
Mapam 143
Marcus, Col. David 113
Mazo, Cpn Shimon 63
Middleton, Hugh 145

Miller, Sgt Arieh 27
Mohammed Amin El Husseine 8
Montgomery, Field Marshal 28
Montgomery, Lt-Col. J B T 56
Moses, Pavel 82
Mosley, Oswald 133
Mossad 11, 127
Mossinson, Corporal Moshe 56
Muscroft, Jack 68
Myers, Brig. E 46

Nabarro, Eric 69-71
Nachson [Operation] 62
Net, the 36, 38, 39, 45, 47, 57, 69, 81, 85, 117, 119, 142
North Irish Horse 59

Obernau 102-4
Odessa [escape route] xii
Ohrenstein, Henry 41
*Old-New Land* 3
*On Parade* 67
Orion, Baruch 64

Pacifici, Rabbi Ricardo 117
Palestine Auxiliary Territorial Service [PATS] 24, 39
Palestine Motor Transport Works Services Company 20
Patterson, Lt-Col. Henry 5, 6
Passover 2, 30, 38, 63, 84
Peel Commission 9
Pelz, Yohanan 61-2, 89
Penn, Galili 135
Popski's Private Army 16

Rabinowitz, Rabbi 30
Rappaport, Maj. Y 111
Rashid Ali, 13
Red Army 101, 102, 104, 115, 118, 142
Reichman, Moshe 68
Reinhart, Col. 78
Reshet *see* Net, the
Return, Law of 31
Roosevelt, Franklin D 10, 100
Rosenberg, Pte Nissel 6
Rosenblum, Corporal 60
Rosette, Maurice 129
Roth, Dr Cecil 109-10
Rothschild, Maj. Edmund de 63, 72
Rovina, Hanna 84
Rubens, Charles 17
Rutenberg, Pinchas 25

Sacharov, Cpn Y 28

Salmond, G P 61-2
Samuel, Sir Herbert 8
Sanitt, Len 66-7, 68, 69, 79, 112, 115, 116, 117, 132-3, 134, 137, 141
Shalit, Cpn Leon 56, 63, 111
Shalit, Memie de 141
Shamir, Shlomo 47
Shapiro, Cpn Jack 71
Shapro, Sraya 65
Sharret, Moshe 18
She'erit Hapleetah [Surviving Remnant] 105
Sheinbaum, Eliezer 68
Shertok, Moshe 25, 37, 39, 55, 64-5, 80
Shugarisky, Ugi 47
Sieff, Marcus 30
Silberstein, Cpn A 27, 40, 59, 111
Six Day War 16
Spector, David 26, 45, 47, 62, 74, 85, 86, 91, 98-9, 118-19, 129-30, 145
Spiegel, Sgt-Maj. Sucher 64
Steele, Sir Christopher 124
Stern Gang xiii, 99, 147

Strabolgi, Lord 42, 84
Struma [SS] 100
Stuart [HMAS] 23
Sutka, Shimon 68

Taiber, Sgt Yehihal 27
Tarachovsky, Nathan 68
Tel Aviv Hospitality Committee 18
Theresienstadt 86
Tito, Marshal 98
Tobias, M 75
Tobruk [siege] 21, 23, 26
Trettner, Maj.Gen. Heinrich 93
Truman, President Harry S 145
Trumpeldor, Joseph 5, 6, 18, 69

United Nations xiv, 148
United Nations Relief and Rehabilitation Administration [UNRRA] 123, 131, 134

van Passen, Pierre 14

Wadel, Moshe 84
Wald, Malachi 103, 106
Weizmann, Chaim 6-7, 12-13, 14, 17, 18, 51, 69
Western Desert campaign xi, 20, 26, 35, 63, 123
Wheels in the Storm 18
Wingate, Charles Orde 9-10, 14-15, 83
Wingate, Sir Reginald 15
Wiseman, Lance-Corporal Shmuel 68
With the Jewish Brigade 54
World Zionist Organisation 17

Yisraeli, Ben Zion 54
Yoselovitch, Berek 2

Zankelis, Pte Zelig 97
Zilberberg, Moshe 91
Zionist Revisionist Party 5
Zion Mule Corps [ZMC] 5, 6
Zola, Emile 3
Zolbi, Rabbi 47
Zorea, Meir xii-xiii, 89, 104
Zweig, Stefan 4